ROBERT J. MARZANO

Becoming a Reflective Teacher

Marzano Research Laboratory

with TINA **BOOGREN**
TAMMY **HEFLEBOWER**
JESSICA **KANOLD-MCINTYRE**
DEBRA **PICKERING**

THE **CLASSROOM** STRATEGIES **SERIES**

555 North Morton Street
Bloomington, IN 47404

888.849.0851
FAX: 866.801.1447

email: info@marzanoresearch.com
marzanoresearch.com

Visit **marzanoresearch.com/classroomstrategies** to download the reproducibles in this book.

Printed in the United States of America

Library of Congress Control Number: 2011944708

ISBN: 978–0-9833512–3-8 (paperback)

978–0-9833512–4-5 (library binding)

16 15 14   6 7 8 9 10

Vice President of Production: Gretchen Knapp

Managing Production Editor: Caroline Wise

Copy Editor: Rachel Rosolina

Proofreader: Elisabeth Abrams

Text and Cover Designer: Amy Shock

MARZANO RESEARCH LABORATORY DEVELOPMENT TEAM

Staff Writer/Researcher

Julia A. Simms

Marzano Research Laboratory Associates

Tina Boogren

Bev Clemens

Jane K. Doty Fischer

Maria C. Foseid

Mark P. Foseid

Tammy Heflebower

Mitzi Hoback

Jan Hoegh

Jessica Kanold-McIntyre

Sharon Kramer

David Livingston

Pam Livingston

Beatrice McGarvey

Margaret McInteer

Diane E. Paynter

Debra Pickering

Salle Quackenboss

Tom Roy

Phil Warrick

Kenneth Williams

Visit **marzanoresearch.com/classroomstrategies**
to download reproducibles from this book.

CONTENTS

Italicized entries indicate reproducible forms.

ABOUT THE AUTHORS

Robert J. Marzano, PhD, is the cofounder and CEO of Marzano Research Laboratory in Denver, Colorado. Throughout his forty years in the field of education, he has become a speaker, trainer, and author of more than thirty books and 150 articles on topics such as instruction, assessment, writing and implementing standards, cognition, effective leadership, and school intervention. His books include *Designing and Teaching Learning Goals and Objectives*, *District Leadership That Works*, *Formative Assessment and Standards-Based Grading*, *On Excellence in Teaching*, *The Art and Science of Teaching*, *The Highly Engaged Classroom*, *Effective Supervision*, and *Teaching and Assessing 21st Century Skills*. His practical translations of the most current research and theory into classroom strategies are known internationally and are widely practiced by both teachers and administrators. He received a bachelor's degree from Iona College in New York, a master's degree from Seattle University, and a doctorate from the University of Washington.

Tina Boogren, MA, is a former classroom teacher, English department chair, instructional coach, digital educator, professional developer, and building-level leader. She is a fellow with the Denver Writing Project and has published numerous articles through the National Writing Project and International Reading Association. Tina has presented at the school, district, state, and national levels and has been a featured speaker at the International Reading Association National Conference and Barnes & Noble Educators' Nights. Tina was a finalist for Colorado Teacher of the Year, and she received the Outstanding Teacher Award seven years in a row. In addition to numerous articles, Tina is author of *In the First Few Years: Reflections of a Beginning Teacher*, published by the International Reading Association. She holds a bachelor's degree from the University of Iowa and a master's degree with an administrative endorsement from the University of Colorado Denver. She is pursuing a doctorate from the University of Denver in educational administration and policy studies.

Tammy Heflebower, EdD, is vice president of Marzano Research Laboratory in Denver, Colorado. She is a consultant with experience in urban, rural, and suburban districts throughout North America. Dr. Heflebower has served as a classroom teacher, building-level leader, district leader, regional professional development director, and national trainer. She has also been an adjunct professor of curriculum, instruction, and assessment courses at several universities. She began her teaching career in Kansas City, Kansas, and later moved to Nebraska, where she received the District Distinguished Teacher Award. She has worked as a national educational trainer for the National Resource and Training Center at Boys Town in Nebraska. A prominent member of numerous educational organizations, Dr. Heflebower has served as president of the Nebraska Association for Supervision and Curriculum Development and was president-elect for the Professional Development Organization for Nebraska Educational Service Units. She was president-elect of the Colorado Association of Education Specialists and legislative liaison for the Colorado Association of School Executives. She is a contributor to *The Teacher as Assessment Leader* and *The Principal as Assessment Leader* and a coauthor of *Teaching and Assessing 21st Century Skills*. Her articles have been featured in the monthly newsletter *Nebraska Council of School Administrators Today*. Dr. Heflebower holds a bachelor of arts from Hastings College in Hastings, Nebraska, a master of arts from the University of Nebraska at Omaha, and an educational administrative endorsement from the University of Nebraska-Lincoln. She also earned a doctor of education in educational administration from the University of Nebraska-Lincoln.

Jessica Kanold-McIntyre, MA, currently serves as a junior high principal in Buffalo Grove, Illinois. She is a proven leader in fostering learning environments where technology is used to enhance current teaching practices. She has experience and expertise in mathematics instruction, technology use tied to sound teaching practices, and district, school, and teacher implementation of technology. Specifically, she is able to train on Promethean and SMART software and the use of learner response systems. Her training style is practical and relevant to the needs of teachers. Jessica holds a bachelor of arts in elementary education from Wheaton College and a master of arts in educational administration from Northern Illinois University.

Debra Pickering, PhD, consults with schools and districts nationally and internationally as a senior scholar for Marzano Research Laboratory. Throughout her educational career, Dr. Pickering has gained practical experience as a classroom teacher, building leader, and district administrator. For many years, she has used this experience to provide training and support to K–12 teachers and administrators as they seek to continually improve student learning. In addition to her work with schools, Dr. Pickering has coauthored (with Dr. Robert Marzano) educational books and manuals, including *Dimensions of Learning*, *Classroom Instruction That Works*, *Classroom Management That Works*, *Building Academic Vocabulary*, and *The Highly Engaged Classroom*. With a combination of theoretical grounding and over three decades of practical experience, she has worked with educators to translate theory into practice. Her work continues to focus on the study of learning and the development of resources for curriculum, instruction, and assessment to help all educators meet the needs of all students. Dr. Pickering holds a master's degree in school administration and a doctorate in curriculum and instruction, with an emphasis in cognitive psychology.

ABOUT MARZANO RESEARCH LABORATORY

Marzano Research Laboratory (MRL) is a joint venture between Solution Tree and Dr. Robert J. Marzano. MRL combines Dr. Marzano's forty years of educational research with continuous action research in all major areas of schooling in order to provide effective and accessible instructional strategies, leadership strategies, and classroom assessment strategies that are always at the forefront of best practice. By providing such an all-inclusive research-into-practice resource center, MRL provides teachers and principals the tools they need to effect profound and immediate improvement in student achievement.

INTRODUCTION

Becoming a Reflective Teacher is part of a series of books collectively referred to as the *Classroom Strategies Series.* This series aims to provide teachers, as well as building and district administrators, with an in-depth treatment of research-based instructional strategies that can be used in the classroom to enhance student achievement. Many of the strategies addressed in this series have been covered in other works such as *Classroom Instruction That Works* (Marzano, Pickering, & Pollock, 2001), *Classroom Management That Works* (Marzano, 2003), *The Art and Science of Teaching* (Marzano, 2007), and *Effective Supervision* (Marzano, Frontier, & Livingston, 2011). Although those works devoted a chapter or a part of a chapter to particular strategies, the *Classroom Strategies Series* devotes an entire book to an instructional strategy or set of related strategies.

Clearly, teaching is a skill, and like any skill, it must be practiced. Just as athletes wanting to improve their skills must identify personal strengths and weaknesses, set goals, and engage in focused practice to meet those goals, teachers must also examine their practices, set growth goals, and use focused practice and feedback to achieve those goals. These reflective processes are essential to the development of expertise in teaching.

We begin with a brief but inclusive chapter that reviews the research and theory on reflective practice. Although you might skip this chapter and move right into those that provide recommendations for classroom practice, we strongly encourage you to examine the research and theory as it is the foundation for the entire book. Indeed, a basic purpose of *Becoming a Reflective Teacher* and others in the *Classroom Strategies Series* is to present the most useful instructional strategies based on the strongest research and theory available.

Because research and theory can provide only a general direction for classroom practice, *Becoming a Reflective Teacher* (and each book in the series) goes one step further to translate that research into applications for the classroom. Specifically, this book addresses how teachers can combine a model of effective instruction with goal setting, focused practice, focused feedback, and observations and discussions of teaching to improve their instructional practices.

Becoming a Reflective Teacher also offers a unique feature, the compendium, located directly after chapter 6 and before the appendices. The compendium matches over 270 specific classroom strategies and behaviors to the forty-one elements of effective teaching described in chapter 2. After a teacher selects specific elements of effective teaching as goals for improvement (described in chapter 3), he or she must engage in focused practice of strategies related to the goal elements (described in chapter 4). To facilitate this process, the compendium provides complete but succinct descriptions of multiple strategies and behaviors for each of the forty-one elements of effective teaching. Without needing to consult other books or sources, a teacher can use the compendium to quickly find and learn about strategies that will help focus practice and growth.

How to Use This Book

Educators can use *Becoming a Reflective Teacher* as a self-study text that provides an in-depth understanding of reflective practice. As you progress through the chapters, you will encounter comprehension questions. It is important to complete these questions and compare your answers with those in appendix A (page 179). Such interaction provides a review of the content and allows a thorough examination of your understanding.

Teams of teachers or entire faculties that wish to examine the topic of reflective practice in depth may also use *Becoming a Reflective Teacher*. When this is the case, teacher teams should answer the questions independently and then compare answers in small- and large-group settings.

As noted, the compendium is designed to be a quick reference tool for teachers and is not intended to be read through from beginning to end. Rather, as you or your team progresses through the chapters of the book, reference those compendium sections that describe strategies related to your growth goals. The strategies in the compendium are designed to be the subject of focused practice and can also add specificity and structure to feedback, observations, and discussions of teaching.

Chapter 1

RESEARCH AND THEORY

It is a well-accepted fact among educators that what a teacher does in the classroom has a direct effect on student achievement (Nye, Konstantopoulos, & Hedges, 2004). In other words, a teacher's pedagogical skill in the classroom is causally linked with how well and how much students learn. A corollary is that teacher reflection improves teacher pedagogical skill. This relationship is depicted in figure 1.1.

Figure 1.1: Relationship between student achievement, teacher pedagogical skill, and teacher reflective practice.

The relationship between classroom strategies and behaviors and student achievement is very straightforward. The causal relationship between reflective practice and pedagogical skill is not as commonly recognized, although the interaction between these elements has been discussed in the research literature for decades.

A Brief History of Reflective Practice

Reflective practice has been recognized as an important component of professional development for some time. Here we consider five generalizations that characterize the research and theory base for reflective practice:

1. Reflective practice is not a new idea.

2. Reflective practice is widely recognized as important.

3. Reflective practice has been greatly influenced by Schön.

4. Reflective practice is critical to expertise.

5. K–12 education has not fully embraced reflective practice.

Reflective Practice Is Not a New Idea

Reflecting on one's experiences is a foundational idea of many ancient Eastern and Western philosophies. Buddhism emphasizes the central role of reflection in an individual's search for insight and truth. In ancient Greece, Socrates taught his students that "the unexamined life isn't worth living" (as quoted by Plato in the *Apology*). According to Jennifer York-Barr, William Sommers, Gail Ghere, and Jo Montie (2006), a common theme throughout the literature on reflective thinking is seeing reflection as "an active thought process aimed at understanding and subsequent improvement" (p. 4).

Early in the 20th century, John Dewey (1910) defined reflective thought as "active, persistent, and careful consideration of any belief or supposed form of knowledge in the light of the grounds that support it, and the further conclusions to which it tends" (p. 8). He emphasized the role of reflection in examining the beliefs and theories that influence our actions.

Reflective Practice Is Widely Recognized as Important

Reflective practice is highly esteemed and widely used in many professions, especially those that require on-the-spot decisions and adaptations. Such endeavors can be difficult for novices who lack practical experience, and reflective practice can help students of those professions build the experience they need in order to be successful. Filippa Anzalone (2010), discussing the role of reflection in the legal profession, stated that reflection helps students

> examine and test beliefs and principles against what is being learned doctrinally. Reflective practice helps students vet their own beliefs and value systems against the mores and norms of the legal profession. Through reflection, they are invited to examine themselves and the profession they are about to enter. (p. 86)

Writing about the nursing profession, Heesook Kim, Laurie Clabo, Patricia Burbank, and Mary Martins (2010) said that reflective practice offers "a way to narrow the gap between theory and practice" and "a way to discover knowledge embedded in practice" (p. 159). In describing the challenges of social work, Marian Murphy, Maria Dempsey, and Carmel Halton (2010) wrote,

> There will be times when students and practitioners will be required to acknowledge the limitations of their knowledge and to respond appropriately. In the immediacy of practice situations, reflection facilitates practitioners to draw from their previous practice experience and to apply that which is relevant to new and unfamiliar practice situations. (p. 177)

In these and in many other fields, reflective practice is acknowledged to be a powerful tool for professional development and growth. Reflective practice facilitates the processing and integration of new knowledge and can help students and practitioners make sound decisions when confronted with unfamiliar situations.

Reflective Practice Has Been Greatly Influenced by Schön

In his 1983 book *The Reflective Practitioner*, Donald Schön applied the concept of reflection to various professions to demonstrate that not only do researchers generate professional knowledge, but practitioners such as doctors, teachers, architects, and engineers do as well. He maintained that "competent practitioners usually know more than they can say" (p. viii), and he labeled this tacit knowledge "knowing-in-action" (p. 49).

Schön (1987) argued that knowing-in-action was what separated skilled practitioners from unskilled ones, and he advocated that practitioners of all levels use what he referred to as "reflection-in-action" as a way to increase their tacit knowledge, and thus their skill. Schön distinguished between *reflection-in-action* (reflecting and changing our behavior in the midst of an action) and *reflection-on-action* (looking back after the fact). When we reflect-in-action, Schön said, "we can still make a difference to the situation at hand—our thinking serves to reshape what we are doing while we are doing it" (1987, p. 26).

Experimentation also plays an important role in reflective practice, according to Schön (1983). "The perception of something troubling or promising," he noted, initiates the experimentation and reflection process, which "is terminated by the production of changes one finds on the whole satisfactory, or by the discovery of new features which give the situation new meaning and change the nature of the questions to be explored" (p. 151).

Reflective Practice Is Critical to Expertise

The research literature on expertise implicitly supports the importance of reflective practice. For centuries, people believed that expertise, or talent, was bestowed on select individuals, and that it was impossible to develop high levels of skill within a given domain unless one had innate talent for that domain. Ancient philosophers believed that extraordinary abilities were gifts from the gods, and experts were simply superior to other humans (Ericsson & Charness, 1994). Even in current times, many people believe that certain characteristics (such as intelligence) are fixed and that successful people simply have more of these traits than others, allowing them to perform at higher levels or produce better products than everyone else.

In contrast to this perspective, and as a result of their examination of the research, K. Anders Ericsson and Neil Charness (1994) deduced that "the traditional view of talent, which concludes that successful individuals have special innate abilities and basic capacities, is not consistent with the reviewed evidence" (p. 744). Ericsson and his colleagues Ralf Krampe and Clemens Tesch-Romer (1993) also observed that

> the search for stable heritable characteristics that could predict or at least account for the superior performance of eminent individuals has been surprisingly unsuccessful. . . . The conviction in the importance of talent appears to be based on the insufficiency of alternative hypotheses to explain the exceptional nature of expert performance. (p. 365)

These findings led Ericsson and his colleagues (1993) to argue:

> The differences between expert performers and normal adults reflect a life-long period of deliberate effort to improve performance in a specific domain. . . . We view elite performance as the product of a decade or more of maximal efforts to improve performance in a domain through an optimal distribution of deliberate practice. (p. 400)

The following list presents examples of people whose accomplishments serve to dispel the "innately gifted or talented" myth. These individuals are commonly thought to be successful because of natural talent or innate giftedness, but they actually worked very hard (usually with coaching from their parents or other experts) over a period of years to become experts in their fields:

- **Yo-Yo Ma**—Ma's father, Hiao-Tsiun, was a music teacher, composer, and conductor, and his mother was a trained opera singer. His older sister studied music from the time she was three, and the Ma family even moved to Paris to pursue Hiao-Tsiun's dream of creating a children's orchestra. Surrounded by music from the moment of his birth, Ma heard hundreds of recordings and live performances of classical music pieces. He desperately wanted to be like his father and sister, and he sought their feedback and criticism about his playing. His father designed teaching techniques specifically for young Ma and allowed him, at age four, to switch from violin to cello (Shenk, 2010).

- **Michelangelo Buonarroti**—Michelangelo grew up in the household of a stone cutter, and he learned to use a hammer and chisel before he learned to read and write. He was apprenticed to the artist Ghirlandaio, for whom he worked long hours each day, sketching, copying, and painting. As a teenager, he worked on frescoes in Florentine churches and was tutored by the master sculptor Bertoldo. Only after eighteen years of practice and work did Michelangelo complete the Pieta, which is considered one of his greatest works (Coyle, 2009).

- **The Brontë Sisters**—During their childhood, Charlotte, Emily, and Anne spent hours and hours writing tiny books, most of which contained passages copied from or modeled after magazine articles and books they had read. Although these early attempts were not very good, they developed skill with character, setting, narrative, and plot, and they gradually became better writers. As adults, all three sisters won acclaim for works such as *Jane Eyre*, *Wuthering Heights*, *Agnes Grey*, and *The Tenant of Wildfell Hall* (Coyle, 2009).

- **Jerry Rice**—Rice played football in high school and college and was successful because of his speed. In the 1985 draft, however, NFL teams didn't think he was very talented, and fifteen teams declined to draft him before the San Francisco 49ers finally signed him. He determined then to work harder than anyone else. After every reception, Rice would sprint to the end zone. He worked out six days a week in the off-season, using a strenuous cardiovascular and strength training regimen that other players tried but couldn't complete because it made them sick. As a result of his hard work, he captured records for total receptions, total touchdown receptions, and total receiving yards, beating previous records by as much as 50 percent (Colvin, 2008).

- **Chris Rock**—Rock's ability to elicit uproarious laughter from audiences caused many people to say he was naturally funny, but he actually spent hours and hours crafting his big shows. He booked warm-up shows with smaller audiences where he tried out new material, evaluated which jokes worked and which didn't, cut unsuccessful bits, and rearranged the good ones until he had a concentrated, finely tuned act, guaranteed to crack up audiences. Only after extensive practice and refinement would he take a show on the road (Colvin, 2008).

- **Warren Buffett**—Buffett's father was a stockbroker during the Great Depression and supported his early interest in investments and finance. Buffett started working in his father's office when he was eleven, but throughout his teens and twenties, he failed both at picking stocks and at trying to time the market. His favorite professor at Columbia Business School refused to give him a job after college. It was only when he opened his first investment business at age twenty-five, after seriously studying business and investing for fourteen years, that he began to experience success (Colvin, 2008).

The concept of *deliberate practice*, identified by Ericsson and his colleagues (1993), flies in the face of what most people think of as practice. Practice is usually thought of as working at a skill until one reaches automaticity with it. For example, when people learn to drive, they first learn the basic rules of driving and how to use the various controls on the car. After they have "practiced" these for a period of time, they begin to show more proficiency and can turn, park, stop, and change lanes smoothly. After more repetition, these actions become automatic, easily executed without much mental effort.

Deliberate practice differs from this popular conception, because individuals engaged in deliberate practice tend to resist automaticity. Their goal is not to avoid thinking about a specific skill or process. Instead, they strive to continuously achieve mastery of "increasingly higher levels of performance through the acquisition of more complex and refined cognitive mechanisms" (Ericsson, Roring, & Nandagopal, 2007, p. 24). In order to achieve these lofty levels of performance, individuals must focus on the "not-yet-attained and challenging tasks that define the desired superior level of performance" (p. 24). In attempting tasks beyond their current level of performance, individuals who engage in deliberate practice often fail.

This frequent failure distinguishes deliberate practice from more pleasurable types of practice, such as playing a sport recreationally. It also differs from the experiences that Mihaly Csikszentmihalyi (1990) referred to as "flow" experiences. Flow occurs when individuals engage in activities at which they are skilled, and it "corresponds to complete immersion and effortless mastery of the activity" (Ericsson, 1996, p. 25). Ericsson observed that "the characteristics of flow are inconsistent with the demands of deliberate practice for monitoring explicit goals and feedback and opportunities for error correction" (p. 25). Whereas flow experiences are motivating and pleasant, "deliberate practice requires effort and is not inherently enjoyable. Individuals are motivated to practice because practice improves performance" (Ericsson et al., 1993, p. 368).

Deliberate practice also requires large amounts of time. Ericsson and his colleagues (1993) examined evidence from a wide range of domains and found that "expert performance is acquired slowly over a very long time as a result of practice and that the highest levels of performance and achievement appear to require at least around 10 years of intense prior preparation" (p. 366). Ericsson (1996) referred to this need for at least a decade of dedicated practice as the "10-year rule" (p. 10).

Harvard University professor John Carroll (1963) created a mathematical ratio that expresses how the amount of time invested in an activity affects a person's level of success with the same activity. He considered the interplay of how long it took a person to learn something (which he called *aptitude*), how long a person was willing to spend with a subject (which he called *perseverance*), and how much time a person was allowed for learning (which he called *opportunity*). Csikszentmihalyi, Kevin Rathunde, and Samuel Whalen (1993) commented on the idea of perseverance, or how motivated a person is to spend time on something: "Unless a person wants to pursue the difficult path that leads to the development of talent, neither innate potential nor all the knowledge in the world will suffice" (pp. 31–32).

The way experts store knowledge also illustrates the importance and consequences of deliberate practice. Michelene Chi (2006) pointed out that one of the key differences between experts and novices is that experts' knowledge is organized and structured differently than that of novices. Robert Weisberg (2006) noted that "the expert acquires a rich, highly complex conceptual structure that is used consciously to represent and reason about situations" (p. 767). In other words, experts' practice causes their brains to develop better systems for storing, organizing, and accessing information in their area of expertise. For instance, before cab drivers can be licensed to work in London, they have to pass a test proving they have acquired something called "the knowledge"—an encyclopedic understanding of the streets, hotels, landmarks, tourist attractions, restaurants, parks, theaters, shops, monuments, businesses, and residential areas of London. A researcher named Eleanor Maguire discovered that learning this knowledge actually caused a specific part of the cabbies' brains (the posterior hippocampus) to grow. The study found that London cabbies with more experience had larger hippocampuses, suggesting they acquired their facility and skill with "the knowledge" over time and improved with experience and practice (Shenk, 2010).

Finally, the research on metacognition supports the importance of reflective practice in developing expertise. Developing expertise through deliberate practice requires a level of metacognition or "knowledge about one's own knowledge and knowledge about one's own performance" (Feltovich, Prietula, & Ericsson, 2006, p. 55). This type of metacognitive control and monitoring can be hard for an individual engaged in deliberate practice to maintain. For this reason, says Geoff Colvin (2008), a coach can be very helpful in providing feedback and direction to someone working to develop expertise. A coach is usually someone whose relationship with the individual allows them to give honest and unbiased assessments of the individual's performance and whose knowledge in the field allows them to choose or design practice activities that will be most effective at helping the subject move to higher and higher levels of skill.

K–12 Education Has Not Fully Embraced Reflective Practice

From one perspective, a case can be made that reflective practice is already a prominent part of K–12 education. For example, a number of researchers (Ball & Cohen, 1999; Cochran-Smith & Lytle, 1999; Darling-Hammond & McLaughlin, 1999; Lyons & LaBoskey, 2002) have reported results that support professional development that "is situated in practice, is ongoing, promotes collaborative inquiry and critical discourse, and is focused on improving student learning" (Mast & Ginsburg, 2010, p. 257). Cheryl Craig and Margaret Olson (2002) observed that effective professional development for teachers should help them "explore the upsides and downsides of experiences, making their practices transparent and their knowledge public in the presence of others" (p. 117). However, in spite of these calls for reflective practice, a 2008 report from the Council of Chief State School Officers (CCSSO) found that a number of teacher development programs in the United States did not meet those standards (Blank, de las Alas, & Smith, 2008). Fred Korthagen and Angelo Vasalos (2010) observed:

> Reflection as it is currently being used in professional settings and in educational programs for professional development, does not always lead to optimal learning or the intended professional development. Sometimes reflection seems to be used by practitioners as merely a technical tool generating quick, but often ineffective, solutions to problems that have been only superficially defined. If we look closely at how many practitioners reflect, we see that if there is any time for reflection at all, work pressure often leads to a focus on finding a "quick fix"—a rapid solution for a practical problem. . . . While this may be an effective short-term measure in a hectic situation, there is a danger that one's professional development may eventually stagnate. (p. 529)

Korthagen and Vasalos (2010) advocated for "structured reflection," arguing that it promotes deep learning, appropriate professional behavior, and a growth competence, which they defined as "the ability to continue to develop professionally on the basis of internally directed learning" (p. 529).

The lesson study model many teachers use in Japan provides one example of structured reflection. In lesson study, a group of teachers (usually from a range of grade levels) sets goals for specific subject areas, units, and lessons, and then writes a research lesson to help students meet those goals. One member of the group presents the research lesson to his or her class while other group members observe. Afterward, the group analyzes the lesson, examining evidence it collected regarding "students' engagement, persistence, emotional reactions, quality of discussion within small-groups, including of group-mates, and degree of interest in the task" (Mast & Ginsburg, 2010, p. 258). The group then draws conclusions to inform its subsequent work. Groups work together for years and sometimes decades, gradually building expertise in "the areas of curriculum expertise, knowledge of student thinking, knowledge of lesson study practices, and collaborative skills and practices" (Mast & Ginsburg, 2010, p. 258). The Change Leadership Group, a Harvard-based organization, has identified lesson study as "the most fully developed model of teacher collaboration to improve practice" (Mast & Ginsburg, 2010, p. 269).

Other attempts to implement elements of reflective practice include the works of Fred Korthagen, Thomas Farrell, Jennifer York-Barr, and others. Korthagen and his colleagues (Korthagen & Kessels, 1999; Korthagen & Vasalos, 2005) presented the ALACT (action, looking back, awareness, creating alternative methods, trial) model as a structure for teacher reflection. They stated that teacher reflection begins with an *action*. Then, as teachers *look back* at the action and identify essential aspects of it, they reflect on how well they performed those essential aspects (*awareness*). Finally teachers *create alternative methods* of performing the action and try them out (*trial*), beginning the cycle again. Figure 1.2 illustrates the process.

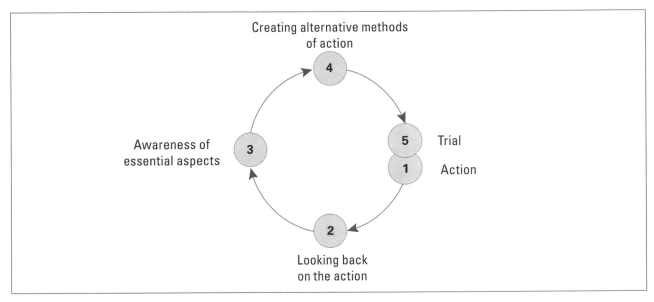

Figure 1.2: The ALACT model, describing a structured process of reflection.

Source: "Levels on Reflection: Core Reflection as a Means to Enhance Professional Growth," F. A. J. Korthagen and A. Vasalos, *Teachers and Teaching: Theory and Practice,* 2005, Taylor & Francis Group, reprinted by permission of the publisher (Taylor & Francis Group, http://www.informaworld.com).

Others have also created models and structures to guide reflection. Thomas Farrell (1999, 2004) provides "an overall framework for teachers to use when reflecting on their work—whether individually, in pairs, or in teams" (2004, p. 36). His framework consists of reflective activities (such as group discussions, classroom observations, teaching journals, and teaching portfolios) supported by the following four components:

1. **Ground rules**—Farrell recommends designing ground rules for group meetings, classroom observations, journal writing, and critical friend relationships.

2. **Categories of time**—Farrell suggests that teachers need to allocate time to engage in reflective activities, individual reflection, skill development, and group reflection.

3. **External input**—Farrell advises that external input might come from other people's observations, reflections, or theories, or from the research and literature on teaching practice.

4. **Affective states**—Farrell acknowledges that reflection can be an uncomfortable experience at times and suggests using structured protocols to alleviate anxiety or embarrassment during reflection.

Jennifer York-Barr and her colleagues (2006) created the reflective practice spiral as a way to "embed reflective practices as a cultural norm in schools" (p. 19). They argue that reflective practice begins with individuals and spreads to larger communities of practice. They describe a number of activities for the following:

- **Individual reflection**—Journaling, case studies, literature review, portfolio development, and video or audio review of one's own teaching

- **Reflection with a partner**—Interactive journaling, cognitive coaching, considering different possibilities for instructional design, using an inquiry cycle to examine specific events, reading and discussing articles and case studies, and examining student work

- **Reflection in a small group or team**—Action research, study groups, grade- or content-specific meetings to design and review instructional designs and assessments, examining student work, examining student data, and reviewing case studies

- **Schoolwide reflection**—Study groups focusing on specific content areas, instructional strategies, or assessment techniques

Max van Manen (1977) proposed three levels of reflection: (1) technical rationality, (2) practical action, and (3) critical reflection. *Technical rationality* is the lowest level and is typical of new teachers whose background knowledge about teaching is limited. It involves figuring out how to make it through a lesson or deal with glaring classroom management issues. At this stage, teachers encounter many problems for the first time. At the second level, *practical action*, teachers reflect on the context of their classrooms and examine their underlying theories and beliefs about teaching. A question typical at this stage is, "Why did I do that?" Here, teachers develop "rules of thumb" that will help them handle different types of situations. During the last stage, *critical reflection*, teachers look at ethical issues related to education in general. Reflection at this level "involves a constant critique of domination, of institutions, and of repressive forms of authority" (van Manen, 1977, p. 227). At this stage, teachers might reflect on why their curriculum focuses on certain topics or events more than others and how that focus affects students' learning and beliefs.

Gillie Bolton (2010) developed a five-stage process to guide teachers as they engage in reflective writing. The five stages are as follows:

1. **The six-minute write**—Here, the reflector writes without stopping for at least six minutes. The goal is twofold: (1) to clear one's head of clutter and (2) to encourage writing to flow. It does not matter what is written down. It can take any form (lists, poetry, prose) and be on any topic. This writing does not need to be reread or shown to anyone else.

2. **The story**—Immediately following the six-minute write, and without rereading what was written during that time, the reflector selects an event and writes down its story. Bolton emphasized writing about the first event that comes to mind and recording as many details as possible about it. She also recommended that the reflector consider the story fictional while writing it, to counter embarrassment or fear of getting details wrong.

3. **Reading and responding**—The reflector goes back and reads everything she has written. While reading, the reflector makes corrections, fills in details, and makes any other changes that she feels are appropriate. The reflector also tries to be aware of her thoughts as she rereads.

4. **Sharing writing with a peer**—Bolton recommended sharing the story with a trusted colleague or peer who can give feedback and ask probing questions about the situation described.

5. **Developing writing**—This stage is designed to help the reflector examine the story she has already written from a different perspective. Bolton suggested rewriting the story from the perspective of another person, writing a commentary on the story, writing a continuation of the story six months or a year later, or zooming in on a specific character's thoughts and feelings.

Several other specific protocols also facilitate teacher reflection in pairs or groups, including cognitive coaching (Costa & Garmston, 2002) and critical friends groups (National School Reform Faculty, 2008).

The Organization of This Book

We have organized our interpretation and translation of the research and theory on reflective practice into five broad categories: (1) having a model of effective teaching, (2) setting growth goals, (3) engaging in focused practice, (4) receiving focused feedback, and (5) observing and discussing teaching.

Having a Model of Effective Teaching

Before reflecting on teaching, a teacher must have a general idea of what constitutes effective teaching. Michael Posner and Mary Rothbart (2007) asserted that the key difference between an expert and a novice is the amount of domain-based knowledge each has accrued. Similarly, Robert Sternberg and Joseph Horvath (1995) reviewed psychological research to determine what features were important to expert teaching. One important feature they identified was domain knowledge. They commented that experts not only *have* more domain knowledge than novices, but they "bring knowledge to bear more effectively on problems within their domains of expertise than do novices" (p. 10). Ericsson and Jacqui Smith (1991) pointed out that experts have "a body of knowledge that not only is more extensive than that for nonexperts but also is more accessible" (pp. 20–21). In other words, experts know which strategies and behaviors are generally effective in their domain of expertise, and they select the best or most effective strategy or behavior for a particular situation.

Ericsson and Charness (1994) pointed out that as the *shared* knowledge base for a domain becomes increasingly well articulated, expertise in that domain becomes accessible to a wider array of people. For example, in the domain of music, certain works by Tchaikovsky and Paganini were considered unplayable when they were first written. However, violinists today perform them with ease. Ericsson and Charness (1994) observed:

> Paganini's techniques and Tchaikovsky's concerto were deemed impossible until other musicians figured out how to master and describe them so that students could learn them as well. . . . In all major domains there has been a steady accumulation of knowledge about the domain and about the skills and techniques that mediate superior performance. (pp. 737–738)

In this book, we use *The Art and Science of Teaching* (Marzano, 2007) as a framework for understanding the nature of effective teaching. Here, we organize the critical design questions from that framework into three broad categories: (1) lesson segments involving routine events, (2) lesson segments addressing content, and (3) lesson segments enacted on the spot. Within these categories, each design question is divided into individual elements that describe specific classroom strategies and behaviors. There are forty-one elements in the framework: five elements for lesson segments involving routine events, eighteen elements for lesson segments addressing content, and eighteen elements for lesson segments enacted on the spot. Table 1.1 depicts this framework of lesson segments, design questions, and elements.

Table 1.1: Organization of *The Art and Science of Teaching* Framework

Lesson Segments Involving Routine Events
Design Question: What will I do to establish and communicate learning goals, track student progress, and celebrate success?
Element 1: What do I typically do to provide clear learning goals and scales (rubrics)?
Element 2: What do I typically do to track student progress?
Element 3: What do I typically do to celebrate success?
Design Question: What will I do to establish and maintain classroom rules and procedures?
Element 4: What do I typically do to establish and maintain classroom rules and procedures?
Element 5: What do I typically do to organize the physical layout of the classroom?

Lesson Segments Addressing Content
Design Question: What will I do to help students effectively interact with new knowledge?
Element 6: What do I typically do to identify critical information?
Element 7: What do I typically do to organize students to interact with new knowledge?
Element 8: What do I typically do to preview new content?
Element 9: What do I typically do to chunk content into "digestible bites"?
Element 10: What do I typically do to help students process new information?
Element 11: What do I typically do to help students elaborate on new information?
Element 12: What do I typically do to help students record and represent knowledge?
Element 13: What do I typically do to help students reflect on their learning?
Design Question: What will I do to help students practice and deepen their understanding of new knowledge?
Element 14: What do I typically do to review content?
Element 15: What do I typically do to organize students to practice and deepen knowledge?
Element 16: What do I typically do to use homework?
Element 17: What do I typically do to help students examine similarities and differences?
Element 18: What do I typically do to help students examine errors in reasoning?
Element 19: What do I typically do to help students practice skills, strategies, and processes?
Element 20: What do I typically do to help students revise knowledge?
Design Question: What will I do to help students generate and test hypotheses about new knowledge?
Element 21: What do I typically do to organize students for cognitively complex tasks?
Element 22: What do I typically do to engage students in cognitively complex tasks involving hypothesis generation and testing?
Element 23: What do I typically do to provide resources and guidance?

Lesson Segments Enacted on the Spot
Design Question: What will I do to engage students?
Element 24: What do I typically do to notice when students are not engaged?
Element 25: What do I typically do to use academic games?
Element 26: What do I typically do to manage response rates?
Element 27: What do I typically do to use physical movement?
Element 28: What do I typically do to maintain a lively pace?
Element 29: What do I typically do to demonstrate intensity and enthusiasm?
Element 30: What do I typically do to use friendly controversy?
Element 31: What do I typically do to provide opportunities for students to talk about themselves?
Element 32: What do I typically do to present unusual or intriguing information?
Design Question: What will I do to recognize and acknowledge adherence or lack of adherence to rules and procedures?
Element 33: What do I typically do to demonstrate "withitness"?
Element 34: What do I typically do to apply consequences for lack of adherence to rules and procedures?
Element 35: What do I typically do to acknowledge adherence to rules and procedures?
Design Question: What will I do to establish and maintain effective relationships with students?
Element 36: What do I typically do to understand students' interests and backgrounds?
Element 37: What do I typically do to use verbal and nonverbal behaviors that indicate affection for students?
Element 38: What do I typically do to display objectivity and control?
Design Question: What will I do to communicate high expectations for all students?
Element 39: What do I typically do to demonstrate value and respect for low-expectancy students?
Element 40: What do I typically do to ask questions of low-expectancy students?
Element 41: What do I typically do to probe incorrect answers with low-expectancy students?

As depicted in table 1.1, the first major category, "Lesson Segments Involving Routine Events," addresses classroom strategies and behaviors that teachers should engage in on a routine basis, including establishing and communicating learning goals, tracking student progress, and celebrating student success and establishing and maintaining classroom rules and procedures. The second major category, "Lesson Segments Addressing Content," involves classroom strategies and behaviors that help students effectively interact with new knowledge, practice and deepen their understanding of new knowledge, and generate and test hypotheses about new knowledge. The third major category, "Lesson Segments Enacted on the Spot," addresses classroom strategies and behaviors for teachers to engage students, recognize and acknowledge adherence or lack of adherence to rules and procedures, establish and maintain effective relationships with students, and communicate high expectations for all students. Chapter 2 discusses this model in depth.

Setting Growth Goals

The road to expertise starts and ends with small steps. For the reflective teacher, this amounts to setting specific goals each year regarding classroom strategies and behaviors. For example, in a given year, a teacher might identify one growth goal related to routines, one growth goal related to content, and one growth goal related to on-the-spot elements. To establish these growth goals, a teacher would conduct a self-audit by rating himself or herself on each of the forty-one elements depicted in table 1.1 (page 12). This might be considered an aspect of what Schön (1987) referred to as "reflection-on-action" because it involves a retrospective examination of one's strengths and weaknesses. Chapter 3 provides tools and a process that allow teachers to score themselves using a scale or rubric with values that range from 0 to 4. As a result of this self-audit, a teacher might write explicit growth goals such as the following:

- By the end of the year, I will raise my score on tracking student progress from a 1 to a 3.

- By the end of the year, I will raise my score on helping students reflect on their learning from a 0 to a 3.

- By the end of the year, I will raise my score on using physical movement from a 1 to a 3.

These goals form the basis for the teacher's development over the course of the year.

Engaging in Focused Practice

Once a reflective teacher identifies growth goals, he or she engages in focused practice of specific strategies and behaviors related to his or her goals. The compendium (page 83) describes over 270 specific instructional strategies and teacher behaviors, organized by element so that teachers can quickly locate and learn about the strategies most relevant to their growth goals.

During this stage of development, the teacher is engaging in what Schön (1987) referred to as "reflection-in-action." There are many approaches a teacher might take. One approach is to *focus on specific steps of an instructional strategy*. For example, a teacher might decide to work with a two-column notes strategy to help her students reflect on their learning. This strategy has two major steps:

1. Ask students to write the important facts and information they recall from the lesson in the left-hand column of their notes.

2. Ask students to reread the facts and information they recorded and to write their reactions, questions, and extended ideas in the right-hand column of their notes.

The teacher might focus her practice on the first step, because it is crucial to successful use of the strategy. Students who have trouble selecting important facts and information for the left-hand column of their notes are unlikely to have meaningful reactions, questions, and extended ideas to record in the right-hand column.

Another approach is to *develop a protocol for a less well-defined strategy*. For example, a teacher might decide to work on using unobtrusive assessments to track student progress. Because this strategy does not have a well-defined set of steps, the teacher might create a protocol, or a set of general rules or guidelines, to specify the most useful actions while applying this strategy. The teacher might generate the following guidelines:

- Schedule time during class (such as during group work or seat work) to make unobtrusive assessments.

- Carry a copy of the scoring scale on my clipboard so I can easily assign a score to what I see students doing.

- Record unobtrusive assessment scores on my seating chart and transfer them to my gradebook every afternoon.

- Try to record at least three unobtrusive assessment scores each day.

A third approach is to *develop fluency with a particular strategy*. For example, a teacher might want to develop fluency with the corners strategy so that he can interact with students during the activity and gauge its effect on their learning. To develop that sort of expertise, the teacher would plan to use the corners strategy many times over the course of a quarter, semester, or year. Each time the teacher used the strategy, the steps of the strategy would become a little more fluid, and he could spend more time and mental energy interacting with students and monitoring their responses.

A fourth approach is to *make adaptations to an existing strategy*. For example, a teacher using the stand-up-and-stretch strategy in her class might notice that when students stand up to stretch, they begin moving around and talking, resulting in a long delay before she can begin teaching again. She might adapt this strategy in different ways to address this problem. One day she might ask her class to do a "silent stretch," and students who talk while stretching have to sit down. On another day, she might do a timed "talk and stretch," during which students are allowed to talk as much as they want until a timer goes off, at which time they are expected to quickly be quiet and sit down. On still another day, she might adapt the strategy to involve teacher-directed stretching motions accompanied by deep breathing exercises to help students relax and refocus.

A final approach is to *integrate several strategies*. For example, a teacher might decide to integrate reflective journals, think logs, and exit slips. Reflective journal questions pertain to the information presented during a lesson, and think log questions help students reflect on specific cognitive skills such as creative thinking, self-regulating, and drawing inferences. The teacher might prepare an exit slip with two reflective questions and two think log questions. The teacher could further integrate this strategy with the strategy of knowledge comparison by saving the exit slips students have turned in and presenting them to students at the end of the unit; students can then compare their previous levels of knowledge with their final levels of knowledge. Chapter 4 describes strategies for engaging in focused practice, and the compendium (page 83) provides a catalog of specific instructional strategies and teacher behaviors associated with each of the forty-one elements from the framework for effective teaching.

Receiving Focused Feedback

To facilitate the growth process, a teacher needs feedback on his or her use of specific instructional strategies and teacher behaviors related to his or her growth goals. This feedback can come from a variety of sources. One powerful source is video data. For example, a teacher might set up a video camera during a lesson in which she practices a specific strategy. After examining the video, the teacher might conclude that she has not yet met her goal for the strategy but is making progress. Another potential source of feedback is student surveys that ask about the extent to which a particular instructional strategy has helped students learn. Still another source is student achievement. Specifically, teacher-designed tests can be used to determine if students learn more when a particular strategy is used. Chapter 5 presents more detail on how this can be done.

The ultimate goal of focused feedback is for teachers to track their progress over time. Figure 1.3 (page 16) depicts this process.

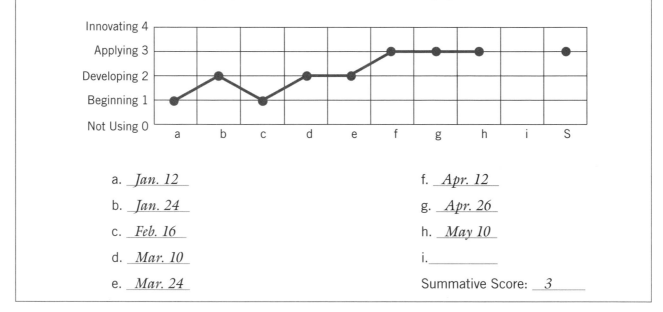

Figure 1.3: Teacher progress over time.

Source: Adapted from Marzano, 2010.

As shown in figure 1.3, this particular teacher chose to focus on using What Is the Question?, an instructional strategy related to her growth goal of using academic games. After considering feedback about her first use of the strategy on January 12, this teacher identified her initial level of performance as Beginning (1). However, as she continued to practice the strategy, the feedback she collected on her performance indicated that her use of the strategy was improving, and her scores gradually increased. She achieved her goal of Applying (3) on April 12, and her subsequent uses of the strategy at the same level on April 26 and May 10 confirmed that she was now at the Applying (3) level for the strategy of using What Is the Question? Therefore, she assigned herself a summative score of 3 for this strategy.

Observing and Discussing Teaching

The final element of our approach to becoming a reflective teacher is observing and discussing teaching. This can be done in a variety of ways. One way is to view videos of other teachers; many of these videos can be found on the Internet. To get the most out of the experience, teachers should view these videos with other teachers. For example, two teachers might view a video of a teacher presenting a lesson on the French Revolution. Since both teachers have articulated growth goals for specific elements of the framework, each can analyze the clip from different perspectives. One teacher might focus on how the teacher in the video clip attempted to increase the response rates of students, while the other teacher might focus on the clarity of the learning goals. After viewing the video clip, both teachers would discuss the strengths and weaknesses of the lesson they observed. Another option is to work with a coaching colleague—a fellow teacher who shares common pedagogical goals. Still a third option is to participate in instructional rounds. Here, groups of teachers visit other classrooms in the school or the district and discuss what they observed. Obviously, this takes a commitment in resources from administrators. Chapter 6 discusses the uses of videos, coaching colleagues, and instructional rounds.

Translating Research and Theory Into Practice

In subsequent chapters, we draw from the research and theory in this chapter and from sources such as *The Art and Science of Teaching* (Marzano, 2007) and *Effective Supervision* (Marzano et al., 2011) to discuss how reflection can be an effective tool for professional growth. As mentioned in the introduction, you will encounter comprehension questions to help you process the content presented as you progress through the remaining chapters. After completing each set of questions, you can check your answers with those in appendix A (page 179).

Chapter 2

HAVING A MODEL OF EFFECTIVE TEACHING

Regardless of the domain in which they operate, all experts have complex models that delineate precisely what to do in specific situations. In other words, they have models of effective performance. The more specific the model, the more nuanced the experts' behavior will be and the higher their level of expertise (Ambady & Rosenthal, 1992, 1993). To illustrate, chess masters can access approximately 10,000 to 100,000 possible moves, effectively forming a model or menu from which they can select the best moves depending on the placement of other pieces on the board (Gobet & Charness, 2006). Expert pilots have complex models that allow them to consider many variables (such as weather conditions and remaining fuel) when taking off, flying, landing, or reacting to unexpected situations (Durso & Dattel, 2006). The complex models that expert writers use to compose poetry or prose allow them to appropriately adapt their compositions to different genres, audiences, and expectations. Expert golfers use a complex model that takes into account ground conditions, obstacles, wind speed, and wind direction when selecting a club or planning a shot. Hockey player Wayne Gretzky's expertise has been attributed not to superior shot-making or skating abilities (Gretzky's shot-making was considered average or below), but to his superior understanding of the game:

> Gretzky can discern the game's underlying pattern and flow, and anticipate what's going to happen faster and in more detail than anyone else in the building. . . . Several times during a game you'll see him making what seem to be aimless circles on the other side of the rink from the traffic, and then, as if answering a signal, he'll dart ahead to a spot where, an instant later, the puck turns up. (McGrath, 1997, para. 28–29)

Gretzky's model of the hockey game allows him to accurately predict and instantaneously react to events during a game.

As mentioned previously, this book uses a specific model of effective teaching from *The Art and Science of Teaching* (Marzano, 2007; Marzano & Brown, 2009). In its entirety, the model addresses four overarching domains: (1) classroom strategies and behaviors, (2) planning and preparing, (3) reflecting on teaching, and (4) collegiality and professionalism. For a discussion of the complete model, see *Effective Supervision* (Marzano et al., 2011). In this book, we focus on the first domain of the complete model, classroom strategies and behaviors, which has three major categories: (1) lesson segments involving routine events, (2) lesson segments addressing content, and (3) lesson segments enacted on the spot.

Lesson Segments Involving Routine Events

As their name implies, elements of lesson segments involving routine events are executed on a regular basis, if not daily. In our model, these routine elements are organized into two design questions: (1) What will I do to establish and communicate learning goals, track student progress, and celebrate success? and (2) What will I do to establish and maintain classroom rules and procedures?

What Will I Do to Establish and Communicate Learning Goals, Track Student Progress, and Celebrate Success?

A teacher might ask this design question periodically to keep in mind the important elements of this particular aspect of good teaching. Specific elements associated with this design question include:

- Providing clear learning goals and scales to measure those goals (for example, the teacher provides or reminds students about a specific learning goal)

- Tracking student progress (for example, using formative assessment, the teacher helps students chart their individual and group progress on a learning goal)

- Celebrating student success (for example, the teacher helps students acknowledge and celebrate their current status on a learning goal as well as knowledge gain)

The central focus of these elements ensures that students clearly and explicitly understand the learning goal and are continually aware of their progress toward that goal. Growth toward the goal and students' final status can and should be celebrated. To illustrate how these elements might manifest in the classroom, consider the following vignettes at the elementary, middle, and high school levels.

Mr. Tucker and his fourth-grade colleagues have been working together to create clear learning goals and corresponding proficiency scales for the language arts content they will teach this year. Mr. Tucker uses these goals to guide his teaching and his expectations for students in his classroom. For example, the learning goal for his current unit is "Students will make logical inferences and defend their conclusions." Mr. Tucker posts this goal in his classroom at the beginning of his language arts block and discusses the corresponding proficiency scale with his students. He also shows exemplars from past classes that illustrate what each level of performance looks like. He refers to the scale regularly, and his students use a graph to track their progress throughout the unit. Justin, a student in Mr. Tucker's class, has just achieved a score of 3.0 for the learning goal by independently creating an appropriate inference during his small reading group discussion. Mr. Tucker takes a moment to celebrate Justin's success, highlighting Justin's progress from a 2.0 earlier that week. Mr. Tucker asks each student in his small group to share a specific compliment about how Justin's inferring skills have improved. Justin takes a copy of the scale home that night to explain his progress to his parents. Before beginning the next unit, Mr. Tucker posts the new learning goals, and his students create new tracking charts and personal learning goals for the next unit.

Ms. Lavold, a middle school language arts teacher, is teaching a creative writing unit with an emphasis on revision for the next two weeks. She is using the learning goals and scales she and her teammates created as a part of their professional learning community. At the beginning of the unit, Ms. Lavold provides students with a handout describing the learning goals for their upcoming work, along with student-friendly proficiency scales. These goals include revising for tense, voice, and point of view, as well as checking for clarity with peer editors. Ms. Lavold spends time directly teaching information about tense, voice, and point of view, and highlights examples of their effective use in writing samples. She also describes what peer editing looks like and models the process with a student volunteer. She reviews the scales with students and explains exactly what each level looks like, assuring students that she will provide the knowledge and support they need to reach a proficient score of 3.0 or 4.0. Next, she asks students to record a personal learning goal for the unit on the back of the handout. She invites students to share their personal goals, and for students who are having trouble coming up with a personal goal, Ms. Lavold previews some of the main ideas of the unit. During the unit, she scores each piece of student writing using the scale, and students track and reflect on their progress along the way. By the end of the unit, nearly every student has shown growth on their goals, and Ms. Lavold celebrates the knowledge gain of the class as a whole and of individual students. Using the scale, students describe their learning and growth to their parents during a student-led conference, highlighting where they started and how they have grown in their understanding of revision and creative writing.

Mr. Garcia is beginning a new unit in his trigonometry course, and though he regularly posts the learning goals for each unit at the front of the classroom, he knows that their technical language can sometimes be confusing and even intimidating to students. Because of this, he takes time at the beginning of class to make connections between students' prior knowledge and the new learning goal. He explains how the new learning goal progresses logically from what they have already learned. He also shares the scale for the current learning goal with them and shows students what performance looks like for each level of the scale, highlighting and explaining new terminology students might not be familiar with.

As the unit progresses, he continually refers to the learning goal, specifically noting which parts the day's lesson will address. He allows students to work in cooperative teams so they can support each other's understanding while he monitors each group's work and checks in with individual students. At the end of the day, his students complete a "ticket out the door" so he can assess each student's progress toward the learning goal. He uses the information from these tickets to plan whole-group, small-group, and individual instruction for the next day. Students have many opportunities to demonstrate their understanding. For example, on each assignment, he includes questions that reflect each level on the scale, so he can clearly see how students are progressing. He also uses planned and pop quizzes to monitor students' learning prior to the unit exam. Students record their scores from each assessment and use their academic notebooks to record what they understand well, what they are getting better at, and what they still need to work on. Throughout the unit, Mr. Garcia meets with students about their progress, pointing out growth and celebrating gains. He uses the school's electronic grading system to communicate student progress to parents, attaching electronic copies of the scale with previous and current student performance levels highlighted.

What Will I Do to Establish and Maintain Classroom Rules and Procedures?

Specific elements associated with this design question include:

- Establishing classroom routines (for example, the teacher reminds students of a rule or procedure or establishes a new rule or procedure)

- Organizing the physical layout of the classroom for learning (for example, the teacher organizes materials, traffic patterns, and displays to enhance learning)

The elements of this design question help ensure a safe, orderly, and predictable classroom. To illustrate how these elements might manifest in the classroom, consider the following vignettes at the elementary, middle, and high school levels.

Miss Bock and her first graders created a set of rules and procedures for their classroom at the beginning of the year. Every couple of weeks, Miss Bock holds a class meeting to monitor how things are going in the classroom.

During one meeting, Keisha says, "Kids at the listening center aren't following the rule that says we're supposed to take care of materials in the classroom. Nobody puts the headphones away when they're done, so the cords get tangled and trip people who are walking by."

Miss Bock asks Keisha for a possible solution, and Keisha suggests making a procedure for the listening center. Miss Bock asks other students for ideas, and eventually the class votes to create a better set of procedures for the listening center. Together, they discuss the necessary steps to a safe and orderly center. Miss Bock asks small groups to draw what the listening center should look like when everything is organized and put away properly. Then the class uses the small groups' drawings to create a single picture showing what the listening center should look like when it isn't being used, and Keisha hangs the picture on the wall next to the center to remind everyone of what is expected. Keisha agrees to be the weekly monitor of the center and to celebrate each time the class follows the rules by adding a star to the class's compliment chart.

Mr. Labron, a middle school mathematics teacher, takes time during the first few weeks of class to establish classroom routines with his students. Rather than trying to talk about all of the class rules and procedures in one class period, he focuses on a new rule or procedure each day for a few weeks. Mr. Labron creates a classroom poster with the rules and procedures that he and the students sign as an indication of understanding and agreement. He also sends a copy of the classroom rules and procedures home to his students' parents. Every few weeks, Mr. Labron spends a few minutes of class reviewing the rules and procedures and asks students if any revisions need to be made.

To facilitate learning, Mr. Labron has organized his classroom to accommodate various groupings. Students usually start the day in a base group, where they can review homework collaboratively. Mr. Labron teaches students how to quickly move from their base groups to new working partners or teams of four. He arranges the students' desks so that every desk is within a few steps of where he stands during whole-group instruction. He also designates baskets in the classroom to hold additional copies of assignments, notes from home, or finished work. Establishing and using these procedures allows Mr. Labron to spend more time teaching and less time answering procedural questions.

Ms. Berry knows that students tend to gravitate to the back of the classroom to avoid participation. To counteract this, she organizes the desks in a large circle. During whole-group instruction, she uses instructional techniques—like Socratic seminar—that work especially well with this configuration. She also reviews rules and procedures regularly, and during the first few weeks of school, she asks students to pick one or two and explain the rationale for the rule or procedure to the class. She emphasizes that the rules and procedures are designed to promote a collaborative atmosphere, rather than to restrict students' freedom. She is careful to monitor her own behaviors and provides more flexibility as students demonstrate responsibility and respect. She sends copies of the class policies home to parents and posts them electronically via her school's parent portal.

Ms. Barry regularly monitors how well students are adhering to the rules and procedures, giving compliments or support as needed.

Lesson Segments Addressing Content

Elements of lesson segments addressing content are organized into three design questions: (1) What will I do to help students effectively interact with new knowledge?, (2) What will I do to help students practice and deepen their understanding of new knowledge?, and (3) What will I do to help students generate and test hypotheses about new knowledge?

What Will I Do to Help Students Effectively Interact With New Knowledge?

Specific elements associated with this design question include:

- Identifying critical information (for example, the teacher provides cues as to which information is important)

- Organizing students to interact with new knowledge (for example, the teacher organizes students into pairs or triads to discuss small chunks of content)

- Previewing new content (for example, the teacher uses strategies such as K-W-L, advance organizers, and preview questions)

- Chunking content into digestible bites (for example, the teacher presents content in small portions tailored to students' level of understanding)

- Processing new information (for example, after each chunk of information, the teacher asks students to summarize and clarify what they have experienced)

- Elaborating on new information (for example, the teacher asks questions that require students to make and defend inferences)

- Recording and representing knowledge (for example, the teacher asks students to summarize, take notes, or use nonlinguistic representations)

- Reflecting on learning (for example, the teacher asks students to reflect on what they understand or what they are still confused about)

As these elements illustrate, lessons devoted to introducing new content employ a direct instruction approach and take quite a bit of preparation. The teacher must organize the content into small, digestible bites. The less students know about the content, the smaller the bites. These are the focus of the lesson. Additionally, the teacher must identify previewing activities, activities to facilitate student interaction after each bite, activities that help students elaborate on what they have learned, activities that facilitate student representation of what they have learned, and activities that allow students to reflect on what they have learned. Finally, throughout the entire process, the teacher points out the most important information. To illustrate how these elements might manifest in the classroom, consider the following vignettes at the elementary, middle, and high school levels.

Mr. Delaney's fifth-grade class is learning about colonial America, specifically about the everyday life of settlers like those in Jamestown. To preview the concept of everyday life in the American colonies, he asks students what they can remember or think they already know about life during colonial times. As students respond, he lists their answers on the board. Then he organizes the students into groups of four and shows a video clip about life in colonial America. After about three minutes, he stops the clip and asks one student in each group to explain what he or she has learned so far to the other members of the group. The other members of the group then ask questions; any questions the group cannot answer are shared with the class, and Mr. Delaney answers them. Then Mr. Delaney plays another two minutes of the video and asks students to repeat the process, with a different group member explaining what has been learned so far.

Mr. Delaney continues to play short chunks of the video until all group members have had a turn summarizing their learning. He then asks questions that were not explicitly addressed in the video, and when students volunteer answers, he asks them to explain how they came to their answers. Finally, Mr. Delaney asks each group to write a short paragraph about what they learned from the video and their discussions and to create a graphic representation of the information from the video. Before students leave, they answer the following two questions in their academic notebooks: (1) What did I learn today? and (2) What am I still confused about?

Mrs. Haskell, a middle school science teacher, looks forward to teaching her students about sea turtles. She begins by engaging students in a K-W-L activity in which students share what they already know about sea turtles and what they'd like to learn during this unit. She then starts showing a short informational video about sea turtles. After four minutes, Mrs. Haskell stops the video and asks students to form random triads by numbering off in 3s.

She asks group member 1 to share everything he or she remembers from the first segment of the video with the other two members of the triad, asks 2 to summarize what 1 said, and asks 3 to fill in other additional information that 1 may have missed. Then Mrs. Haskell shows another three minutes of the video and asks students to discuss, in their groups, three inferential questions based on what they have learned so far. After the final few minutes of the video, Mrs. Haskell asks each student to draw a nonlinguistic representation of his or her new learning and post it on the bulletin board at the front of the room. She then reads a series of summary statements and questions and has students use green, yellow, and red cards to indicate their current level of understanding (green = solid; yellow = a bit unsure; red = confused). After class, Mrs. Haskell uses feedback from this activity to design the next day's lesson, making sure that she addresses any misunderstandings or areas where students seemed unsure or confused.

Ms. Houser's family and consumer science class is beginning a unit on preparing food in healthy ways. Her students already understand how to identify healthy and unhealthy foods, but she knows they also need to understand that the nutritional value of various foods can change based on how they are cooked. She begins by reviewing basic information students already know about cooking—which methods (such as frying) tend to be unhealthy and which methods (such as steaming or grilling) are usually healthier. She then asks two preview questions about the new content: (1) Are green vegetables healthier when eaten raw or when steamed? and (2) Why can some fish be eaten raw while other fish cannot? Next, she teaches students about the chemical changes meat and vegetables undergo when they are exposed to heat. She breaks this content into small segments. After each segment, students interact in pairs to summarize what they have just heard and to speculate on what they might hear next. At the end of class, students make graphic representations of what they have learned and explain their representations to other students.

What Will I Do to Help Students Practice and Deepen Their Understanding of New Knowledge?

Specific elements associated with this design question include:

- Reviewing content (for example, the teacher briefly reviews related content addressed previously)

- Organizing students to practice and deepen knowledge (for example, the teacher organizes students into groups designed to review information or practice skills)

- Using homework (for example, the teacher uses homework for independent practice or to elaborate on information)

- Examining similarities and differences (for example, the teacher engages students in comparing, classifying, and creating analogies and metaphors)

- Examining errors in reasoning (for example, the teacher asks students to examine informal fallacies, propaganda, and bias)

- Practicing skills, strategies, and processes (for example, the teacher uses massed and distributed practice)

- Revising knowledge (for example, the teacher asks students to revise entries in notebooks to clarify and add to previous information)

Lessons designed to practice and deepen knowledge typically begin with a review of the previously introduced content. After the review, the teacher uses a number of techniques that can help students deepen their understanding of content. For many of these activities, which include examining similarities and differences and examining errors in reasoning, students are organized into groups. If the focus of a lesson is a skill or process, the teacher facilitates practice activities. These activities commonly start in class but are then completed as homework. Finally, many of these lessons end with students revising previous notes about the content or adding to entries in their academic notebooks. To illustrate how these elements might manifest in the classroom, consider the following vignettes at the elementary, middle, and high school levels.

> Mr. Su's kindergarten class has been learning about sound and how it is caused by vibrations. After students watch a short video clip of a harpist playing, Mr. Su says, "Did you see how the strings moved when the lady plucked them? Who remembers the word we use to describe something moving back and forth very quickly?"
>
> "Vibration!" the class answers.

"That's right," says Mr. Su, "and remember how we talked about how vibrating things often make a noise? Put your hand on your throat, and make a noise like this: 'Ahhhhhhh.' What do you feel?"

"My insides are shaking," says Rianna.

"Is there a word we could use to describe that shaking feeling, class?" asks Mr. Su.

"Vibration!" replies Jimmy.

Mr. Su then groups students around several xylophones he borrowed from the music teacher and has them compare the sound the bigger pipes make when they vibrate to the sounds the smaller pipes make when they vibrate.

"I think that bigger things vibrate and smaller things don't," says Seann. "I can see the big pipes moving, but the smaller ones aren't."

To help Seann clear up his misconception, Mr. Su says, "Remember, sometimes you can't see everything that is happening, so you have to use your other senses to get information."

For homework that night, he asks students to find three things in their house that make a sound when they vibrate.

Mrs. Haskell's class is continuing their unit on sea turtles. At the end of class one day, Mrs. Haskell asks students to create summaries of what they have learned so far. After reading the summaries, she realizes she needs to clear up a few misconceptions at the beginning of class the next day. She moves students into pairs and asks them to compare sea turtles to gray wolves, another endangered species being studied, using a Venn diagram. After creating diagrams, pairs share them with other groups using a give one, get one strategy. Mrs. Haskell asks students to write two paragraphs about the similarities and differences of sea turtles and gray wolves for homework that evening. Mrs. Haskell then returns to the K-W-L chart from the beginning of the unit and asks the class to revise anything that needs to be changed and to add to the column representing what students have learned about sea turtles.

In his current issues class, Mr. Milano's students are studying a series of revolutions that have occurred in several African nations. At the beginning of the lesson, Mr. Milano asks students what they remember about revolutions from the previous lesson. As students volunteer answers, Mr. Milano lists them on the board. Then Mr. Milano selects two revolutions from the list and has students examine how the situations in which they began are similar to or different from current situations in the African nations. Next, he presents a series of statements that revolutionaries in both situations made and asks students to look for errors in reasoning in the statements. Students complete this activity in small groups and share their conclusions during a whole-class discussion. For homework, Mr. Milano asks students to revise the revolutionaries' statements to reflect more logical claims and reasoning. Before leaving class, students record new insights in their academic notebooks and revise previous entries in light of what they learned that day.

What Will I Do to Help Students Generate and Test Hypotheses About New Knowledge?

Specific elements associated with this design question include:

- Organizing students for cognitively complex tasks (for example, the teacher organizes students into small groups to facilitate cognitively complex tasks)

- Engaging students in cognitively complex tasks involving hypothesis generation and testing (for example, the teacher engages students in decision-making tasks, problem-solving tasks, experimental inquiry tasks, and investigation tasks)

- Providing resources and guidance (for example, the teacher makes resources available that are specific to cognitively complex tasks and helps students execute such tasks)

Lessons devoted to generating and testing hypotheses are much more student-directed than the other two types of lessons addressing content. The driving force behind lessons that involve generating and testing hypotheses is that students apply what they have learned—they predict the results of specific tasks and then carry out the tasks to determine if their predictions are correct. Here the teaching role is one of guide and resource provider. To illustrate how these elements might manifest in the classroom, consider the following vignettes at the elementary, middle, and high school levels.

Mrs. Wills's fifth-grade class is learning to use an algorithm to multiply two- and three-digit numbers. In order to help students extend their knowledge, Mrs. Wills asks them to experiment with different ways to multiply numbers. For example, she asks, "What would happen if you just multiplied each number by the one beneath it and added up the answers?" In small groups, students predict an outcome and experiment with different ways to multiply larger numbers. Felicia's group comes up with a new algorithm that involves breaking numbers down into hundreds, tens, and ones and multiplying each part separately. Sam's group creates a strategy that uses similar principles but is expressed differently. As students predict and experiment, Mrs. Wills circulates around the classroom, asking questions and clarifying misconceptions. Afterward, she facilitates a class discussion in which groups share what they learned or discovered and whether or not their predictions were correct.

After studying a number of different endangered species, Mrs. Haskell asks her students to design projects to generate and test hypotheses about the topic. She poses the following questions to help them figure out what to focus on: Is there a particular problem you would like to examine using the information we have been studying regarding endangered species? Is there a particular decision you would like to examine using the information we have been studying regarding endangered species? Is there a particular concept, past event, or hypothetical event you would like to examine using the information we have been studying? Mrs. Haskell confers with students individually about their projects, helping them clarify their action plans and identify potential resources as they design their studies. She also makes sure that students predict what they will find as a result of their projects. After projects are completed, students will revisit their predictions. As students work on their projects over the next three days, Mrs. Haskell acts as a guide and a coach, moving around the room, checking in with and assisting each student. At the end of the week, she invites students to share their projects with one another during a project fair, where each student presents his or her research and learning and provides feedback to other students using specific criteria.

Ms. Munro's high school students are studying World War II. After assigning them to groups of three, she asks each group to conduct an investigation of an event or concept related to the war. Natalie's group decides to focus on the Battle of Midway and to examine what would have happened if the United States had not broken the Japanese code warning of the attack. They speculate that the United States might not have completed the necessary repairs to its aircraft carriers and that the Japanese might have won the battle and even the war. They predict ways that life in the United States today would be different if that hypothetical outcome were true. Then they collect information about the Battle of Midway and use it to determine how probable or improbable their predicted outcome would be.

Other groups of students select different events that occurred during World War II. Ms. Munro assists each group by providing or helping them find the resources and information they need to complete their projects. She also helps them plan their next steps and stay on schedule. After each group finishes their project, Ms. Munro asks students to go back and examine their original prediction to see if their findings are consistent or inconsistent with it. Each student then journals about how his or her thinking has changed over the course of the project.

Lesson Segments Enacted on the Spot

Elements of lesson segments enacted on the spot are those a teacher is prepared to use but has not necessarily planned for a specific day or lesson. These on-the-spot elements are organized into four design questions: (1) What will I do to engage students?, (2) What will I do to recognize and acknowledge adherence or lack of adherence to rules and procedures?, (3) What will I do to establish and maintain effective relationships with students?, and (4) What will I do to communicate high expectations for all students? An effective teacher consistently scans the classroom to determine if students are engaged, if students are being acknowledged for adherence to rules and procedures as well as lack of adherence, if students are being treated in a manner that indicates the teacher cares for them, and if the students are being sent signals that the teacher believes they can all do well in class. If these messages are not being conveyed, the teacher adjusts his or her behaviors.

What Will I Do to Engage Students?

Specific elements associated with this design question include:

- Noticing when students are not engaged (for example, the teacher scans the classroom to monitor students' level of engagement)

- Using academic games (for example, when students are not engaged, the teacher uses adaptations of popular games to re-engage them and focus their attention on academic content)

- Managing response rates during questioning (for example, the teacher uses strategies such as response cards or response chaining and voting technologies to ensure multiple students respond to questions)

- Using physical movement (for example, the teacher uses strategies that require students to move physically, such as voting with their feet, and physical reenactments of content)

- Maintaining a lively pace (for example, the teacher slows and quickens the pace of instruction in such a way as to enhance engagement)

- Demonstrating intensity and enthusiasm (for example, the teacher uses verbal and nonverbal signals to show enthusiasm about the content)

- Using friendly controversy (for example, the teacher uses techniques that require students to take and defend a position about content)

- Providing opportunities for students to talk about themselves (for example, the teacher uses techniques that allow students to relate content to their personal lives and interests)

- Presenting unusual or intriguing information (for example, the teacher provides or encourages the identification of intriguing information about the content)

The first element in this list is the starting place for effective engagement. Simply stated, to stimulate and maintain student engagement, a teacher must constantly evaluate the extent of students' attention. If students are engaged, the teacher continues on with the lesson. If not, the teacher uses one of the other elements listed to re-engage students. To illustrate how these elements might manifest in the classroom, consider the following vignettes at the elementary, middle, and high school levels.

> Mrs. Harvey is an elementary school music teacher. While teaching a unit on reading and notating music, she uses a variety of engagement strategies whenever she notices that her fourth graders seem disengaged. Sometimes she has them stand up and create body representations for a whole note, a half note, a quarter note, and an eighth note. Other times she uses a game in which one student creates a grouping of four notes, rests, or other musical notation symbols, and another student decides which one doesn't belong and explains why. She frequently passes out small dry-erase boards so students can respond to her questions simultaneously. When she sees that all of the students are answering her questions correctly, she speeds up the pace of instruction and adds extension activities so they can explore specific elements of notation that interest them. Several students use computer composition software to alter the duration of each note in a well-known song, creating an entirely new song. When they disagree about "what sounds good," they engage in a friendly controversy activity called "opposite point of view" to develop alternative perspectives. She also inserts interesting details into many of her lessons. For example, one day she tells students about John Cage, a composer who flipped a coin to make composition decisions, wrote music for the "prepared piano" (a piano with different objects placed beneath its strings), and composed a piece of music called "4'33"," which is simply four minutes and thirty-three seconds of silence.

> Mrs. Colton, an eighth-grade art teacher, continually scans her classroom to check on students' levels of engagement. She also maintains a high level of enthusiasm for the content and presents important information with lots of intensity. If the energy level in her classroom feels a bit low, Mrs. Colton uses academic games to help students practice and review content. Because she uses games regularly, students understand the rules clearly and know what behavior is expected of them. They also know that Mrs. Colton won't use points from the game for their grades. One popular game that students often request is Talk a Mile a Minute. Mrs. Colton writes a category

on the board above a list of words that fit in that category. When the student looking at the list has gotten his or her partner (facing away from the list) to say all the words, the pair stands up. Mrs. Colton encourages students to incorporate physical movement into the game by allowing them to use gestures or body representations to communicate with their partners. When students are working on projects, Mrs. Colton helps them make connections to their own lives by selecting subjects or themes that are important to them. Mrs. Colton knows that students remember content at a deeper level when they've made connections to their own interests.

Mr. Roy is a master at engaging students in his AP language arts class. He maintains a lively pace when he teaches but is careful not to move so fast that he frustrates students. He walks around the room while teaching, and his eye contact has become legendary. "It's impossible not to pay attention when he's looking at you. . . . It's like he's so excited about what he's saying, and he wants you to be excited, too!" one of his students comments. He loves to share wacky, interesting, and unusual anecdotes about the authors and books they study, and his students know they will never have to sit still through a class period. He always has them up out of their chairs, acting out scenes from novels or moving around the classroom to express different opinions. One of his favorite activities is to "fold" a line. Students line up according to their opinion (from "strongly disagree" to "strongly agree"). Next, Mr. Roy asks one side of the line to fold, so that the students with the strongest opposing opinions become partners. Partners each get thirty seconds to share their perspective while the other partner listens. Then they switch roles. As a follow up, Mr. Roy asks each student to write a persuasive essay on the topic, keeping in mind the opposite perspectives they were exposed to. Finally, students find connections between authors and characters in the books they are reading and their own lives.

What Will I Do to Recognize and Acknowledge Adherence or Lack of Adherence to Rules and Procedures?

Specific elements associated with this design question include:

- Demonstrating withitness (for example, the teacher is aware of variations in students' behavior that might indicate potential disruptions and attends to them immediately)

- Applying consequences for lack of adherence to rules and procedures (for example, the teacher applies consequences for lack of adherence to rules and procedures consistently and fairly)

- Acknowledging adherence to rules and procedures (for example, the teacher acknowledges adherence to rules and procedures consistently and fairly)

Teachers apply these elements as needed. For example, if the teacher senses a possibility of disruptive behavior in the classroom, then he employs strategies associated with withitness. However, if everything is running smoothly, then he does not employ the strategies. To illustrate how these elements might manifest in the classroom, consider the following vignettes at the elementary, middle, and high school levels.

During a centers activity, Mr. Young has noticed a group of his second graders whispering and giggling together at the literature center. He moves closer to the group and makes eye contact with them. Most of them then get back on task, but two students are still being noisy and are looking at something written on a piece of paper. Mr. Young quietly approaches these students and collects the piece of paper.

"Please rejoin your group's activity at the center," he requests. "You may be able to help them solve the problem they're working on."

The boys re-engage and soon focus on the task at hand. When the group shares their work at the end of the center rotation, Mr. Young recognizes the work of all the groups, adding a marble to the class compliment jar as recognition for a job well done. Before centers the next day, Mr. Young reminds the group from the literature center of the rules and procedures for on-task work during center rotations, and he arranges a signal to let them know if their behavior is becoming inappropriate.

Students in Mrs. Song's Chinese classes say she has eyes in the back of her head. She is keenly aware of what's happening throughout her classroom at all times and can usually head off any problems quickly. She has noticed that the sooner she catches a situation, the better. She respects her students and teaches them to respect her in return. In situations in which unobtrusive corrections don't work, Mrs. Song uses more direct methods or meets privately with students to discuss problems they are having in class. She notices that when middle school students are not in front of their peers, they tend to be more honest and willing to cooperate. Mrs. Song regularly recognizes good behavior by thanking students for specific things they have done to create a well-functioning classroom, and she often follows up with a positive note or phone call to their parents. Students appreciate being honored for what they're doing well, and an atmosphere of calmness and safety permeates Mrs. Song's classes.

Mrs. Norris, a high school physical education teacher, has noticed that her students have not been following the procedure for putting their jerseys and basketballs away after class. The next day, she points this out to them and takes time at the beginning of class to review the procedure. When it is time to put equipment away, she reminds them again about the procedure and their discussion. Her students do an excellent job of following the procedure that day and the next. She recognizes the class as a whole for this adherence, but also stands at the door and thanks specific students who were particularly careful to put the equipment away neatly. She points out that their efforts not only help the equipment last longer but also allow other students to find what they need quickly.

What Will I Do to Establish and Maintain Effective Relationships With Students?

Specific elements associated with this design question include:

- Understanding students' interests and backgrounds (for example, the teacher seeks out knowledge about students and uses that knowledge to engage in informal, friendly discussions with students)

- Using verbal and nonverbal behaviors that indicate affection for students (for example, the teacher uses humor and friendly banter appropriately with students)

- Displaying objectivity and control (for example, the teacher behaves in ways that indicate he or she does not take infractions personally)

These elements are typically an aspect of every lesson. That is, the teacher always strives to communicate that he or she understands students' interests, likes each student, and so on. To illustrate how these elements might manifest in the classroom, consider the following vignettes at the elementary, middle, and high school levels.

Miss Faden, a physical education teacher, is working to develop relationships with the students at her elementary school. Every morning, she stands at the front door and greets students by name and with a high five as they enter the building. At six foot four, she is very tall, and sometimes playfully challenges students to try to jump up and touch her outstretched hand. When she has time, she attends after-school activities like athletic events, recitals, or award ceremonies for students with whom she is having difficulty developing a relationship or who seem alienated in her class. In class, she talks about how the fitness skills they develop in PE will help them perform better in sports and in other activities as they continue to grow. When students behave inappropriately in class, Miss Faden calmly asks them if they need to take a time-out or if they want to participate fully in what the class is doing. She never acts annoyed or angry when she corrects students. She is respectful and kind, yet clearly communicates her expectations for everyone to improve their personal fitness.

Mrs. Swanson works hard to establish and maintain effective relationships with her homeroom students. She can often be heard saying, "I believe in each and every one of you and am here to provide you with the guidance necessary to be successful at school both academically and behaviorally." Mrs. Swanson greets each student at the door, checking in with them and asking them questions. She also makes sure she knows the names of all her students within the first week of school and asks students to fill out interest surveys so she can learn unique facts about each of them. Mrs. Swanson uses these facts to personalize the learning activities in her classroom and connect the content to students' lives.

Mr. Rodriguez has always prided himself on his objectivity and control in the classroom. One day, however, his coaching colleague, Ms. Jackson, observes very little levity in his class.

"The students seem almost afraid to approach you with questions," she says. "How would you describe your relationship with your students?"

Mr. Rodriguez realizes that he doesn't really have relationships with his students beyond what is necessary to maintain order in his classroom. He also realizes that his impersonal demeanor may prevent students from coming to him with problems or questions. Ms. Jackson invites him to observe her classroom, where students regularly laugh and joke with the teacher in a respectful way, and where students feel comfortable bringing up aspects of the content that are confusing or unclear to them. In his own class, Mr. Rodriguez decides to lighten the atmosphere by incorporating humor and friendly banter with students into his lessons. He also starts reading the school newspaper and eating lunch in the cafeteria one day a week to try to learn more about his students' interests and achievements, and he incorporates those interests into lessons whenever he can. He discovers that he can maintain an orderly classroom environment while helping his students feel more welcome and comfortable in class.

What Will I Do to Communicate High Expectations for All Students?

Specific elements associated with this design question include:

- Demonstrating value and respect for low-expectancy students (for example, the teacher demonstrates the same positive affective tone with low-expectancy students as with high-expectancy students)

- Asking questions of low-expectancy students (for example, the teacher asks questions of low-expectancy students with the same frequency and level of difficulty as with high-expectancy students)

- Probing incorrect answers with low-expectancy students (for example, the teacher inquires into incorrect answers from low-expectancy students with the same depth and rigor as those from high-expectancy students)

Like the elements for maintaining effective relationships, teachers should consider using those listed here in every lesson. Each student should receive the tacit message from the teacher daily that they are expected to accomplish great things in class and that the teacher is there to help them. To illustrate how these elements might manifest in the classroom, consider the following vignettes at the elementary, middle, and high school levels.

Mrs. Pennell teaches a combination fourth- and fifth-grade class. Although she thought that she was basing her expectations for students on their grade level, when she took time to analyze her expectations for each individual student, she realized that each student's ethnicity, socio-economic status, and personality played a subtle role in determining her level of expectation for that student's achievement. Although this realization distressed her, she decided to take steps to help communicate high expectations to all students. On her seating chart, she identified those students for whom she had lower expectations, and she now makes a point to elicit the same depth of responses from them as from her high-expectancy students. She has also started calling on students randomly and using response chaining strategies to make sure she requires *all* students to listen and participate in class discussions.

At the beginning of each quarter, Mr. Rundle uses an informal observation form to examine his behavior toward students for whom he realizes he doesn't have high expectations. As embarrassed as he is about finding that he has different expectations for different students, he is determined to treat all students the same. He uses a video camera to tape himself during several class periods, and he reviews the tape to look for differential treatment. Mr. Rundle monitors his affective tone as well as the quality of his interactions with all students, but especially for those that he has identified as low-expectancy students. Mr. Rundle focuses on making frequent eye contact with these students, smiling at them, and engaging them in informal dialogue about their lives, their families, and their interests. Later in the year, Mr. Rundle tapes himself again and pleasingly discovers that his behavior has indeed changed. Remarkably, so have the academic behaviors of the students!

Mr. Giokas has identified low-expectancy students in his class, and he uses specific strategies to involve them in class discussions. He plans specific higher-level questions for these students ahead of time and makes sure to use random questioning strategies. When he asks a question, he always states the question first, without drawing anyone's name, provides three to five seconds of wait time, and then provides a chance for students to think about their question responses in groups. He also allows students to answer using their group's answer (instead of an individual response), so that all students can feel publicly successful. He regularly asks probing questions to help students elaborate on why they believe their answer is correct. When a student answers a question incorrectly, he makes sure to identify what parts of the answers are correct and to thank the student for his or her contribution. If a student gets flustered, he lets him or her off the hook, but follows up to make sure that the student understands the information being studied.

Summary

This chapter presented a model of effective teaching derived from *The Art and Science of Teaching* (Marzano, 2007), which forms the basis for engaging in reflective practice. Three major categories comprise the model: (1) lesson segments involving routine events, (2) lesson segments addressing content, and (3) lesson segments enacted on the spot. We discussed the specific elements of each category and provided vignettes to illustrate the use of these elements in elementary, middle, and high school settings.

Chapter 2: Comprehension Questions

1. Why is a model of effective performance in a domain important to the development of expertise in that domain?

2. What is the overall structure of the model of effective teaching presented in this chapter?

3. What is the difference between elements of lesson segments involving routine events, elements of lesson segments addressing content, and elements of lesson segments enacted on the spot?

4. How are lessons where students generate and test hypotheses different from the other types of lessons addressing content?

Chapter 3

SETTING GROWTH GOALS

Reflective teachers systematically set annual growth goals for themselves. For example, during a given year, a particular teacher might decide to work on one element from each of the three broad categories (lesson segments involving routine events, lesson segments addressing content, and lesson segments enacted on the spot) described in chapter 2. From the category of routine segments, the teacher might work on tracking student progress. From the category of content segments, the teacher might work on engaging students in cognitively complex tasks. From the category of on-the-spot segments, the teacher might work on noticing and reacting when students are not engaged. Strategic selection of what to work on begins with an audit of a teacher's strengths and weaknesses.

Conducting a Self-Audit

Conducting a self-audit involves determining one's level of competence for each of the forty-one elements described in chapter 2. To do this, a teacher needs a rubric or scale for each element. Scales for the forty-one elements are provided in appendix B (page 185). To understand the nature of the scale, consider its generic form shown in table 3.1.

Table 3.1: Generic Form of the Scale

4 Innovating	3 Applying	2 Developing	1 Beginning	0 Not Using
The teacher adapts or creates a new version of the strategy or behavior for unique student needs and situations.	The teacher uses the strategy or behavior and monitors the extent to which it affects student outcomes.	The teacher uses the strategy or behavior but does so in a somewhat mechanistic way.	The teacher uses the strategy or behavior incorrectly or with parts missing.	The teacher should use the strategy or behavior but does not.

In the generic form of the scale, Not Using (0) means that strategies or behaviors related to an element are called for in the classroom, but the teacher does not use them. A teacher who scores himself as Not Using (0) for an element indicates that he is unaware of strategies and behaviors related to that element. At the Beginning (1) level, a teacher recognizes that strategies or behaviors related to an element are called for and attempts to use them but executes the strategies or behaviors incorrectly or with parts missing. A teacher at the Developing (2) level uses strategies and behaviors related to an element in the classroom but in a somewhat mechanistic way (that is, she fails to monitor how students respond to the strategies or behaviors and how they affect desired student outcomes). Applying (3) means that the teacher not only effectively uses strategies or behaviors related to an element but also monitors the extent to which they affect student outcomes. Finally, an Innovating (4) teacher adapts or creates new versions of existing strategies or behaviors related to an element in response to unique student needs and situations.

For each of the scales in appendix B, we have written the values of Developing (2) and Applying (3) specifically for the element that is their focus. The values Not Using (0), Beginning (1), and Innovating (4) are the same in every scale. Not Using (0) always means the teacher does not use strategies or behaviors related to an element even though they are called for in class. Beginning (1) always means the teacher does employ strategies or behaviors related to an element, but parts are missing or errors are made. Innovating (4) always means the teacher knows strategies or behaviors related to an element so well that he has adapted them to meet students' specific needs. To illustrate, consider table 3.2, which is a scale specific to the element of managing response rates. Managing response rates is one of the elements of the design question, What will I do to engage students?—an on-the-spot lesson segment.

Table 3.2: Scale for Managing Response Rates

	4 Innovating	3 Applying	2 Developing	1 Beginning	0 Not Using
Managing response rates	I adapt and create new strategies for unique student needs and situations.	I use response-rate techniques to maintain student engagement in questions, and I monitor the extent to which the techniques keep students engaged.	I use response-rate techniques to maintain student engagement in questions, but I do so in a somewhat mechanistic way.	I use the strategy incorrectly or with parts missing.	I should use the strategy, but I don't.

Notice that the scale value for Developing (2) says, "I use response rate techniques to maintain student engagement in questions, but I do so in a somewhat mechanistic way." At the Applying (3) level, the scale value says, "I use response-rate techniques to maintain student engagement in questions, and I monitor the extent to which the techniques keep students engaged." Here the teacher not only uses strategies that engage more students in answering questions, but she monitors the extent to which students are actually answering the questions thoughtfully.

To understand the logic of the scales in appendix B, it is useful to understand the stages a teacher goes through when learning a new strategy. The research and theory from cognitive psychology (Marzano, 1992) inform us that a teacher progresses through at least three stages: (1) the cognitive phase, (2) the shaping phase, and (3) the autonomous phase.

The first stage, the *cognitive phase*, occurs when a teacher tries to understand a strategy and gathers information about it. During this stage, a teacher is not actually using the strategy but becomes aware of it, observes its use, or reads about its proper execution. On the scale, the beginning of the cognitive stage corresponds to the Not Using (0) level, when a teacher is not using a strategy because he or she is unaware of it. As the teacher's awareness of a strategy grows, he or she moves toward the Beginning (1) level of the scale.

The second stage, referred to as the *shaping phase*, occurs when a teacher begins to use a new strategy. During this stage, the teacher's execution of the strategy might still contain significant errors or omissions. Moving through this phase, the teacher gradually addresses errors or omissions until he or she can perform the strategy successfully, but the performance will still require the teacher to consciously think about and focus on the execution of the strategy. When a teacher uses the strategy, but with significant errors or omissions, performance is at the Beginning (1) level. As the teacher corrects errors and begins to perform the strategy successfully, he or she moves to the Developing (2) level of the scale.

The final stage a teacher experiences when learning a new strategy, the *autonomous phase*, occurs when the teacher performs the strategy with ease and fluency. During this stage, the teacher focuses on the strategy's effect on students' learning and adapts the strategy to fit particular situations or meet specific student needs. The autonomous phase of teacher learning corresponds to the Applying (3) and Innovating (4) levels. It is important to remember that for the reflective teacher, the autonomous phase is not synonymous with automaticity. Rather, the reflective teacher continues to examine his or her use of a strategy or behavior even when fluent with it.

The scales in appendix B also contain descriptions of teacher and student behavior for each element. For example, table 3.3 shows teacher evidence and student evidence associated with the element of managing response rates.

Table 3.3: Teacher and Student Evidence for Managing Response Rates

Teacher Evidence	Student Evidence
❏ Teacher uses wait time. ❏ Teacher uses response cards. ❏ Teacher has students use hand signals to respond to questions. ❏ Teacher uses choral response. ❏ Teacher uses technology to keep track of students' responses. ❏ Teacher uses response chaining.	❏ Multiple students or the entire class respond to questions the teacher poses. ❏ When asked, students can describe their thinking about specific questions the teacher poses.

The teacher and student evidence listed in table 3.3 aim to provide rich detail to perform a self-audit with. For example, table 3.3 lists teacher behaviors such as use of wait time, use of response cards, and so on. These items provide teachers with examples of how specific strategies and behaviors might manifest. In addition, table 3.3 includes student behaviors such as responding to and describing their thinking about questions the teacher posed. Measuring these specific types of evidence allows teachers to obtain a more accurate sense of their strengths and weaknesses when performing a self audit.

A Compendium of Strategies for Reflective Practice

In addition to the scales in appendix B and their accompanying lists of teacher and student evidence, over 270 strategies and behaviors for reflective practice are listed in the compendium (page 83). The compendium allows teachers to quickly locate and learn about specific instructional strategies and teacher behaviors that correspond to each element of *The Art and Science of Teaching* framework (Marzano, 2007). In the compendium, each strategy or behavior is described succinctly but with enough detail to allow a teacher to use it immediately in his or her classroom. The compendium is designed to give teachers the look and feel of a strategy without having to reference other books or resources. To investigate a strategy more thoroughly, visit **www.marzanoresearch.com /classroomstrategies** for links to other works in which the strategy and its research base are described in greater detail.

The compendium is meant to be a quick reference tool for teachers, helping them easily plan and implement strategies specific to their growth goals. As an example of how the compendium is organized, table 3.4 shows the strategies it lists for managing response rates.

Table 3.4: Strategies for Managing Response Rates

Random names	The teacher writes each student's name on a separate slip of paper or tongue depressor and selects one at random after asking a question. The teacher should put the selected name back into the jar or hat before the next question.
Hand signals	Students use a thumbs-up to indicate they understand the content being addressed, a thumbs-down to indicate they do not understand, and a flat palm to indicate they understand some of the content but are also confused about some of the content. Students can also use hand signals to indicate responses to multiple-choice questions. For example, one finger indicates that response A is correct, two fingers indicate response B, three fingers indicate response C, and four fingers indicate response D.
Response cards	Students write their answers on small (for example, 12 × 12–inch) whiteboards or chalkboards and reveal them to the teacher simultaneously.
Response chaining	After a student responds to a question, the teacher asks a second student to explain why the initial answer was correct, partially correct, or incorrect. The teacher might also ask the second student to paraphrase the initial answer before responding. The teacher can call on a third student to respond to the second student's response.
Paired response	Students confer in pairs to answer a question. The teacher then calls on a pair. One student can verbalize the answer for the pair, or both can contribute.
Choral response	The teacher presents target information in a clear and concise statement and asks the class to repeat the information as a group. The goal is to form an "imprint" of important information.
Wait time	The teacher allows a pause of at least three seconds after posing a question. The teacher also allows for a pause of at least three seconds if a student stops speaking in the middle of an answer and teaches students to allow a three-second pause between student answers.

Elaborative interrogation	After a student answers a question, the teacher probes the answer by asking, "How do you know that to be true?" and "Why is that so?" The teacher might also ask the student to provide evidence to support his or her conclusions.
Multiple types of questions	The teacher uses a combination of retrieval, analytical, predictive, interpretive, and evaluative questions such as the following:
	• **Retrieval questions**—These require students to recognize, recall, and execute knowledge that was directly taught.
	• **Analytical questions**—These require students to take information apart and determine how the parts relate to the whole.
	• **Predictive questions**—These require students to form conjectures and hypotheses about what will happen next in a narrative or sequence of information or actions.
	• **Interpretive questions**—These require students to make and defend inferences about the intentions of an author.
	• **Evaluative questions**—These require students to use criteria to make judgments and assessments of something.

Table 3.4 lists different strategies for managing response rates: random names, hand signals, response cards, response chaining, paired response, choral response, wait time, elaborative interrogation, and multiple types of questions. Each includes a brief description. Visit **marzanoresearch.com/classroom strategies** for a list of sources that teachers can consult for more information on each strategy.

The compendium also includes a Technology Links section for each of the forty-one elements. This section describes ways in which technology can augment or enhance the strategies for that element. For example, learner response system technologies allow teachers to simultaneously gather and display data about an entire class's answers to a question. Teachers can display initial answers anonymously (for example, in bar graph form) and then ask students to discuss an issue in light of their peers' perspectives. After a discussion, students might vote again. This questioning strategy can teach students both to defend and reconsider their initial answers to a question. Table 3.5 shows the Technology Links section for managing response rates.

Table 3.5: Technology Links for Managing Response Rates

- Use learner response systems or voting websites (such as www.polleverywhere.com) to give more students an opportunity to answer questions and increase students' attention and engagement during questioning.
- Ask students to respond to questions posted on a class website, blog, or wiki. Monitor student participation and the complexity of responses generated.

Creating a Personal Profile

To begin a self-audit, teachers score themselves on each of the forty-one scales in appendix B. Table 3.6 (page 42) reports one teacher's self-ratings. Visit **marzanoresearch.com/classroomstrategies** for a blank reproducible version of the personal profile.

Table 3.6: Teacher Self-Ratings on the Personal Profile

Lesson Segments Involving Routine Events					
Design Question: What will I do to establish and communicate learning goals, track student progress, and celebrate success?					
Element	4 Innovating	3 Applying	2 Developing	1 Beginning	0 Not Using
1. What do I typically do to provide clear learning goals and scales (rubrics)?					
2. What do I typically do to track student progress?					
3. What do I typically do to celebrate success?					
Design Question: What will I do to establish and maintain classroom rules and procedures?					
Element	4 Innovating	3 Applying	2 Developing	1 Beginning	0 Not Using
4. What do I typically do to establish and maintain classroom rules and procedures?					
5. What do I typically do to organize the physical layout of the classroom?					
Lesson Segments Addressing Content					
Design Question: What will I do to help students effectively interact with new knowledge?					
Element	4 Innovating	3 Applying	2 Developing	1 Beginning	0 Not Using
6. What do I typically do to identify critical information?					
7. What do I typically do to organize students to interact with new knowledge?					
8. What do I typically do to preview new content?					
9. What do I typically do to chunk content into digestible bites?					

Element	4 Innovating	3 Applying	2 Developing	1 Beginning	0 Not Using
10. What do I typically do to help students process new information?					
11. What do I typically do to help students elaborate on new information?					
12. What do I typically do to help students record and represent knowledge?					
13. What do I typically do to help students reflect on their learning?					

Design Question: *What will I do to help students practice and deepen their understanding of new knowledge?*

Element	4 Innovating	3 Applying	2 Developing	1 Beginning	0 Not Using
14. What do I typically do to review content?					
15. What do I typically do to organize students to practice and deepen knowledge?					
16. What do I typically do to use homework?					
17. What do I typically do to help students examine similarities and differences?					
18. What do I typically do to help students examine errors in reasoning?					
19. What do I typically do to help students practice skills, strategies, and processes?					
20. What do I typically do to help students revise knowledge?					

Continued on next page →

Design Question: What will I do to help students generate and test hypotheses about new knowledge?					
Element	**4** **Innovating**	**3** **Applying**	**2** **Developing**	**1** **Beginning**	**0** **Not Using**
21. What do I typically do to organize students for cognitively complex tasks?					
22. What do I typically do to engage students in cognitively complex tasks involving hypothesis generation and testing?					
23. What do I typically do to provide resources and guidance?					

Lesson Segments Enacted on the Spot

Design Question: What will I do to engage students?					
Element	**4** **Innovating**	**3** **Applying**	**2** **Developing**	**1** **Beginning**	**0** **Not Using**
24. What do I typically do to notice when students are not engaged?					
25. What do I typically do to use academic games?					
26. What do I typically do to manage response rates?					
27. What do I typically do to use physical movement?					
28. What do I typically do to maintain a lively pace?					
29. What do I typically do to demonstrate intensity and enthusiasm?					
30. What do I typically do to use friendly controversy?					
31. What do I typically do to provide opportunities for students to talk about themselves?					
32. What do I typically do to present unusual or intriguing information?					

Design Question: What will I do to recognize and acknowledge adherence or lack of adherence to rules and procedures?

Element	4 Innovating	3 Applying	2 Developing	1 Beginning	0 Not Using
33. What do I typically do to demonstrate withitness?					
34. What do I typically do to apply consequences for lack of adherence to rules and procedures?					
35. What do I typically do to acknowledge adherence to rules and procedures?					

Design Question: What will I do to establish and maintain effective relationships with students?

Element	4 Innovating	3 Applying	2 Developing	1 Beginning	0 Not Using
36. What do I typically do to understand students' interests and backgrounds?					
37. What do I typically do to use verbal and nonverbal behaviors that indicate affection for students?					
38. What do I typically do to display objectivity and control?					

Design Question: What will I do to communicate high expectations for all students?

Element	4 Innovating	3 Applying	2 Developing	1 Beginning	0 Not Using
39. What do I typically do to demonstrate value and respect for low-expectancy students?					
40. What do I typically do to ask questions of low-expectancy students?					
41. What do I typically do to probe incorrect answers with low-expectancy students?					

Notice that the teacher depicted in table 3.6 has rated herself Innovating (4) on three elements, Applying (3) on fourteen elements, Developing (2) on eleven elements, Beginning (1) on nine elements, and Not Using (0) on four elements. Self-ratings provide an initial profile of a teacher's strengths and weaknesses. Certainly, scores of 3 and 4 indicate strengths and should be celebrated. Scores of 1 and 0 represent weaknesses and form a pool of elements from which teachers can select yearly growth goals. While thirteen scores are Beginning (1) or Not Using (0) in table 3.6 (page 42), it is not recommended that the teacher work on all of these in a given year. Rather, the teacher should select two or three elements for each year. To make a selection, the teacher should select elements for which she has low scores (that is, 1s and 0s) and in which she is interested. In this case, the teacher might select the following three elements:

1. What do I typically do to celebrate success?

2. What do I typically do to help students examine errors in reasoning?

3. What do I typically do to use friendly controversy?

For each of these three selected elements, the teacher would write specific growth goals for the year, such as the following:

1. By the end of the year, I will raise my score on celebrating success from 1 to 3.

2. By the end of the year, I will raise my score on helping students examine errors in reasoning from 0 to 3.

3. By the end of the year, I will raise my score on using friendly controversy from 0 to 3.

These three goals provide a set of targets around which the teacher can engage in focused practice. The following vignette depicts how a teacher might set growth goals using a self-audit.

> Mrs. Conners is excited about the beginning of the school year, and in addition to preparing for her students and planning instruction, she also sets aside time to prepare for her own professional growth. To begin, she conducts a self-audit. Using a five-point scale, she examines forty-one different elements of effective teaching. She is encouraged to see that her ratings for the areas she identified last year as growth goals have increased substantially, but she still has six Beginning (1) ratings and four Not Using (0) ratings. Out of these ten elements, she looks for one element that involves routine events in the classroom that she would like to work on, one element that addresses content, and one on-the-spot element. This year, she selects these three elements: (1) What do I typically do to organize the physical layout of the classroom?, (2) What do I typically do to help students elaborate on new information?, and (3) What do I typically do to maintain a lively pace? Mrs. Conners then converts each question into a specific growth goal and writes them on an index card:
>
> 1. By the end of the year, I will raise my score on organizing the physical layout of the classroom from 1 to 3.
>
> 2. By the end of the year, I will raise my score on helping students elaborate on new information from 0 to 3.
>
> 3. By the end of the year, I will raise my score on maintaining a lively pace from 1 to 4.
>
> She makes three copies of the card and puts one copy on the bulletin board by her desk, staples another copy inside her plan book, and tapes the third to the podium that she normally uses while teaching. She knows that having specific growth goals is the first step toward engaging in focused practice.

Summary

This chapter presented and explained scales, teacher and student evidence, and strategies for each of the forty-one elements. The chapter also illustrated the use of a personal profile to conduct a self-audit and provided guidelines for selecting two to three specific elements as focus areas for growth each year. This process allows teachers to write specific growth goals for the elements they have chosen to focus on each year.

Chapter 3: Comprehension Questions

1. Describe the five performance levels from the scales explained in chapter 3: Not Using (0), Beginning (1), Developing (2), Applying (3), and Innovating (4).

2. Describe the three phases that a teacher goes through when learning a new strategy.

3. Why is it important to select only a few elements to focus on in a given year?

4. What are the important elements of a good growth goal?

Chapter 4

ENGAGING IN FOCUSED PRACTICE

At an intuitive level, most people commonly think of practice as performing an action multiple times. As we saw in chapter 1, simply doing something over and over again does not necessarily increase one's skill with it. What we refer to as focused practice goes well beyond the common conception of practice. As the name implies, focused practice involves repeating a specific strategy with attention to improving detailed aspects of the strategy. A golfer involved in focused practice would choose to practice a specific type of shot (for example, putting, driving, or chipping) using a specific type of club (putter, driver, wedge) in a specific situation (uphill, downhill, or across a slope). A gymnast might focus practice on a specific part of a move (for example, landing a cartwheel) on a specific apparatus (like the balance beam). Pilots often use a simulator to replicate specific weather conditions (such as dry, windy, rainy, or snowy) in which they can practice specific elements of specific flight sequences like taxiing, taking off, approaching an airport, or landing.

As these examples indicate, the hallmark of focused practice is specificity. In a classroom, this usually means that a teacher selects a specific strategy for practice, along with a specific aspect of that strategy. To this end, the compendium (page 83) can be very useful. Teachers can use the compendium to select and learn about specific strategies related to the elements they have chosen as growth goals. There are a number of ways that a teacher might focus his or her practice: focusing on specific steps of a strategy, developing a protocol, developing fluency with a strategy, making adaptations to a strategy, or integrating several strategies to create a macrostrategy.

Focusing on Specific Steps of a Strategy

Some strategies or behaviors have a rather well-defined set of steps. To illustrate, consider the strategy of using comparison matrices to examine similarities and differences. Table 4.1 depicts a comparison matrix.

Table 4.1: Comparison Matrix

	Element 1	Element 2	Element 3
Attribute 1	Similarities:	Similarities:	Similarities:
	Differences:	Differences:	Differences:

Continued on next page →

	Element 1	Element 2	Element 3
Attribute 2	Similarities:	Similarities:	Similarities:
	Differences:	Differences:	Differences:
Attribute 3	Similarities:	Similarities:	Similarities:
	Differences:	Differences:	Differences:
Summary:			

The steps to using a comparison matrix might be described as follows:

1. Identify the elements you wish to compare, and write them at the top of each column.

2. Identify the attributes on which you wish to compare the elements, and write them in the rows.

3. In each cell, record how the elements are similar (note that similarities will be the same for multiple cells). In each cell, also record how the elements are different (note that differences will not be the same in each cell).

4. Summarize what you have learned about the elements.

To illustrate the process, consider table 4.2, which depicts how a teacher might organize a comparison activity involving solids, liquids, and gases.

Table 4.2: Comparison Matrix for Solids, Liquids, and Gases

	Solids	Liquids	Gases
Shape	Similarities: Solids and liquids are not easily compressible because there is little free space between their particles. Solids and gases cannot be poured from one container to another.	Similarities: Solids and liquids are not easily compressible because there is little free space between their particles. Liquids and gases both flow easily and take the shape of their containers.	Similarities: Liquids and gases both flow easily and take the shape of their containers. Solids and gases cannot be poured from one container to another.
	Differences: Solids keep their shape unless they are broken. Solids do not flow easily.	Differences: Liquids do not spread out from their initial position in a container. Liquids can be poured from one container to another.	Differences: Gases are easily compressible because there is free space between their particles. Gases spread out from their initial position in a container (diffusion).

	Solids	Liquids	Gases
Particle Behavior	Similarities: Solids, liquids, and gases are all composed of atoms. The particles in solids, liquids, and gases vibrate. The particles in solids and liquids are close together.	Similarities: Solids, liquids, and gases are all composed of atoms. The particles in solids, liquids, and gases vibrate. The particles in solids and liquids are close together. The particles in liquids and gases are able to move around. The particles in liquids and gases do not have a regular arrangement.	Similarities: Solids, liquids, and gases are all composed of atoms. The particles in solids, liquids, and gases vibrate. The particles in liquids and gases are able to move around. The particles in liquids and gases do not have a regular arrangement.
	Differences: The particles in solids usually have a regular arrangement. The particles in a solid vibrate but do not move around.	Differences: The particles in liquids move by sliding past one another.	Differences: The particles in gases move freely at high speeds.
Reaction to Changes in Temperature	Similarities: When solids and liquids are heated, they change state.	Similarities: When solids and liquids are heated, they change state. When liquids and gases are cooled, they change state.	Similarities: When liquids and gases are cooled, they change state.
	Differences: When solids are heated, they turn into liquids (melting). When solids are cooled, they do not change state.	Differences: When liquids are heated, they turn into gases (evaporation). When liquids are cooled, they turn into solids (freezing).	Differences: When gases are heated, they change volume and expand. When gases are cooled, they turn into liquids (condensation).

Summary: Understanding the shape, particle behavior, and reactions to temperature changes of solids, liquids, and gases helps me predict how different elements and compounds will behave under different amounts of pressure and heat. If I were designing a device that needed to be used at very cold temperatures or under extreme pressure, understanding the similarities and differences between these attributes of the different states of matter would allow me to select the best materials for my device.

During step 1, the teacher had students record the elements of *solid*, *liquid*, and *gas* at the top of each column. She then identified three attributes on which students were to compare solids, liquids, and gases, and students filled in one attribute for each row. In table 4.2 (page 50), the attributes are shape, particle behavior, and reaction to changes in temperature. Alternatively, she might have had students select their own attributes. Next, the teacher asked students to find similarities between solids, liquids, and gases for each of the three attributes and record their observations in the appropriate cells. The teacher then asked students to identify differences that set each element apart from the others and to record those differences in the appropriate cells. After completing the matrix, the teacher asked each student to summarize what they had learned about the elements.

Quite obviously, the comparison matrix is a complex strategy, and a teacher might decide to focus attention on one or more of the steps. For example, a teacher might identify the second step as the most critical to the overall success of the strategy, because the attributes used in the matrix govern the depth or superficiality of the similarities and differences students identify. For example, if the attribute "hardness" was selected for inclusion in the matrix depicted in table 4.2, the similarities and differences identified might be superficial. With "shape" as an attribute in the comparison matrix, however, the similarities and differences identified are quite substantive. Over time, the teacher would seek to develop explicit guidelines regarding how to select the best attributes to use in comparison matrices. The following vignette depicts how this focus might manifest for a particular classroom teacher.

Mr. Shenk, a middle school math teacher, is having his students use comparison matrices to identify similarities and differences between several types of triangles. His specific focus is helping students select attributes that will lead to meaningful, rather than superficial, comparisons. His students are currently comparing obtuse, acute, and right triangles. Before they select the attributes for their comparisons, he reviews a set of three guidelines he developed to help them choose attributes that lead to insightful comparisons:

1. Think about what you already know about the general topic. What facts stand out to you?

2. Do a quick mental comparison of two of the elements. What differences do you immediately see?

3. Think about all of the elements. What do you look at or think about to tell them apart?

"What do we already know about triangles, class?" asks Mr. Shenk.

"The measurement of the inner angles is important," offers Keisha.

"And the length of the sides helps determine what kind of triangle it is!" adds Kevin.

"That's right," says Mr. Shenk. "So what attributes could we use to compare them based on what we already know?"

"Maybe the measurement of the inner angles and the length of the sides," volunteers Stanley.

Mr. Shenk records these two things on the board and then moves to the second guideline. Students point out that what separates an obtuse triangle from an acute triangle is the measurement of the biggest inner angle. So Mr. Shenk adds "measurement of biggest inner angle" to the list of potential attributes. Finally, Mr. Shenk prompts his students to follow the last guideline and think about how they tell the three kinds of triangles apart.

"I can always tell a right triangle because it has a boxy corner," says Lynne.

"Yeah, and even though I don't use it to tell them apart, I just remembered that triangles can be isosceles or scalene, and some are equilateral," replies Evan.

"Okay," says Mr. Shenk, and he adds "boxy corners" and "can be isosceles, scalene, or equilateral" to the list on the board. He asks the class to discuss the list on the board, and they agree to eliminate "length of sides" from the list because it is similar to the item about isosceles, scalene, or equilateral triangles. Finally, he asks each student to use the three attributes listed on the board in their comparison matrices.

Developing a Protocol

Some strategies or behaviors do not have well-developed sets of steps. For example, consider the behavior of commenting on student achievement or areas of importance (see compendium, page 83)—one of the possible strategies a teacher might use to understand students' interests and backgrounds. This element is part of the design question, What will I do to establish and maintain effective relationships with students? If a teacher had selected this particular behavior for focused practice, he would most likely want to develop a protocol to guide his actions. One way of thinking about a protocol is as a set of general rules or guidelines. Such specificity would guide the teacher's focused practice. To begin, the teacher might generate the following protocol:

- I will focus on students who seem disenfranchised in my class and those with whom I don't have a good rapport yet.

- When a student does something well, I will compliment him or her.

- I will find out information about my students and use that knowledge in my interactions with them.

For each of these general rules in this protocol, the teacher might articulate more specific actions. For example, consider the second rule in this protocol ("When a student does something well, I will compliment him or her"). The teacher might research this topic and determine that there are optimum ways to provide praise, such as tailoring the compliment to the work the student did well. To illustrate, as opposed to telling a student he is good at something or smart, the teacher might say, "You did an excellent job on this test. I looked at your other scores this semester and this was the highest one. Congratulations." The teacher might also learn that specific praise is more effective than general praise. For example, instead of simply telling a student that he or she did well on the test, the teacher might say, "You did very well on the essay question about local river pollution. It was obvious that you put a lot of thought into your answer, and you wrote very clearly about it." The following vignette depicts how this focus might manifest for a particular teacher.

Mrs. Southy, a high school science teacher, has decided to focus on complimenting her students regarding their academic and personal accomplishments. Specifically, she wants to focus on one aspect of the protocol she has created for that strategy: I will find out information about students and use that knowledge in my interactions with them. To do this, she writes down the names of any students who might feel alienated in her class or with whom it is awkward for her to interact. She decides that over the next week, she will work to find out something special about each of these students. From talking to other students, she discovers that Emilie loves to cook.

While reading the school newspaper, she notices that Jose and Nathan are both on the school's baseball team, and that they have a home game coming up. She overhears one of Chandra's other teachers talking about how much progress she's made this year, and finds out from the counselor that Luis aspires to be a pilot when he grows up. In response to the information she's collected, Mrs. Southy makes plans to interact with these students.

On Monday, she finds Emilie in the cafeteria and sits at her table to eat lunch. The conversation inevitably turns to food, and Mrs. Southy asks Emilie about her cooking. She finds out that Emilie just won a cooking competition at the local recreation center, and all the other students at the table excitedly tell Mrs. Southy about how great Emilie's food is. Mrs. Southy has to stay at school for an evening meeting on Tuesday, so she tells Jose and Nathan that she'll be at their game (which is after school but before her meeting) cheering for them. Their team wins, and she gets the chance to briefly congratulate them before heading to her meeting. On Wednesday, her physics class is studying the Bernoulli principle, and she asks Luis to explain how it creates lift for an airplane. He describes his recent flying lessons, telling the class what it feels like to hold the yoke (the plane's steering wheel) and feel the resistance as the plane takes off. On Thursday, while working individually with Chandra, Mrs. Southy passes on the compliment she overheard from the other teacher and praises her hard work and effort.

Developing Fluency With a Strategy

As described in chapter 3, fluency means a teacher can perform a strategy or execute a behavior with ease. In other words, a fluent teacher is skilled enough with a strategy or behavior to employ it without having to think about the steps involved. This is not to say that the teacher is not mindful of the strategy. Indeed, when fluency has been fully developed, the reflective teacher both executes the strategy or behavior and monitors its effect. For example, assume that a teacher is working on the previewing strategy of K-W-L (What do I *know?*, What do I *want* to know?, What have I *learned?*). That strategy involves the following three elements:

1. Students identify what they know about the topic, and the teacher records this information under *K* on a chart.

2. Students list what they want to know about a topic, and the teacher records this information under *W* on a chart.

3. After a lesson, the students identify and list things that they have learned, and the teacher records this under *L*.

Each element of the strategy has an intended outcome. For example, during the first phase—What do I know?—the intended outcome is to activate students' background knowledge regarding a specific topic. This step also primes students to make connections between prior knowledge and new knowledge that will be presented. During the second phase—What do I want to know?—the intended outcome is student engagement. It stands to reason that students will be more highly engaged if they are learning about aspects of the content they are genuinely interested in. During the third phase—What have I learned?—the intended outcome is to highlight knowledge gain.

Even though a particular strategy (for example, K-W-L) might seem simple, a teacher must engage in extended practice to develop fluency with it (Ackerman, 2007; Bloom, 1986; Gaschler & Frensch, 2007; Holt & Rainey, 2002; James, 1890; Jenkins & Hoyer, 2000; Logan, 1988, 1992; Logan & Etherton,

1994; Rawson, 2004; Rawson & Middleton, 2009; Rawson & Touron, 2009; Schneider & Shiffrin, 1977; Shiffrin & Schneider, 1977; Touron & Hertzog, 2004). The most effective practice occurs regularly over a period of time, with breaks between practice sessions. Nicholas Cepeda, Harold Pashler, Edward Vul, John Wixted, and Doug Rohrer (2006) found that an interval of at least one day between practice sessions maximizes the benefits of practice. Additionally, practice that continues after a person has achieved proficiency, referred to as *overlearning*, has been shown to be effective. James Driskell, Ruth Willis, and Carolyn Copper (1992) found that 100 or 150 percent overlearning was most effective. This means that if it takes four practice sessions to become proficient, it would take eight practice sessions to overlearn to the 100 percent level and ten sessions to overlearn to the 150 percent level.

Fluency allows people to think about other things while they execute a skill or process. Reading, riding a bicycle, and driving are all common tasks that most people perform fluently. When a person reads fluently, he does not individually examine each letter or even each word. Instead, he automatically decodes the words, which allows him to focus his cognitive attention on comprehension. When riding a bicycle, a person somewhat effortlessly performs the tasks of pedaling and balancing, leaving her attention free to deal with potholes, uphill or downhill slopes, and other obstacles. Experienced drivers have developed fluency with the basic rules of driving (for example, traffic signal colors and the meanings of road signs) and the basic functions of the car (such as braking, parking, and shifting gears) so they can make quick, subconscious decisions about these elements. This fluency allows them to focus their attention on variable factors, such as changing road conditions or the behavior of other drivers.

The teacher who has selected the K-W-L strategy might find that consciously practicing the strategy three times allows her to feel proficient. However, she adds another three sessions to overlearn it. At this point, the teacher knows the strategy so well that she can focus her attention on monitoring students' reactions. As we saw in chapter 3, this means the teacher has reached the Applying (3) level on the scale. The following vignette depicts how this focus might manifest for a particular teacher.

> Ms. Washoe, a fifth-grade teacher, has been practicing the K-W-L strategy as a way to preview upcoming information with her students. Her grade level uses a departmentalized system for teaching science and social studies, so she can practice a strategy multiple times over the course of a week with different groups of students. Last week, she used the K-W-L strategy with each of her four classes to preview information about the thirteen original colonies. She feels like she's getting good at it, but knows that if she wants to focus her attention on the students and not on the strategy, she needs to stick with it. So she uses it again to preview critical content about the American Revolution. She finds that as she uses the strategy for the sixth, seventh, and eighth times, she doesn't really have to think much about how to record student responses, what order to use when calling on students, or what to do if students forget what they were going to say. As her attention shifts from the strategy to the students, she finds herself really listening to what they say, correcting misconceptions when they arise, and helping students clarify their meaning using probing questions.

Making Adaptations to a Strategy

Even when a teacher has reached the level of Applying (3) for a strategy or behavior (that is, he or she has developed fluency), the teacher might want to create new versions of the strategy for special situations. In fact, this is the defining characteristic of the Innovating (4) level in the scales for the forty-one elements of the model. Consider the strategy of homework. A teacher realizes that he must make adaptations for students who come from homes with fewer resources. When he assigns homework that requires students to create presentations or dramatizations of what they learned in class, he notices that the quality of a student's presentation varies according to his or her family's socioeconomic level. When students from more affluent families create PowerPoint slide shows with color handouts and stage elaborate skits with props and costumes, and students from lower-income families give presentations that obviously lack these extra touches, it creates a sense of discomfort and unfairness in his class. The teacher reconsiders the types of assignments that he gives as homework, adapting his homework strategy to meet the needs of his students. Instead of asking students to create presentations or performances for homework, he has them complete those activities in class, and saves text- and writing-based activities for homework assignments. He also realizes that students may have different levels of parent support at home and provides time at the end of class for students to review homework assignments in small groups. If students realize they have questions or are going to need help, they can request his assistance then. The following vignette depicts how this focus might manifest for a specific teacher.

> Mr. Cleery, a middle school language arts teacher, has decided he needs to adjust the strategy he uses for homework to maintain a more equitable environment in his classroom. To this end, he reviews his revised homework policy with parents during fall conferences.
>
> "I'm going to start asking students to work on presentations and performances in class," he tells them. "I want everyone to have access to the technology and resources they need in order to be and feel successful."
>
> When he gives parents the list of novels that students will be studying, he also lets them know that he is accepting donations for his "costume and prop closet" to help students dramatize scenes from *The Call of the Wild, A Christmas Carol,* and various stories by Rudyard Kipling. One parent contacts him to let him know that his company is replacing some of their employees' laptops and would like to donate the old ones for students to use when creating presentations. In class, Mr. Cleery begins to assign homework that doesn't require outside resources and makes sure that he provides everything students might need to complete each assignment. Additionally, he institutes "Homework Hounds" during the last ten minutes of any class in which he assigns homework. Students meet in preassigned groups to talk about the homework and to clarify things they are unsure about. Additionally, each student in class has a homework buddy, a friend with whom they exchange phone numbers, so that if students get stuck on the homework, they can contact their buddy for help.

Integrating Several Strategies to Create a Macrostrategy

A teacher might choose to integrate strategies as the subject of focused practice. At this stage of development, a teacher is competent with most, if not all, of the strategies for a particular element but wishes to combine some of those strategies into a composite or macrostrategy. Focused practice that involves integrating usually means a teacher is at the Innovating (4) level on the scale. To illustrate, consider the strategies from the compendium (page 83) for the element of previewing, which is within the design question, What will I do to help students effectively interact with new knowledge? Table 4.3 lists these strategies.

Table 4.3: Strategies for Previewing New Content

What do you think you know?	The teacher asks students to individually write down what they already know about an upcoming topic. After each student has created an individual list, the teacher asks students to pair up and discuss their previous knowledge and ideas. Each pair creates a list of its most original or most important knowledge and ideas, using examples where appropriate. Finally, each pair shares its list, and the teacher creates a whole-class list of what is already known about upcoming content.
Overt linkages	The teacher helps students make overt links between content they have previously studied in class and new content being presented by simply explaining the connections. For example, the teacher might say, "When you read the section in the chapter about percolation, keep in mind that it is similar to what happened in our last experiment, where the soil acted as a filter as the water seeped through it."
Preview questions	The teacher asks questions about upcoming content to pique students' curiosity and activate their prior knowledge. Although students may not know the answers to the questions because they have not yet learned the new content, the questions help signal what information they should be listening for as the teacher presents new content.
Brief teacher summary	The teacher provides students with an oral or written summary of content that is about to be presented. This helps students see key ideas and patterns and follow those ideas as the teacher presents more detailed information.
Skimming	The teacher helps students skim written information on an upcoming topic by teaching them to look at major section headings and subheadings and asking them to analyze those headings to pick out main ideas and important concepts in the passage. The teacher might also ask students to try to summarize a passage after skimming it, record how well they think they already understand the new content, and predict what they will learn during an upcoming presentation of the new content.
Teacher-prepared notes	The teacher provides an outline of the content to students before beginning to present new information. The teacher should allow students to ask questions after the teacher presents new information and reviews the outline. This can help clear up initial confusion or misconceptions that students have about new content.
K-W-L strategy (Ogle, 1986)	The teacher uses a K-W-L strategy before presenting new content. First, students identify what they know about the topic, and the teacher records this information under *K* on a chart. Then students list what they want to know about a topic, and the teacher records this information under *W* on a chart. Finally, after a lesson, students identify and list things they have learned, which are recorded under *L*. At this point, the teacher and students examine what was written in the *K* column in an attempt to identify initial misconceptions about the content.
Advance organizers	The teacher creates a visual representation (often called a graphic organizer) showing the structure and organization of new content and illustrating how new content connects to information previously learned in class. Students can use this organizer to ask questions before the presentation of new content, to identify what they already know about new content, and to connect new content to their personal interests.

Anticipation guides	Before presenting new content, the teacher has students respond to a series of statements that relate to upcoming information. After students respond to the statements, the teacher leads the class in a discussion about how students responded. This activates students' prior knowledge about a topic and helps them consider issues and ideas associated with new content.
Word splash activity	The teacher uses this strategy to help students preview vocabulary terms and concepts associated with new content. The teacher prepares a number of words and short phrases associated with the new content and presents them to students. Students try to sort the terms into categories that make sense to them. The teacher then allows students to share their categories and sorting strategies and leads the class in a discussion of how the terms and concepts relate to each other and to students' prior knowledge and individual interests.
Preassessment	The teacher administers a preassessment to students before presenting new content. This strategy exposes students to the most important information in an upcoming presentation, and the teacher can use preassessment results to gain an understanding of which students have a lot of prior knowledge about upcoming content and which do not.

Instead of considering each of these eleven strategies as isolated activities, a teacher might decide to integrate or combine them. For example, if a teacher discovers after administering a preassessment that her students have very little prior knowledge about upcoming content, she might decide to combine the first part of the strategy for skimming with the middle part of the What do you think you know? strategy. In this case, she asks students to skim text about the upcoming content and make a list of what they think might be main ideas and important concepts. She then asks them to pair up and discuss their lists, creating a new list of what they agree are the most important ideas and concepts. Finally, she leads a class discussion about what students found out and makes a whole-class list of what they expect to be the important ideas and concepts in the upcoming content. The following vignette depicts how this focus might manifest for a particular classroom teacher.

> Mrs. Abelson considers herself fluent with all the strategies for previewing new content. She thinks she can combine pieces and parts of the various strategies into a macrostrategy for previewing. The first part of her macrostrategy involves a preview page—a handout with three preview questions, a brief teacher summary of the upcoming content, and a graphic representation showing how the segments of information she is about to present fit together. She asks students to read the page and then form small groups to discuss their answers to the preview questions. The second part of her macrostrategy involves asking the students to write down three statements about the upcoming content. After students write, a volunteer reads one statement and the class discusses it. The final part of Mrs. Abelson's macrostrategy involves reviewing key vocabulary terms related to the upcoming content using a word splash.

Summary

This chapter centered on the principles of focused practice. By focusing on specific steps within a chosen strategy, developing a protocol for a strategy, developing fluency with a strategy, making adaptations to a strategy, or integrating several strategies, teachers can engage in focused practice designed to enhance their expertise. When a teacher is skilled enough to make adaptations to a particular strategy or behavior, he or she can begin combining and integrating different strategies within an element to create various macrostrategies.

Chapter 4: Comprehension Questions

1. How is focused practice different from the common conception of practice?

2. What are the benefits of focusing on specific steps of a strategy or developing a protocol for a strategy?

3. What is overlearning, and what role does it play in the development of fluency?

4. What are the similarities and differences between focused practice at the Applying (3) level and focused practice at the Innovating (4) level?

Chapter 5

RECEIVING FOCUSED FEEDBACK

Feedback is essential to determining the success of focused practice. Specifically, feedback tells teachers if their efforts are actually developing expertise. At a very basic level, focused feedback simply means continually examining one's progress toward the desired goal. Recall from the discussion in chapter 3 that reflection begins with a self-audit and the identification of improvement goals for specific elements of effective teaching. Next the teacher engages in focused practice, as we saw in chapter 4. Focused feedback involves keeping track of progress on growth goals that are the subject of focused practice. To this end, we strongly recommend that teachers maintain a reflection log like that in figure 5.1.

9/12	I used a free-flowing web to introduce the writing process. It was not very effective at first because I explained how the web works instead of showing students how to use it. The class seemed to like the exercise, though, so I would like to keep trying to use the webs.
9/21	Today we used free-flowing webs to brainstorm ideas for an essay. Once my students had selected topics for their essays, they mapped out main ideas and details using another web. It worked well, but the circles tended to get disorganized.
10/5	Today I tried asking students to use free-flowing webs to compare two things, and it worked really well. They drew the two things they were comparing in two big circles on the left and right of a page and wrote descriptors and facts in smaller circles around them. Then they connected the big circles to all the descriptors and facts that applied to them. There were some really interesting webs that helped the kids see connections they hadn't realized before.
10/14	Today the counselor came in to do a career lesson, and I asked her to use a free-flowing web as a part of her lesson, because the kids were already familiar with it. They really caught on to the idea of putting themselves in the center circle and then filling in their life goals in the surrounding circles. Some of them even made circles to show what they would have to do to achieve their goals.
10/20	Now that my students are comfortable with free-flowing webs, we've started using them to show relationships, and a few of my students even adapted the web for use with pictures. Almost like a storyboard, they planned out narrative pieces by drawing different events from their stories, and then found connections between the events and characters by drawing lines.

Figure 5.1: Sample reflection log for the strategy of using a free-flowing web.

In figure 5.1, the teacher has recorded anecdotal comments about her performance with a specific strategy for helping students record and represent knowledge, called a free-flowing web (see compendium, page 83). Figure 5.1 (page 61) represents a six-week period of time during which the teacher simply recorded impressions about her use of the strategy. The following vignette depicts how the use of reflection logs might manifest for a specific teacher.

> Mrs. Ferwerda teaches high school chemistry and has started using a reflection log to document her use of nonlinguistic representations to record and represent knowledge. She is a little nervous about writing her reflections because she has never considered herself a good writer, but she reminds herself that she is the only one who will ever read her entries. She begins her log in September and quickly realizes how easy it is to forget to make entries, especially when things get busy. In October, she looks back and realizes she only made two entries in September. She'd like to make at least one entry a week, so she decides to dedicate Thursday afternoons to a treat at her favorite coffee shop and half an hour to write in her log. As she writes, she tries to let her words flow and records her thoughts as they occur, without worrying about spelling, conventions, or organization too much. In November, she looks back over her past six reflections and realizes she has made a lot of progress. By reviewing her thinking, she sees that she has developed fluency with using nonlinguistic representations, and she decides to focus on using academic notebooks next.

There are a number of other ways that a teacher might gather information about her continuing progress, including video data, student survey data, and student achievement data.

Video Data

One powerful way for teachers to obtain focused feedback about their progress is to watch video recordings of themselves using specific strategies in class. A number of research studies indicate that viewing video augments teachers' reflection and performance (Armstrong & Curran, 2006; Cunningham & Benedetto, 2002; Goldman, 2004; Griswold, 2005; Miyata, 2002; Powell, Francisco, & Maher, 2003; Sheard & Harrison, 2005; Sherin & van Es, 2005; Sorenson, Newton, & Harrison, 2006; Spurgeon & Bowen, 2002; Storeygard & Fox, 1995).

Gavriel Salomon and Frederick McDonald (1970) found that self-viewing helped teachers evaluate how much their performance differed from self-expectations, and that self-viewing was enhanced if the viewing was focused (for example, the teacher watched for the use a specific strategy). John Lyle (2003) and Sandra Griswold (2005) suggested that self-viewing is helpful for teachers because it provides a rich, detailed account of classroom events and stimulates teachers to recall events they would not have otherwise remembered or reflected on. Miriam Sherin (2001, 2004; Sherin & Han, 2004) found similar results.

Cheryl Rosaen, Mary Lundeberg, Marjorie Cooper, Anny Fritzen, and Marjorie Terpstra (2008) found that preservice teachers who engaged in reflection after watching video of their teaching (compared to those who simply reflected from memory) wrote more specific comments about their teaching, focused on instruction rather than on classroom management, and examined their teaching rather than themselves. Tina Seidel and her colleagues (2005) compared teachers who watched video of themselves with teachers who watched video of other teachers and found that the teachers who watched video of themselves reported higher levels of learning. Elizabeth van Es and Sherin (2006) found that as teachers watched video of their teaching regularly over a period of time, they shifted from noticing themselves to noticing their students and from making evaluative comments to making interpretive comments.

Mary Lundeberg and her colleagues (2008) compared teachers who watched video of their own teaching with teachers who watched videos of their colleagues and of unfamiliar teachers. They found that teachers reported the greatest benefits from watching video of their own teaching and that simply watching videos of one's teaching is less effective than doing careful analysis of the video and viewing videos multiple times. Others have reported similar results (Brophy, 2004; Calandra, Gurvitch, & Lund, 2008; Hennessy & Deaney, 2009).

Perhaps the most useful aspect of video data is that teachers can examine them multiple times (van Es, 2009). They can rewind and replay videos repeatedly, each time focusing on different aspects of their teaching. For example, the first time a teacher watches a video segment, he might examine his use of verbal and nonverbal behaviors that indicate affection for students. The second time, he might pay attention to how the physical layout of the classroom affects pacing and classroom routines (such as moving into groups or passing out and collecting papers). The following vignette depicts how a teacher might use video as a form of focused feedback.

> Mr. Beuchen, a middle school social studies teacher, has videotaped himself teaching a lesson about the Constitution. As he reviews it the first time, he watches to see how well his classroom setup facilitates group work—something he has targeted as a growth goal. He notices that the way he has grouped desks in pods is helpful, but he realizes that students keep leaving their groups to go get materials and supplies, and when they come back, it takes the group a long time to get back on task. He thinks, "Maybe I'll make a supply caddy for each pod so everything the group needs is right in front of them."
>
> The second time he watches the tape, he looks for how well he helped students make overt links between content related to the Constitution and the unit his class just completed on different forms of government. This is another area he has decided to focus on. He listens carefully to students' responses to his questions and realizes that although the links students were making were good, they were all verbal. He realizes he needs to make links in the future using different media like video clips, pictures, art, and visual representations. He reviews the tape one more time, because he wants to focus on his level of withitness, the third and final element for which he has set growth goals. He notices that he did a great job of moving around the room and making eye contact with each student, but he realizes that on several occasions, he didn't deal with potential problems when he first noticed them. He knows that ignoring problems won't make them go away and decides to focus on nipping issues in the bud in the future.

Student Survey Data

Student survey data can be used as a powerful form of focused feedback. Figure 5.2 depicts one form of a student survey.

Directions: For each question, circle "I disagree," "I agree," or "I strongly agree."
Learning Goals and Feedback
1. My teacher clearly communicates what I am supposed to be learning during lessons.

I disagree	I agree	I strongly agree

2. My teacher helps me see how well I am doing during each unit.

I disagree	I agree	I strongly agree

3. My teacher notices when I do well.

I disagree	I agree	I strongly agree

Figure 5.2: Student survey.

Continued on next page →

Rules and Procedures

4. My teacher tells me how he or she expects me to behave in class.

   I disagree   I agree   I strongly agree

5. My classroom is organized for learning.

   I disagree   I agree   I strongly agree

New Information

6. My teacher tells me what information is most important.

   I disagree   I agree   I strongly agree

7. My teacher asks me to work in a group when I am learning new information.

   I disagree   I agree   I strongly agree

8. My teacher helps me think about what I already know.

   I disagree   I agree   I strongly agree

9. My teacher teaches me new information a little bit at a time.

   I disagree   I agree   I strongly agree

10. My teacher gives me time to think about what I have learned.

    I disagree   I agree   I strongly agree

11. My teacher helps me learn things that he or she didn't teach in class.

    I disagree   I agree   I strongly agree

12. My teacher asks me to show my learning using pictures, charts, and diagrams.

    I disagree   I agree   I strongly agree

13. My teacher asks questions that make me think about my learning.

    I disagree   I agree   I strongly agree

Practicing and Deepening Knowledge

14. My teacher reminds me of what I already know.

    I disagree   I agree   I strongly agree

15. My teacher expects students in this class to help each other learn.

    I disagree   I agree   I strongly agree

16. My teacher gives me homework that helps me learn.

    I disagree   I agree   I strongly agree

17. My teacher asks me to think about how things are like each other and different from one another.

    I disagree   I agree   I strongly agree

18. My teacher asks me to look for errors in the information I hear or read.

    I disagree   I agree   I strongly agree

19. My teacher asks me to practice things over and over until I get good at them.

    I disagree   I agree   I strongly agree

20. My teacher asks me to think about what I might have misunderstood or what I am still confused about.

    I disagree   I agree   I strongly agree

Applying Knowledge

21. My teacher asks me to solve problems in teams.

       I disagree   I agree   I strongly agree

22. My teacher asks me to make predictions and test them to see if they are true.

       I disagree   I agree   I strongly agree

23. My teacher is always willing to help me and provide guidance.

       I disagree   I agree   I strongly agree

Engagement

24. My teacher notices when I'm not interested in what he or she is teaching.

       I disagree   I agree   I strongly agree

25. My teacher makes learning interesting and fun.

       I disagree   I agree   I strongly agree

26. My teacher wants everyone to participate in class discussions.

       I disagree   I agree   I strongly agree

27. My teacher asks me to move around during class.

       I disagree   I agree   I strongly agree

28. My teacher keeps class moving.

       I disagree   I agree   I strongly agree

29. My teacher is excited about what he or she is teaching me.

       I disagree   I agree   I strongly agree

30. My teacher encourages me to disagree with other students in a respectful way.

       I disagree   I agree   I strongly agree

31. My teacher wants to know about me.

       I disagree   I agree   I strongly agree

32. My teacher tells me interesting or unusual facts about what I am learning.

       I disagree   I agree   I strongly agree

Management

33. My teacher knows about everything that happens in our classroom.

       I disagree   I agree   I strongly agree

34. My teacher gives consequences when students break the rules.

       I disagree   I agree   I strongly agree

35. My teacher notices when I follow the rules.

       I disagree   I agree   I strongly agree

Relationships

36. My teacher wants to know about the things I am interested in.

       I disagree   I agree   I strongly agree

37. My teacher likes me.

       I disagree   I agree   I strongly agree

Continued on next page →

38. My teacher is very self-controlled.		
I disagree	I agree	I strongly agree

Expectations

39. My teacher thinks that I can succeed.		
I disagree	I agree	I strongly agree

40. My teacher expects me to answer difficult questions.		
I disagree	I agree	I strongly agree

41. My teacher asks me to explain the thinking behind my answers to questions.		
I disagree	I agree	I strongly agree

Visit **marzanoresearch.com/classroomstrategies** for a reproducible version of this figure.

The questions in figure 5.2 directly ask students about each of the forty-one elements in the model. Readers can access versions of the survey for primary (grades K–2), upper elementary (grades 3–5), middle school (grades 6–8), and high school (grades 9–12) students online at **marzanoresearch.com /classroomstrategies**. Student responses to these surveys provide teachers with feedback on the entire model.

Another option is to ask students only a few questions that are specific to the strategies the teacher has selected for growth goals. For example, a teacher who has been trying to increase wait time after asking a question as a way to give more students time to think about their answers might ask, "As your teacher, I've been trying to wait a little while before calling on someone to answer a question. How does this change the way you think when questions are asked?" Following are sample responses from students.

- **Student 1**: "Sometimes it's a little awkward. I feel like you're waiting for some magic signal before you call on anybody. But now that I know that you're just giving us time to think, I'll probably be more comfortable."

- **Student 2**: "I like it. It gives me some time to think. Usually I don't bother to think about questions in class because I know someone else will probably figure out the answer before me."

- **Student 3**: "I don't need you to wait. I always know the answer right after you ask the question."

- **Student 4**: "I wish you had told us that was what you were doing. I thought that you were mad at us and you were taking that time to cool down. But knowing you're doing it so we can all have a better chance of answering questions makes me like it more."

- **Student 5**: "Please keep doing that thing where you wait. It's so annoying that some kids always have their hands up right after you ask a question. When you wait it gives them some time to chill out, and then the rest of us have a chance to participate."

- **Student 6**: "It makes class boring. I'm not going to answer questions in class anyway, so I don't know why you think giving more time is going to help."

The teacher would analyze these responses and then make an entry in a reflection log. Figure 5.3 depicts a sample entry in a reflection log.

2/6	I surveyed my students today to find out how they were feeling about my use of wait time after I ask questions. Overall, I think my students are grateful for the time to think. They seem to like the idea that it evens the playing field and gives more students a chance to answer.
	I had a few students who didn't like it, and I may want to follow up with them. I'm thinking of seeing if I can find some strategies for my students whose hands always shoot up right after I ask a question. I don't want them to lose enthusiasm, but I want other students to have a chance to participate. Perhaps I'll ask that group (who are always the first to raise their hands) to keep their academic notebooks out during class and respond in them when I ask a question. That way they are still engaged, and they have a chance to formulate more extended answers. I'd want to meet with them regularly to review their answers and provide feedback.
	I had a few responses from students who said they didn't want to answer questions regardless of how long I waited. I'd like to come up with a strategy that encourages them to answer questions even if they're not comfortable speaking in front of the group.
	I think in the future, I want to be more open with my students when I'm trying out a new strategy. I had several responses indicating that students were confused when I used wait time, and some who felt uncomfortable because they didn't know what I was doing or why I was doing it. I could have alleviated that discomfort by explaining the strategy to my class before I started using it.

Figure 5.3: Sample entry in reflection log.

The following vignette depicts how a teacher might use student survey data.

Miss Tso wants to start using student survey data to collect information about her teaching, but she is concerned that her first graders might have trouble filling out the surveys. In light of this, she decides to use her interactive whiteboard's learner response system. She selects survey questions pertaining to her growth goals for the trimester and displays each question on the board as she reads it aloud to her students. The students push the following buttons on their response devices to indicate the particular response: (A) Yes, I feel like that!, (B) I'm not sure how I feel, or (C) No, that's not how I feel. The students love using the technology, and Miss Tso's software program reports data for individual students and the class as a whole. Afterward, Miss Tso looks at the survey data and sees several questions for which a majority of students answered, "No, that's not how I feel." One is "I know exactly what we're learning in class right now," a question designed to measure how well the teacher communicates clear learning goals. In response, Miss Tso spends some more time talking to students about their target learning goal for each unit and decides to start asking students to help her translate each goal into their own words, a language she calls "first-gradish."

Student Achievement Data

Ultimately, the most valid information a teacher can use to determine the extent to which a specific strategy has been effective is data about student achievement. Obtaining this type of data takes preparation and planning, but such information is well worth the effort. We recommend the following process for studying the impact of a specific strategy on student achievement.

1. **Identify two groups of students with whom you can teach the same content.**

   This is a fairly easy process if a school is departmentalized (that is, a teacher teaches more than one class). For example, if a teacher teaches seventh-grade mathematics, she would identify two classes to which she teaches the same content.

If a teacher works in a self-contained classroom (that is, one teacher is responsible for all subjects taught to students), she would randomly assign students to two groups. To illustrate, an elementary teacher in a self-contained classroom could randomly split his class in half to create two similar groups. When the class is split into two, the teacher must arrange for the students in one group to be somewhere other than the classroom for at least one class period. A teacher might make arrangements for half of the class to go to the library for one class period. The next day, the other half of the class would visit the library for one class period.

2. **Teach the same content to both classes using a selected strategy in one class but not in the other.**

When two different classes are employed, more than one class period can be used to try the strategy under investigation. When students in a single class have been organized into two groups, it is probably best if only a single class period is used to try the target strategy.

As much as is possible, everything in the two classes should be the same except that in one class the target strategy is used, but in the other class it is not. To illustrate, a teacher who is working on clearly communicating learning goals might begin a unit in one class with a discussion of the learning goal and provide time for students to ask clarifying questions about the goal. Each day, the teacher would also post the learning goal on the whiteboard. With the other class, the teacher would not mention a learning goal but would do everything else in the class exactly the same.

In this example, the teacher uses two different classes of students. Therefore, the teacher's experiment with the effects of setting class learning goals can extend over a number of lessons. However, if the teacher were in a self-contained classroom and had to split her class into two groups, a single lesson would be employed. While one half of the students were in the library, the other half would be taught the lesson with a clear focus on the learning goal. The next day, those students would go to the library, and the other half of the class (who were previously in the library) would be taught the same lesson without the benefit of a clear learning goal.

3. **Administer the same pretest and posttest to both groups and compare the results.**

To determine whether the strategy has worked, the teacher would give the same pretest and the same posttest to both groups—the students for whom the target instructional strategy was used (called the *experimental* group) and the group of students for whom the target instructional strategy was not used (called the *control* group). The teacher would subtract each student's pretest score from his or her posttest score to compute gain scores. At Marzano Research Laboratory, over 490 studies with teachers have been conducted using gain scores for which the pretest and posttests both involved a 100-point scale (that is, the highest score a student could receive is 100). Table 5.1 displays the distribution of these gain scores.

In table 5.1, the median gain score (that is, the 50th percentile) is 25.9. That means, on the average, that in these studies, students gained 25.9 points from the pretest to the posttest. The 40th percentile average gain score is 22.6, the 60th percentile average gain score is 31.7, and so on.

Table 5.1: Distribution of Gain Scores Across 493 Classes

Percentile	Gain Score
1st	0.0
5th	1.2
10th	4.9
15th	8.8
20th	11.7
25th	15.4
30th	17.8
35th	20.0
40th	22.6
45th	24.2
50th	25.9
55th	28.5
60th	31.7
65th	34.9
70th	37.7
75th	41.1
80th	43.8
85th	48.4
90th	56.7
95th	68.2
99th	89.6

To determine if the target strategy enhances student achievement, a teacher simply compares the average gain scores of the two groups of students. For example, if the average gain score for the students who were exposed to the strategy (the experimental group) was 32.5 and the average gain score for students who were not exposed to the strategy (the control group) was 22.1, that indicates that the strategy had a positive impact on student learning. Of course, this is not a rigorous statistical treatment of the data, but it is evidence that the strategy has generated positive effects. If desired, a teacher can also send the pretest and posttest data to Marzano Research Laboratory (www .marzanoresearch.com) for a more sophisticated analysis.

Looking at Specific Types of Students

Another use of achievement data is to examine the differences in scores between groups of students in class. For example, a teacher might compare those students who are English learners (ELs) and those who are not. Such comparisons commonly interest school and district administrators because they can be used to determine the effectiveness of instruction across different subgroups of students. To illustrate, figure 5.4 depicts the gain scores for students classified as ELs and those not classified as ELs for the experimental and control classes for one teacher.

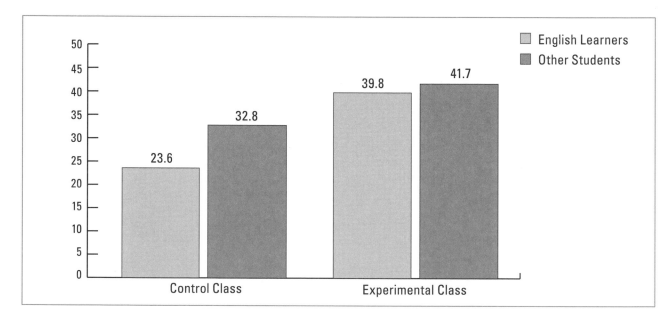

Figure 5.4: Average gain scores for English learners compared to other students.

Notice that in the experimental class, the average gain scores for the EL students and the other students are very close, whereas in the control class, the average gain scores are much lower for the EL students. Such evidence is an indication that the strategy has had an effect; it appears to help English learners. Students' average gain scores might also be compared according to gender, ethnicity, or level of teacher expectation. The following vignette depicts how a teacher might use student achievement data.

> Ms. Rozetti, a high school English teacher, is focusing on helping her students revise their knowledge as they read *A Tale of Two Cities* by Charles Dickens. She teaches two periods of sophomore students and decides to use academic notebooks with one class but not with the other. To begin, she administers the same pretest to both classes. Then she teaches exactly the same content to both classes, but in the experimental class, she asks them to write in their academic notebooks during the last five minutes of class each day. Once a week, students review their notebooks with peers to correct errors or misconceptions and add additional information or conclusions they may have drawn over the past week.

At the end of the unit, Ms. Rozetti administers the posttest and computes a gain score for each student. She finds that the average gain score for the control group (without academic notebooks) was 22.8, and the average gain score for the experimental group was 30.5. She also compares the average gain scores for her EL students with other students' scores in both classes, and she finds that in the experimental class, there was only a 0.8 difference between the two groups, compared with a 4.8 difference in the control class. She is very enthusiastic about her findings, as are her principal and other district administrators.

Putting the Data Together

The ultimate goal of focused feedback is to allow teachers to track their progress over time. Figure 5.5 depicts this feedback for a teacher working on using the class vote strategy, one of the strategies for the element of using friendly controversy. Visit **marzanoresearch.com/classroomstrategies** to access a blank reproducible version of the Teacher Progress Chart.

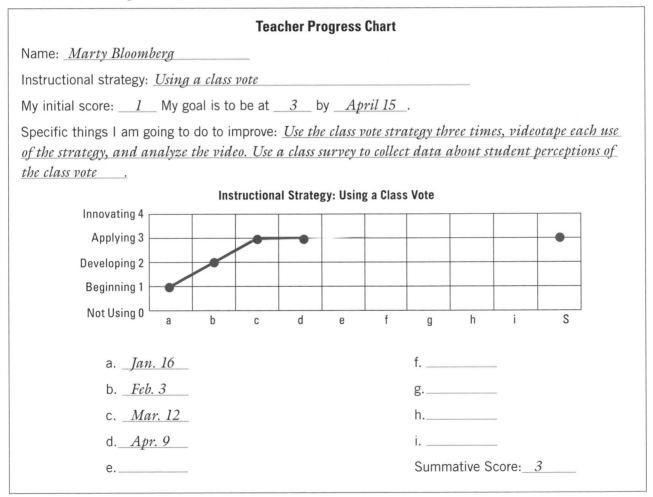

Figure 5.5: Teacher progress for the strategy of using friendly controversy.

Notice the different scores over the four months shown on the chart. To obtain these scores, the teacher used the various types of data previously described to estimate his status at each point in time. It is important for teachers to record their logic in assigning scores. Figure 5.6 (page 72) depicts the way a teacher can record these descriptions.

1/16	I assigned myself a 1 after watching a videotape of myself using a class vote to incorporate friendly controversy. I tried the strategy, but I feel like I got important parts of it wrong. I had the students vote, but when I asked them to move to different parts of the room according to how they voted, they got really noisy, and it was almost impossible to lead a discussion about their opinions. I didn't have them vote again at the end, because I was so tired from asking them to be quiet during the discussion.
2/3	I videotaped myself using the class vote strategy again. I assigned myself a 2, because I feel like I got better. I followed a protocol I designed to help the discussion be more orderly (I had students take chairs and sit down after they had voted), and we had a discussion of students' opinions and the class voted again after the discussion. I think the discussion was a little superficial, but I was busy making sure everyone was paying attention, and I couldn't focus all my attention on what students were saying.
3/12	I used the class vote strategy again today and videotaped myself. After watching the tape and thinking about how it went, I gave myself a score of 3. I felt like this time I didn't have to focus as much on my protocol or the steps of the strategy, and I was able to pay attention to what students were saying. I asked probing questions and even helped students ask each other questions and respectfully comment on other people's opinions.
4/9	I used a survey to collect information from my students on how well they feel I am doing with the class vote strategy. Based on the results, I gave myself a 3 for this strategy. Most of the responses indicated that students were learning from the class vote strategy and that they appreciated the way it helped them clarify and discuss their views on an issue. A few students pointed out they are sometimes uncomfortable taking a position on an issue prior to the discussion, so I may incorporate some aspects of seminars when I do this next to give students time to collect information and form an opinion on the topic before we discuss it in class.

Figure 5.6: Teacher descriptions concerning why scores were assigned.

On January 16, the teacher rated himself at the Beginning (1) level. He explained that he still made mistakes while executing the strategy. By March 12, however, he had assigned himself a score of Applying (3). He explained that he was able to monitor the strategy's effect on students while using the strategy. The following vignette depicts how a teacher might put data together to track his or her progress.

> Mr. Falls has been tracking his progress on helping his students examine similarities and differences. Since he started tracking his progress in January, he has used several different comparison strategies, including sentence stem comparisons, Venn diagrams, and comparison matrices. However, his scores are still usually 1s and 2s. He's feeling a little frustrated, but as he looks at his scores, he realizes skipping around from strategy to strategy doesn't allow him to get really good at any of them. He decides to focus exclusively on using sentence stem comparisons with his fourth graders. He videotapes himself teaching several lessons where he models making these comparisons and asks his students to generate them, and he also surveys his students to see how the strategy is helping them. He plans a unit with his cooperating teacher, where he teaches the content using sentence stem comparisons, and she teaches the same content without any comparison activities. They collect pretest and posttest data and see that the sentence stems made a difference in student achievement. He plots his scores on his tracking chart for all these activities, and in several months, he has scored at the Applying (3) level several times.

Summary

This chapter discussed the elements of focused feedback. Feedback allows teachers to gauge how effective their practice has been. Reflection logs and self-viewing using video footage are both ways teachers can view their practice from an outside, more objective perspective. Pairs and teams of teachers can also watch videos together to provide each other with feedback about specific elements of performance. Students are also excellent sources of feedback. They can provide data by answering survey questions about their teacher's use of specific strategies. Additionally, student achievement data can provide insightful feedback. It stands to reason that when students are achieving at higher levels, a teacher's practice has had the desired effect.

Chapter 5: Comprehension Questions

1. What are ways to obtain focused feedback?

2. What guidelines should a teacher follow when watching video of his or her teaching?

3. How might you go about collecting student achievement data for a specific strategy in your own classroom?

4. How might a teacher organize and track multiple sources of feedback?

Chapter 6

OBSERVING AND DISCUSSING TEACHING

The final element important to the development of teaching expertise is observing and discussing teaching. By definition, such activities require interaction with other teachers. In this chapter, we briefly discuss three ways that teachers might interact: (1) videos of other teachers, (2) coaching colleagues, and (3) instructional rounds. Two or more teachers can fairly easily set up the first two techniques. The third technique requires administrative support.

Videos of Other Teachers

In chapter 5, we discussed how teachers might examine videos of their own teaching as a form of personal feedback. In this section, we consider how teachers might examine videos of other teachers and discuss the effectiveness of the strategies they observe. This simply requires two or more teachers who agree to meet and discuss instructional strategies and behaviors.

There are a number of sources that can be used for this type of professional interaction. Table 6.1 lists videos from YouTube that might be used to observe and discuss other teachers. These are free to all users of the Internet. When using videos from YouTube, it is important to remember that they are raw footage of classroom activities, and there is no guarantee that they exhibit effective teaching. Visit **marzanoresearch.com/classroomstrategies** for live versions of all links mentioned in the text.

Table 6.1: List of Teaching Videos From YouTube

Level	Video Links
Primary (Grades K–2)	Reading (read-aloud): www.youtube.com/watch?v=pInDSYAiNPA
	Reading (reading workshop): www.youtube.com/watch?v=BWDZqopREwg&feature=related
	Reading (phonics): www.youtube.com/watch?v=2YwMY5sn9t8
	Writing (mini-lesson): www.youtube.com/watch?v=WQVNL3F67Q8&feature=related
	Math (measurement): www.youtube.com/watch?v=HHDyxTRCwQ0&feature=related
	Math (calendar): www.youtube.com/watch?v=UXkGzjeFH88&feature=related
	Science: www.youtube.com/watch?v=b133AGFcICY

Continued on next page →

Level	Video Links
Upper Elementary (Grades 3–5)	Classroom management: www.youtube.com/watch?v=S4QbG4dZErng Reading: www.youtube.com/watch?v=jgUvNnkGZhM&feature=related Math: www.youtube.com/watch?v=j8nwgjHJiIO Writing: www.youtube.com/watch?v=OPw_O8knKmg Science: www.youtube.com/watch?v=HVrYOFDKSrM Social studies: www.youtube.com/watch?v=RV4y9PP_g80 Social studies: www.youtube.com/watch?v=JXYOUZbGVFU
Middle School (Grades 6–8)	Language arts (similes, metaphors, and descriptive writing): www.youtube.com/watch?v=X5xFMmK5Ujs Math: www.youtube.com/watch?v=pi7ED4wqfSY&feature=related Math (order of operations): www.youtube.com/watch?v=XroJtR9gQc8&NR=1 History/social studies: www.youtube.com/watch?v=h2pHiWJtmrw&feature=related Science: www.youtube.com/watch?v=tFY3zJvyw50&feature=related Science: www.youtube.com/watch?v=k48AZn9q5rs
High School (Grades 9–12)	Math: www.youtube.com/watch?v=h6WJdsbOdfM Math (AP calculus): www.youtube.com/watch?v=fe6eQp8avDg&feature=related Language arts (writing): http://www.youtube.com/watch?v=RY3t2sijb4M Language arts (writing mini-lesson): www.youtube.com/watch?v=NtXn9JaxcTA Science (physics): www.youtube.com/watch?v=MLW5LsgEe8g Social studies: www.youtube.com/watch?v=WuNJTeIN79Y
To find more videos, search YouTube using grade-level and subject-area key words (for example, "third-grade math lesson").	

A number of humorous video clips from television shows and movies are also available on the Internet. Following is a list of such videos.

- **Ben Stein in *Ferris Bueller's Day Off*:** www.youtube.com/watch?v=dxPVyieptwA

- **Robin Williams in *Dead Poets Society*:** www.youtube.com/watch?v=qQtmGcdSDAI&feature=related

- **Jerry Seinfeld on *Saturday Night Live*:** www.dailymotion.com/video/xa83cm_snl-seinfeld-school-sketch_fun

- **Rodney Dangerfield in *Back to School*:** www.youtube.com/watch?v=YlVDGmjz7eM

- **David Spade in *8 Simple Rules*:** www.youtube.com/watch?v=0WXhtyVs9Gk

When examining videos from YouTube or from television shows and movies, it is useful to determine what was done well by the teacher and what was not. To illustrate, consider the video segment from *Dead Poets Society* (Haft, Witt, Thomas, & Weir, 1989). In that movie, actor Robin Williams plays a teacher at a private boys' school. In the particular scene listed, Williams takes his students to the foyer of the school to stand in front of a giant display case with photos, trophies, and awards that past students earned. Using the first stanza of a poem by Robert Herrick, he urges them to seize the day ("Carpe diem!") and make the most of their lives, especially since they will someday die, just as the people in the photographs in front of them have died.

In this scene, Williams's character demonstrates several effective strategies. For example, he gets the boys physically moving by taking them out of the classroom and into the foyer of the school. He uses quotations and visual aids to capture students' attention and engage them, and his intensity and enthusiasm are palpable as he makes eye contact with every student. He directly connects the content to students' lives, and although the students later describe his voice fluctuations (from a loud shout to a quiet whisper) as "spooky," they also recognize that he is different and interesting.

There are also other strategies that Williams's character could have employed but did not. For example, when a student answers one of his questions with a short and shallow answer, Williams's character responds "No!" and goes on to tell the class what the answer should be. He could have used elaborative interrogation to probe this student's answer in order to elicit a more meaningful response.

In general, discussing the effective strategies demonstrated in a video segment, as well as strategies that could have or should have been employed, make almost any video segment a useful vehicle for observing and discussing teaching. The following vignette depicts how two teachers might use video segments.

> Ms. Brown and Mrs. Selgis are watching videos of teachers. They start with one they found on the Internet of an eighth-grade teacher using hand signals and tone of voice to teach her students about the order of operations. They each identify things she did well (demonstrating intensity and enthusiasm, using gestures, using verbal cues) and then discuss what they think she could have done to improve. They both agree that she could have asked the students to do more to practice and develop fluency with using the order of operations, and students might have understood the principles behind the process better if she had asked them to engage in friendly controversy or perspective-taking activities. Then they watch a humorous video clip from the movie *Ferris Bueller's Day Off*. They are already familiar with the scene in which actor Ben Stein teaches a high school social studies class, but they want to see if they can identify any positive strategies. They have a great time laughing at how excruciatingly dull his teaching is, but they do notice that he must have had good classroom management and withitness, since there don't seem to be any behavior problems in the room. They also observe that the teacher seems to have a thorough knowledge of the content, but they note that he could do a better job of identifying critical-input experiences, and he could have used some friendly controversy activities to help his students discuss the Laffer curve.

Coaching Colleagues

Coaching colleagues are pairs or trios of teachers who agree to provide each other with honest feedback regarding their use of instructional strategies. Coaching has been used in a variety of ways in K–12 education, but *coaching colleagues* (also called peer coaching) refers specifically to "a confidential process through which two or more professional colleagues work together to reflect on current practices; expand, refine, and build new skills; share ideas; teach one another; conduct classroom research; or solve problems in the workplace" (Robbins, 1991, p. 1). Bruce Joyce and Beverly Showers (2002) concluded that coaching has a dramatic impact on a teacher's skills. Specifically, they found that "a large and dramatic increase in transfer of training—effect size of 1.42—occurs when coaching is added to an initial training experience" (p. 77). In other words, training with coaching (as opposed to training alone) produced a 42 percentile point gain with regard to transfer of training among teachers. They also found that, compared to uncoached teachers with the same initial training, coached teachers practiced new strategies more frequently, developed greater skill with strategies, used strategies more appropriately, exhibited greater long-term retention of strategies, and were more likely and better able to explain new strategies to their students.

Peer coaching, where two or more teachers provide coaching to one another, has demonstrated benefits in a variety of venues and a variety of ways. It can promote more effective instructional practices (Ponticell, Olson, & Charlier, 1995), it helps teachers learn and refine new strategies (Gordon, Nolan, & Forlenza, 1995), it leads to better instruction for linguistically and culturally diverse students (Galbraith & Anstrom, 1995), it prompts teachers to adopt new instructional strategies (Slater & Simmons, 2001), and it enhances teachers' early literacy instruction for at-risk students (Swafford, Maltsberger, Button, & Furgerson, 1997).

Rosanne Zwart, Theo Wubbels, Theo Bergen, and Sanneke Bolhuis (2009) found that teachers in a peer coaching program benefitted the most if they felt some pressure to experiment with new instructional practices and methods in their classrooms and if they felt their peer coaching relationship was safe, constructive, and trustworthy. Pam Robbins (1991) stated that "to be effective and sustained over time, coaching activities must have a deliberate focus. And the focus must be one that matters to the individuals involved" (p. 6).

While *peer coaching* is a popular term in K–12 education, we prefer *coaching colleagues*. Coaching colleagues can be assigned or selected using several different methods. A teacher might simply choose a colleague or colleagues with whom he or she already has an established respectful and trusting relationship. Alternatively, a teacher could identify colleagues who demonstrate strengths in the particular areas in which that teacher wants to improve. Yet another method might be to have the teachers in a school randomly draw names to form peer coaching pairs or triads. All three methods are acceptable, depending on the comfort level of staff and the collegial atmosphere in a building. Once peer coaching relationships have been established, norms should be generated for each small group or pair of colleagues. Norms might include the following:

- Observations and feedback are confidential and should stay within the peer coaching group.

- Information obtained as a result of the peer coaching relationship should not be shared or used for formal evaluative purposes.

- Peer coaching colleagues should ask clarifying questions and use communication techniques that are honest and supportive.

The following vignette depicts how coaching colleagues might be employed.

> Debbie, Latisha, and Li are elementary teachers who have agreed to be coaching colleagues. Debbie, a third-grade teacher, seeks assistance on her use of routines. Specifically, she wants assistance in setting up clear rules and procedures, as well as acknowledging adherence or lack of adherence to the established rules and procedures. She notices that her students tend to follow rules and procedures less and less as the year progresses. By the end of the year, she struggles. Latisha, a fifth-grade teacher, is strong in this area and has some great ideas for Debbie. Latisha wants help with her questioning strategies. Li, the music teacher, struggles with setting and describing clear learning goals. She finds that she gets so focused on classroom

activities that she neglects to make sure her students know what they are expected to learn by the end of the unit. Li and Debbie think they can provide Latisha with specific help in the area of questioning. The three meet to share their personal growth goals. They set up their first class observation session, and Debbie agrees to be observed first, because rules and procedures are important to establish early in the year. After the observation, the group meets and Latisha and Li pose reflective questions to Debbie and give her some suggestions based on the scales, teacher evidence, and student evidence associated with clearly defining and communicating rules and procedures. They limit the number of suggestions to keep the interaction focused. At the end of each quarter, the group members reflect on their personal improvement and record their progress toward their goals.

Instructional Rounds

One of the most powerful ways to observe and discuss teaching is to engage in instructional rounds (see Marzano, 2011; Marzano et al., 2011). Teachers can examine videos of other teachers and interact with coaching colleagues with little or no administrative support, but instructional rounds are usually a schoolwide effort that requires administrative support and involvement.

During instructional rounds, groups of teachers visit classrooms in their school to observe their colleagues in action. The goal of instructional rounds is for the observing teachers to compare their own practices to the practice of the observed teacher. After visiting classrooms, the observing teachers engage in group discussion and reflection and draw conclusions about their own practices. Unlike many teacher observations, the focus of instructional rounds is not on evaluation. Although the observed teacher *can* request feedback from the observing teachers, instructional rounds are primarily designed to enhance the pedagogical skills of the observing teachers and encourage collaboration among colleagues. Many schools that use instructional rounds have found that they create a sense of energy and excitement about professional growth and empower teachers to examine and improve their instructional practice.

In a well-designed instructional rounds program, every teacher in a school should have the opportunity to participate as an observing teacher once a semester. A lead teacher facilitates groups of observing teachers. The lead teacher is a highly professional individual who is well respected as an exceptional teacher and who guides the group's observations, discussions, and reflections. Although an administrator can fill the lead teacher's role, everyone involved must clearly understand that the administrator acts in a nonevaluative role during instructional rounds. Ideally, groups of observing teachers should visit the classrooms of veteran teachers whose ability to enhance student achievement is well proven. The lead teacher might select a number of these teachers at a school and request that the group be allowed to observe in their classrooms. Alternatively, any teachers might volunteer their classroom for observation, in which case the group would observe teachers with various levels of expertise.

In the first phase of instructional rounds, the observed teacher alerts the class that a group of teachers will be visiting their classroom that day. The observed teacher might let students know that the purpose of their visit is to help teachers learn from each other, in the same way that students are asked to learn from each other. The observing group of teachers should knock before entering the room, find seats that do not interrupt the flow of instruction (usually at the back of the room), and take notes about specific instructional strategies that they observe the teacher using. When the observation is complete, the observing group of teachers should thank the observed teacher and class and quietly exit the room.

The lead teacher facilitates the second phase of instructional rounds, involving discussion and reflection. This occurs right after the observation, usually in the hallway outside the classroom. To begin, the lead teacher reminds all participants that the focus is not on evaluating the observed teacher. Rules or norms (established before the observation) should also be reviewed before the discussion. Following is one set of rules that the group might use:

- Information gathered and recorded during classroom observations is confidential and should not be shared with anyone outside the group.

- All comments made during the discussion are confidential and should not be shared with anyone outside the group.

- Suggestions should not be made to observed teachers unless they explicitly ask for feedback.

- Observed teachers should be thanked and acknowledged for their contributions to the collective pedagogical knowledge of the school.

To begin the discussion, teachers share the positive events or outcomes (sometimes called *plusses*) they observed in a classroom and what teacher practices or strategies they thought led to those events or outcomes. For example, one participant might share that students in a social studies class seemed engaged and excited about the class discussion. This participant might then suggest that the teacher's use of the friendly controversy strategy contributed to those high levels of engagement and excitement. Another participant might say she noticed from students' responses that they seemed to be processing the content deeply and making connections with their prior knowledge, and she might attribute this outcome to the teacher's use of "small chunks."

Teachers can also share questions or concerns (sometimes called *deltas*) that they had about how the observed teacher used strategies in the classroom. Using the previous example, the participant who observed the teacher's use of friendly controversy might note that some students seemed reluctant to join in the class discussion, perhaps because they weren't sure what they thought about the issue being discussed or felt overpowered by the more vocal members of the class. When each participant has shared their plusses and deltas for one specific classroom, the team moves on to observe another classroom.

The final step of instructional rounds is for participants to each summarize the conclusions they drew from the first two phases. This last sharing session occurs at the end of the rounds cycle. In their conclusions, participants should identify the following three elements:

1. Strategies and instructional practices they already use and that they saw others use effectively

2. Strategies and instructional practices they already use but would like to re-examine or modify based on their observations

3. Strategies or instructional practices they don't use but will try because they saw others use them effectively

For example, an observing teacher might state the following conclusions:

> I already use think-pair-share as a processing strategy and I saw another teacher use it with great success. That confirms to me that it is a highly effective strategy, and I will keep using it. I already use academic notebooks, but I saw another teacher ask students to create nonlinguistic representations in their academic notebooks, in addition to writing text, and it seemed like they understood the content better as a result. I've really only asked my students to *write* in their academic notebooks, so I'd like to begin asking them to use nonlinguistic representations like charts, graphs, graphic organizers, flowcharts, and pictures in their notes as well. I'm not currently asking my students to engage in friendly controversy activities, but I'd like to start doing it. I don't want students to feel

left out if they are quiet or if they don't have fully formed opinions on the topic, so I think I'll use the vote-with-your-feet strategy to give everyone a voice and to incorporate some physical movement into my instruction.

The following vignette depicts how a school might use instructional rounds.

Mrs. Aubmeyer, the principal of Sunset Middle School, has asked one of her most seasoned and professional teachers, Mr. Jenkins, to lead instructional rounds at the school. Mr. Jenkins explained instructional rounds at the first staff meeting of the year, and several teachers have volunteered to be observed. Additionally, Mr. Jenkins and Mrs. Aubmeyer have identified several veteran teachers whose students consistently attain high levels of achievement and have requested that they allow observations in their classrooms. Most of the teachers were comfortable with being observed once Mr. Jenkins reiterated that the observations are not evaluative. Mr. Jenkins created a schedule showing which teachers will participate in rounds on specific days, and Mrs. Aubmeyer arranged for those teachers' classes to be covered.

On the first day of rounds, Mr. Jenkins meets with the participating teachers before school starts to review how teachers should act during observations, what they should look for, and what they should be prepared to share during the discussion phase. Mr. Jenkins and his group observe three classrooms that morning. Each observation lasts for ten to fifteen minutes. Immediately afterward, teachers share the plusses and deltas they observed. Discussions about these observations are brief but focused. The observing teachers seem to be very engaged in the process. After the third observation and debriefing, teachers summarize their conclusions from the morning by identifying instructional strategies they saw that are similar to the strategies they already use, questions or concerns they may have about their own instructional practice, and new ideas about instructional strategies they have as a result of the morning's observations. All of the observing teachers agree that the morning was very beneficial to their professional development.

Summary

This chapter discussed ways that teachers can observe and discuss teaching. Teachers can examine videos of other teachers in pairs or small groups and look for instructional strategies they used well and strategies they might have used but did not. Coaching colleagues can observe each other and meet together to offer feedback and suggestions, and instructional rounds offer a formalized structure for teachers to observe their colleagues and reflect on their own practice.

Chapter 6: Comprehension Questions

1. What things should teachers keep in mind when watching videos of other teachers?

2. How might you use coaching colleagues to enhance your own professional development?

3. What is the purpose of instructional rounds?

4. How might you use instructional rounds in your school?

COMPENDIUM

STRATEGIES FOR REFLECTIVE PRACTICE

The first six chapters of this book discussed a model of reflective practice that can be a powerful tool for professional growth and developing teaching expertise. The model of effective teaching outlined in chapter 2 can be used to set growth goals, engage in focused practice, receive focused feedback, and observe and discuss teaching to promote self-awareness and self-reflection for K–12 teachers.

Throughout the book, we have referred to instructional strategies and teacher behaviors related to each of the forty-one elements of effective teaching in *The Art and Science of Teaching* model (Marzano, 2007; Marzano et al., 2011) presented in chapter 2. These instructional strategies and teacher behaviors provide a unique level of specificity for the reflective practice model described in *Becoming a Reflective Teacher*. To facilitate teachers' awareness and knowledge of these instructional strategies and teacher behaviors, we provide this compendium of strategies for reflective practice.

The compendium contains over 270 strategies for reflective practice, organized according to the forty-one elements of effective teaching outlined in *The Art and Science of Teaching* framework. The compendium is intended to be a quick reference for teachers, allowing them to locate, learn about, plan, and implement instructional strategies and teacher behaviors that correspond to their personal growth goals. Here, we describe each strategy briefly but with enough detail to allow a teacher to use the strategy or behavior in the classroom right away. For those who wish to learn more about any of the strategies or behaviors listed here, visit **marzanoresearch.com/classroomstrategies** for links to other works that describe each strategy and its research base in greater detail.

For additional tips and advice about using the strategies in this compendium, visit **marzanoresearch .com/classroomstrategies** for the online appendix, *MRL Associate Tips for Reflective Practice*. These tips, which MRL associates compiled based on their experiences in schools and districts, give advice about implementing the strategies in this compendium.

COMPENDIUM CONTENTS

Lesson Segments Involving Routine Events

Design Question: What will I do to establish and communicate learning goals, track student progress, and celebrate success?

Element 1: What do I typically do to provide clear learning goals and scales (rubrics)?

Strategies

Clearly articulating learning goals, being careful not to confuse them with activities or assignments

The teacher clarifies learning goals that state what students will know or be able to do at the end of a lesson, unit, or semester. Activities and assignments are the tasks that the teacher asks students to do in order to achieve the learning goals. The teacher translates general statements from standards documents into the following learning goal formats:

Declarative knowledge: Students will understand _____.

Procedural knowledge: Students will be able to _____.

Once the teacher is familiar with the distinction between declarative and procedural knowledge, more flexible language and phrasing can be used to write learning goals, such as the following: students will be able to describe and exemplify the relationship between color and the intensity of light.

Creating scales or rubrics for learning goals

The teacher creates a scale for each target learning goal. This is done by articulating a simpler learning goal and a more complex learning goal (relative to the target learning goal) and putting the three statements into a scale such as the following (see table C.1).

Table C.1: Five-Value Scale

Score 4.0	More complex learning goal For example: Students will be able to compare and contrast the process of mitosis with other cell division processes, such as meiosis.
Score 3.0	Target learning goal For example: Students will be able to create a diagram showing the process of mitosis.
Score 2.0	Simpler learning goal For example: Students will be able to identify accurate statements about the process of mitosis.
Score 1.0	With help, partial success at score 2.0 content and score 3.0 content
Score 0.0	Even with help, no success

Note that the statements for scores 1.0 and 0.0 do not change from scale to scale.

Student-friendly scales

The teacher asks students to translate scales into student-friendly language. After the teacher explains the target, simpler, and more complex learning goals to students, students work in small groups to create their own wording for the 2.0, 3.0, and 4.0 content statements. The teacher then compiles the students' suggestions, presents the rewritten scale to students for feedback and comments, and revises as necessary.

Individual student learning goals

The teacher asks students to identify a personal learning goal that interests them and that relates to the teacher-identified learning goals. Students state their personal learning goals using the following formats:

When this unit is completed, I will better understand _____.

When this unit is completed, I will be able to _____.

Students can use the following scale to track their progress on individual learning goals (see table C.2).

Table C.2: Student Self-Assessment Scale for Individual Learning Goals

4 = I did even better than the goal I set.
3 = I accomplished my goal.
2 = I didn't accomplish everything I wanted to, but I learned quite a bit.
1 = I tried, but I didn't really learn much.
0 = I didn't really try to accomplish my goal.

Technology Links

- Throughout a presentation, include slides that restate the learning goal.

- When using learner response systems, include questions that ask students how well they think they are achieving the learning goal.

- When students are working on the Internet, remind them to consider whether a website will help them achieve the learning goal.

- Encourage students to explore websites related to the learning goal to help them identify personal learning goals.

Element 2: What do I typically do to track student progress?

Strategies

Formative assessments

To create formative assessments, the teacher designs assessment tasks that correspond to 2.0, 3.0, and 4.0 content (as specified on the scale for each learning goal). For 2.0 content, forced-choice or selected-response tasks (multiple-choice, matching, true/false, or fill-in-the-blank items) are most appropriate. For 3.0 and 4.0 content, short or extended constructed-response tasks (short written or oral responses, essays, oral reports, demonstrations, or performances) are most appropriate.

The teacher can grade these assessments using a simplified scale (without half-point scores, see table C.1, page 89) or a complete scale. Following is the generic form of the complete scale (see table C.3).

Table C.3: Generic Form of the Complete Scale

Score 4.0	More complex learning goal
Score 3.5	In addition to score 3.0 performance, partial success at score 4.0 content
Score 3.0	Target learning goal
Score 2.5	No major errors or omissions regarding score 2.0 content, and partial success at score 3.0 content
Score 2.0	Simpler learning goal
Score 1.5	Partial success at score 2.0 content, but major errors or omissions regarding score 3.0 content
Score 1.0	With help, partial success at score 2.0 content and score 3.0 content
Score 0.5	With help, partial success at score 2.0 content, but not at score 3.0 content
Score 0.0	Even with help, no success

The following scale has specific content filled in for score values 2.0, 3.0, and 4.0 (see table C.4).

Table C.4: Complete Scale With Learning Goals for Specific Content

Score 4.0	Students will be able to explain why Europeans explored and established settlements on other continents including Africa, Asia, and Australia.
Score 3.5	In addition to score 3.0 performance, partial success at score 4.0 content
Score 3.0	Students will be able to explain why Europeans explored and established settlements in the Americas.
Score 2.5	No major errors or omissions regarding score 2.0 content, and partial success at score 3.0 content

Continued on next page →

Score 2.0	Students will be able to recognize facts about European exploration and settlement in the Americas.
Score 1.5	Partial success at score 2.0 content, but major errors or omissions regarding score 3.0 content
Score 1.0	With help, partial success at score 2.0 content and score 3.0 content
Score 0.5	With help, partial success at score 2.0 content, but not at score 3.0 content
Score 0.0	Even with help, no success

Response patterns

The teacher identifies response patterns by deciding which items on an assessment represent 2.0, 3.0, and 4.0 content and scoring each item using a coding scheme (for example, C = correct, I = incorrect, P = partially correct). A score can then be assigned using the following guidelines:

- All items correct = 4.0

- All 3.0 and 2.0 items correct, partial credit for 4.0 items = 3.5

- All 3.0 and 2.0 items correct, no 4.0 items correct = 3.0

- All 2.0 items correct, partial credit for 3.0 items and/or 4.0 items = 2.5

- All 2.0 items correct, no 3.0 or 4.0 items correct = 2.0

- Partial credit for 2.0 items, partial or no credit for 3.0 and/or 4.0 items = 1.5

If a student does not answer any items correctly or does not complete any items, the teacher should meet with that student to determine his or her score, using the following guidelines:

- Independently, no items correct; with help, partial credit for 2.0 and 3.0 items = 1.0

- Independently, no items correct; with help, partial credit for 2.0 items but not for 3.0 items = 0.5

- Independently, no items correct; with help, no items correct = 0.0

If the pattern of responses does not fit any of the previous guidelines, the teacher might drop flawed items from the assessment, reclassify items at a higher or lower score value (based on the class's responses), or meet with a student and ask the student to verify his or her understanding of the content from specific items the student missed. The student might complete exercises or design a task that shows his or her understanding.

Individual score-level assessments

The teacher uses assessments that evaluate only one level of a scale (for example, only 2.0 content) to measure students' procedural knowledge (which builds on itself and requires competency at one level before progressing to the next) or to allow students to progress at their own pace through the levels of a scale.

Different types of assessments

The teacher uses obtrusive assessments (which interrupt the flow of classroom activity), unobtrusive assessments (which do not interrupt classroom activities), or student-generated assessments. Obtrusive assessments might be paper-and-pencil tests, demonstrations and performances, oral reports, or probing discussions (one-on-one conversations between the teacher and a student). Unobtrusive assessments are usually observations when the teacher sees the student demonstrating a particular type of knowledge and records a score for that student. Student-generated assessments involve students proposing tasks that will demonstrate their level of knowledge for a specific learning goal.

Formative grading

The teacher uses one or more of several different approaches to grading, each of which is summarized as follows:

- **Approach 1**—Each assessment in a unit allows students to score at the 2.0, 3.0, or 4.0 level. The students graph their scores throughout the unit, and the teacher uses that group of scores to assign a summative score at the end of the unit.

- **Approach 2**—The first assessment in a unit allows students to score at the 2.0, 3.0, or 4.0 level. After the first assessment, students move at their own pace, taking individual score-level assessments to move up to the next level.

- **Approach 3**—The teacher administers individual score-level assessments to the entire class, only moving up to the next level once the majority of students in the class has mastered the content at the current level.

- **Approach 4**—The teacher assigns students scores at the end of each unit, but they are allowed to improve those scores at any time during the year by demonstrating their competence at higher score levels, usually using student-generated assessments.

Charting student progress

The teacher provides students with charts on which they can record their progress on a learning goal over time, such as the following (see fig. C.1, page 94).

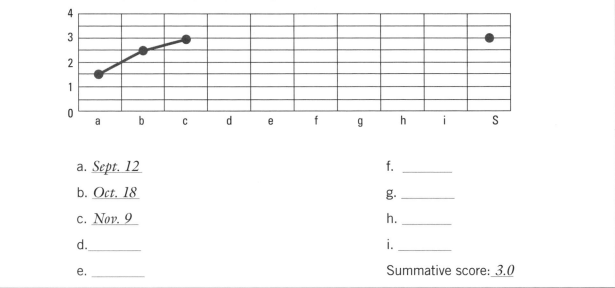

Student Progress Chart

Keeping Track of My Learning

Name: _Courtney_

Learning goal: _Make and defend inferences about the causes of the Civil War_

My score at the beginning: _1.5_. My goal is to be at _3.0_ by _November 17_.

Specific things I am going to do to improve: _Work 15 minutes three times a week_.

Learning Goal: Making and Defending Inferences About the Causes of the Civil War

a. _Sept. 12_   f. _____

b. _Oct. 18_   g. _____

c. _Nov. 9_   h. _____

d. _____   i. _____

e. _____   Summative score: _3.0_

Figure C.1: Student progress chart.

Source: Adapted from Marzano, 2010.

The student sets a learning goal at the beginning of the unit and then tracks her scores on that learning goal throughout the unit. At the end of the unit, the teacher assigns a final or summative score to the student for the learning goal being tracked (see column S in the figure).

Charting class progress

The teacher uses a whole-class tracking chart to create a snapshot of the progress of a group of students, such as the following (see fig. C.2).

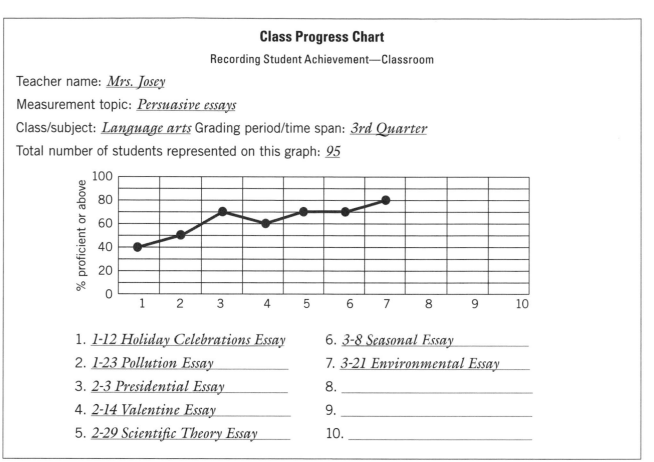

Class Progress Chart

Recording Student Achievement—Classroom

Teacher name: *Mrs. Josey*

Measurement topic: *Persuasive essays*

Class/subject: *Language arts* Grading period/time span: *3rd Quarter*

Total number of students represented on this graph: *95*

1. *1-12 Holiday Celebrations Essay*
2. *1-23 Pollution Essay*
3. *2-3 Presidential Essay*
4. *2-14 Valentine Essay*
5. *2-29 Scientific Theory Essay*
6. *3-8 Seasonal Essay*
7. *3-21 Environmental Essay*
8. _____
9. _____
10. _____

Figure C.2: Class progress chart.

Source: Adapted from Marzano, 2010.

Technology Links

- Use learner response systems or voting websites (such as www.polleverywhere.com) to collect evidence of students' levels of learning.

- When using learner response systems, display voting results anonymously, and ask students to suggest activities that will help the class achieve the learning goals.

- Use social networking and other communication websites and devices to allow students to post and discuss what they understand and what they need more help with.

- Allow students to submit their work electronically (by email or as an online post). The teacher can provide feedback electronically, and students can respond to the feedback and resubmit their work.

- Use audio and video recordings to provide verbal feedback or to record teacher-student conferences for students to review later.

Element 3: What do I typically do to celebrate success?

Strategies

Final status celebration

The teacher celebrates each student's final status (or summative score) at the end of each unit. The teacher might recognize all the students who achieved a final score of 3.0, all the students who achieved a final score of 3.5, and all the students who achieved a final score of 4.0. Students could stand for a round of applause from their peers, or the teacher could display their names on a poster in the classroom.

Knowledge gain celebration

The teacher celebrates knowledge gain, which is the difference between a student's initial and final scores for a learning goal. To do this, the teacher recognizes the growth each student has made over the course of a unit. The teacher recognizes a student who started at a 1.5 and ended at 3.0 in the same way as a student who began with a score of 2.5 and ended with a score of 4.0; the teacher recognizes both students for a knowledge gain of 1.5. The teacher can recognize students with knowledge gains of .5, 1, 1.5, 2.0, 2.5, 3.0, and on up as applicable.

Verbal feedback

The teacher emphasizes each student's effort and growth by specifically explaining what a student did well on a task. The teacher should avoid attributing students' accomplishments to innate intelligence, talent, or other fixed characteristics. Appropriate phrases to use when giving verbal feedback include the following:

- You tried very hard on this—good job.

- You put a lot of effort into this—nice work.

- You were very focused while working on this—way to go.

- You were well prepared for this; keep up the good work.

- You really thought through this, and it paid off.

- You came very well informed about this—excellent work.

- You were ready for this—very good.

Technology Links

- Use email or text messages to send celebratory messages about students' work. Encourage students to share the positive messages with their parents.

- Use displays from learner response systems or voting websites (such as www.polleverywhere.com) to celebrate class progress.

- Use spreadsheet software (such as Excel) to create graphs and other visual displays to highlight individual and group progress.

Design Question: What will I do to establish and maintain classroom rules and procedures?

Element 4: What do I typically do to establish and maintain classroom rules and procedures?

Strategies

Using a small set of rules and procedures

The teacher maintains rules and procedures by limiting these to only five to eight per class. The teacher can construct these rules and procedures around any of the following areas:

- General classroom behavior

- Beginning and ending the period or school day

- Transitions and potential interruptions

- Group work

- Seat work and teacher-led activities

- Use of common materials, supplies, and equipment

Explaining rules and procedures to students

At the beginning of the school year or term, the teacher discusses the need for rules and procedures with students, presents a set of teacher-designed rules, and explains the logic behind the presented rules. The teacher and students might make rules more explicit by creating procedures (how-to steps) for them.

Modifying rules and procedures with students

The teacher invites students to modify existing rules and procedures by suggesting changes. In small groups, students create a list of modified rules. The teacher lists the groups' suggestions on the board and leads the class in a discussion of them. Finally, students vote on each suggestion. Those that gain consensus are then applied to the original set of rules and procedures.

Generating rules and procedures with students

After a whole-class discussion about the need for rules and procedures, the teacher asks students to form small groups and create initial lists of suggestions for rules (the teacher might display class rules from previous years to facilitate the process). The teacher then aggregates the lists into one set of rules, which the class discusses. Then they vote on each rule. The teacher adds the rules that obtain a consensus to the class's final list of rules. In a subsequent discussion, students might design procedures for rules that need further clarification.

Language of responsibility and statements of school beliefs

The teacher leads a discussion about concepts like *freedom, equality, responsibility, threats, opinions,* and *rights*. Students can then create written statements of their beliefs about their rights and responsibilities at school. The class might also discuss real-life situations that require rules and procedures.

Posting rules around the room

The teacher posts rules near relevant locations. For example, he or she might post group-work rules and procedures near group-work spaces, rules for leaving the classroom by the door, and rules for the use of equipment and supplies near storage areas.

Class pledge or classroom constitution

Students write a class pledge or constitution based on the classroom rules and procedures. This document describes what the ideal classroom looks like and what behaviors are necessary to achieve that ideal. All students sign the final copy, and the teacher displays it in the classroom.

Posters and graphics

Students create posters and graphics that emphasize the importance of specific rules and procedures or specific character traits important to proper classroom functioning (integrity, emotional control, and so on).

Gestures and symbols

The teacher and students collaborate to establish gestures or symbols that communicate basic messages in the classroom. For example, a raised hand might indicate a need for quiet or attention, turning the lights off and on could signal that group work has become too noisy, a raised book or pencil could show that a student needs help from the teacher, and words or phrases such as *groups* might be used to send students to preassigned work areas or groups.

Vignettes and role-playing

Students write vignettes or role-play situations in which the classroom rules apply. Students should model what appropriate behavior looks and sounds like.

Reviewing rules and procedures with students

If students seem to systematically violate or ignore rules and procedures, the teacher calls the lapse to students' attention and asks for suggestions about how to get behavior back on track. Students might work with the teacher to design a procedure to make a rule more explicit, suspend a rule for a period of time, or drop a rule entirely.

Classroom meetings

Teachers and students designate time to discuss classroom issues. Classroom meetings should be governed by a set of guidelines. For example:

- Classroom meetings will be held for ten minutes at the end of class every other Friday.

- Students and the teacher will sit so that everyone can see everyone else's face.

- Students and the teacher will avoid using people's names to emphasize a focus on issues.

Issues for discussion might be raised verbally or submitted ahead of time using a suggestion box.

Student self-assessment

The teacher periodically asks students to assess their own level of adherence to classroom rules and procedures. Students might use a list of the classroom rules and procedures and rate themselves on a scale from 1 (not adhering very well) to 4 (exemplary adherence) for each rule or procedure.

Technology Links

- Use technology to post procedures (such as warm-ups or agendas) for the day or to post rule reminders. Including reminders at the beginning of a presentation allows the teacher and students to review, modify, update, or highlight rules and procedures.

- Post rules and procedures on the class website, blog, or wiki so that parents and students can access them easily.

- As new technology equipment is added to the classroom, work with students to establish rules and procedures for its use. For example, rules for laptop use might state when lids need to be partially closed so students can focus on other things in the classroom.

Element 5: What do I typically do to organize the physical layout of the classroom?

Strategies

Learning centers

The teacher places learning centers away from major traffic patterns. They should be easy for the teacher to see and monitor from all parts of the room and should be close to books, resources, and other materials that may be required to complete tasks at the center.

Computers and technology equipment

The teacher places computers away from major traffic patterns and where the teacher can see all of the screens to monitor students' activity. Printers should be easy for students to access and convenient for teachers to monitor. Computers and printers should be located close to storage areas for accessories (like headphones, data storage devices, and extra paper). Projectors should be located so that they are easy to use during whole-group instruction and close to storage areas (for markers, transparencies, laptop computers, and other accessories).

Lab equipment and supplies

When thinking about storage and student access to plant and animal specimens, chemicals, and laboratory equipment (such as glassware and Bunsen burners), the teacher considers student safety, protection of the equipment, and ease of access and use for students.

Bookshelves

The teacher places bookshelves where they will provide support for individual, small-group, and whole-group learning activities.

Wall space

The teacher posts materials on the walls of the classroom to highlight current learning goals, assignment timelines, and announcements. The teacher also leaves empty space on the walls at the beginning of the year for later use and to post student work. Bulletin boards might display learning goals, classroom rules and procedures, assignments, school announcements, or school spirit paraphernalia. Calendars might display daily schedules or assignment timelines. Other learning resources on the walls could include the alphabet (in elementary classrooms), poems, vocabulary lists, historical timelines, information on current topics of study, the correct format for assignments (headings, page numbers, and so on), or exemplars and prototypes for assignments.

Displaying student work

The teacher displays student work using clear 8½ × 11–inch pockets into which students slide their exemplary assignments or compositions. Student mailboxes can be made using laminated envelopes on a poster.

Classroom décor

The teacher considers the following questions when designing the overall appearance of the classroom:

- What will students see as they enter and leave the room?

- What will students see when they are seated at their desks?

- What will students see when they are in group-work areas?

- What will students see in learning center areas?

- What could be distracting?

- Is the room welcoming?

- Does the room communicate an overall focus on learning?

Classroom materials

The teacher uses the following list as a guide to necessary classroom materials (Marzano et al., 2005, p. 140):

- Pens, pencils, and paper

- Paper clips, staplers, and staples

- Music and a CD player

- Band-Aids, tissues, and any other first-aid equipment your school requires

- Attendance materials, class sheets, and seating charts

- In/out boxes for collected papers and transparencies

- An extra bulb for the overhead projector

- Sticky notes and name tags

The teacher makes sure that work spaces are located close to materials and that materials are organized in a fashion that allows students to find what they need quickly and independently. The teacher might also consider when specific materials will be needed throughout the year and thus order them at the proper times.

Teacher's desk

The teacher places his or her desk to accommodate access to materials for whole-group instruction, eye contact with students, and monitoring during seat work.

Student desks

The teacher considers how many students will be in the class when arranging classroom furniture. The teacher places student desks to accommodate pairings and groupings during whole-group instruction and allows walkways to each student's desk (to monitor behavior and for individual assistance).

Areas for whole-group instruction

The teacher designs areas for whole-group instruction to include storage for frequently used materials, a blackboard or whiteboard, a document camera or projector, and a projection screen. The teacher should be able to make eye contact with all students while teaching, and students should be able to see the teacher, the projector screen, and the board at all times during instruction. All students should be able to hear the teacher easily.

Areas for group work

The teacher designs areas for group work to include easy access to the materials needed for collaboration (such as chart paper and markers) and arranges seating to facilitate student discussion and productive interaction.

Technology Links

- Look online or consult technology specialists to discover how to arrange and store technology equipment to maximize students' access and productivity.

- Periodically take video of students while they use technology equipment in class to assess the effectiveness and safety of its location and use. Adjust the classroom layout, if needed.

Lesson Segments Addressing Content

Design Question: What will I do to help students effectively interact with new knowledge?

Element 6: What do I typically do to identify critical information?

Strategies

Identifying critical-input experiences

The teacher identifies segments of content that are critical to students' abilities to achieve the learning goal, with only two to three critical-input experiences likely for each learning goal. Singling out these experiences provides focus for the students and teacher.

Visual activities

The teacher uses storyboards, graphic organizers, and pictures to highlight critical information.

Narrative activities

The teacher uses stories to help anchor information in memory and signal to students that certain information is important.

Tone of voice, gestures, and body position

The teacher raises or lowers his or her voice to signal critical information or create suspense about upcoming information. The teacher might also communicate excitement about the information by making eye contact with students, using hand gestures, moving around the room, and smiling (or using other appropriate facial expressions). These actions should be used with discretion, as overuse can diminish their effectiveness.

Pause time

The teacher pauses at key points during the presentation of new content to give students time to think about information and signal that it is important.

Technology Links

- Use presentation software, images from the Internet, or interactive whiteboard tools to create visual displays that highlight critical information.

- Use videos to augment narrative activities.

- Ask students to explore interactive websites related to critical information (such as www .nationalgeographic.com or www.coolmath.com).

- Schools and districts can purchase subscriptions to websites that help students focus on essential knowledge (for example, www.explorelearning.com or www.brainpop.com).

Content

Element 7: What do I typically do to organize students to interact with new knowledge?

Strategies

Grouping for active processing

When students process new information in groups, the teacher exposes them to ways other students process information, some of which might enhance their own information processing. Groups can consist of as few as two students and as many as five. Groups might have operating rules such as the following:

- Students should be willing to add their perspective to each discussion.

- Students should respect the opinions of other group members.

- Students should make sure they understand what others are saying.

- Students should be willing to ask questions if they don't understand something.

- Students should be willing to answer questions that other group members have about their ideas.

Groups can convene for a specific purpose (ad hoc groups) or form as long-term partnerships. The teacher can assign students to groups randomly or based on current levels of understanding, mixing students who appear to understand something quite well with those who don't.

Group norms

In order to ensure that student groups (especially long-term groups) function smoothly, the teacher asks students to create a list of norms (common attitudes and beliefs) to govern the group's functioning. The teacher might give each team member several index cards and have them write down the norms that are most important to them. Students then aggregate and classify them to create a list of the beliefs and attitudes that will help guide the behavior of group members.

Fishbowl demonstration

The teacher gives students a visual representation of what effective group work looks like by asking students to form a circle ("fishbowl") around a group that demonstrates what effective group work looks like. The demonstration group might model behaviors such as paraphrasing, pausing, clarifying, questioning, brainstorming, and using respectful language.

Job cards

The teacher uses job cards to designate specific roles that students are to take within their groups. Examples of different jobs include facilitator, summarizer, questioner, and note-taker. This strategy can also help equalize participation when students work in groups.

Predetermined "buddies" to help form ad hoc groups

The teacher gives students a blank chart showing a clock (with twelve blanks, one for each hour), the seasons (with four blanks), or another theme-based graphic with blanks. The teacher asks students to find a partner for each blank and fill in the partner's name on their chart. For example, if Maddie and John agreed to be "summer" partners, Maddie would sign the summer blank on John's chart, and John would sign the summer blank on Maddie's chart. When the teacher wants to form quick, ad hoc groups, she asks students to find their summer (or, for example, "two o'clock") buddies, and students quickly pair up.

Contingency plan for ungrouped students

The teacher designates a meeting spot for "singles" and can then help those students pair up or join existing groups. This helps avoid some students being left ungrouped when groups are student selected.

Grouping students using preassessment information

After administering a preassessment, the teacher uses the information gained about individual students' prior knowledge to assign students to groups. In some cases, the teacher might want to mix students with high prior knowledge and students with low prior knowledge together. In other cases, the teacher might want to differentiate by grouping students with high prior knowledge together and creating separate groups of students with medium and low prior knowledge.

Technology Links

- Use websites that allow students to collaborate while working in groups. Some websites are designed to facilitate online conversations, while others allow students to collect information and work together to produce papers and presentations (for example, www.wikispaces.com or https://docs.google.com).

- Use technology tools like dice and spinners (available in interactive whiteboard software or online) to assign students to groups.

Content

Element 8: What do I typically do to preview new content?

Strategies

What do you think you know?

The teacher asks students to individually write down what they already know about an upcoming topic. After each student has created an individual list, the teacher asks students to pair up and discuss their previous knowledge and ideas. Each pair creates a list of its most original or most important knowledge and ideas, using examples where appropriate. Finally, each pair shares its list, and the teacher creates a whole-class list of what is already known about upcoming content.

Overt linkages

The teacher helps students make overt links between content they have previously studied in class and new content being presented by simply explaining the connections. For example, the teacher might say, "When you read the section in the chapter about percolation, keep in mind that it is similar to what happened in our last experiment, where the soil acted as a filter as the water seeped through it."

Preview questions

The teacher asks questions about upcoming content to pique students' curiosity and activate their prior knowledge. Although students may not know the answers to the questions because they have not yet learned the new content, the questions help signal what information they should be listening for as the teacher presents new content.

Brief teacher summary

The teacher provides students with an oral or written summary of content that is about to be presented. This helps students see key ideas and patterns and follow those ideas as the teacher presents more detailed information.

Skimming

The teacher helps students skim written information on an upcoming topic by teaching them to look at major section headings and subheadings and asking them to analyze those headings to pick out main ideas and important concepts in the passage. The teacher might also ask students to try to summarize a passage after skimming it, record how well they think they already understand the new content, and predict what they will learn during an upcoming presentation of the new content.

Teacher-prepared notes

The teacher provides an outline of the content to students before beginning to present new information. The teacher should allow students to ask questions after the teacher presents new information and reviews the outline. This can help clear up initial confusion or misconceptions that students have about new content.

K-W-L strategy (Ogle, 1986)

The teacher uses a K-W-L strategy before presenting new content. First, students identify what they know about the topic, and the teacher records this information under *K* on a chart. Then students list what they want to know about a topic, and the teacher records this information under *W* on a chart. Finally, after a lesson, students identify and list things they have learned, which are recorded under *L*. At this point, the teacher and students examine what was written in the *K* column in an attempt to identify initial misconceptions about the content.

Advance organizers

The teacher creates a visual representation (often called a graphic organizer) showing the structure and organization of new content and illustrating how new content connects to information previously learned in class. Students can use this organizer to ask questions before the presentation of new content, to identify what they already know about new content, and to connect new content to their personal interests.

Anticipation guides

Before presenting new content, the teacher has students respond to a series of statements that relate to upcoming information. After students respond to the statements, the teacher leads the class in a discussion about how students responded. This activates students' prior knowledge about a topic and helps them consider issues and ideas associated with new content.

Word splash activity

The teacher uses this strategy to help students preview vocabulary terms and concepts associated with new content. The teacher prepares a number of words and short phrases associated with the new content and presents them to students. Students try to sort the terms into categories that make sense to them. The teacher then allows students to share their categories and sorting strategies and leads the class in a discussion of how the terms and concepts relate to each other and to students' prior knowledge and individual interests.

Preassessment

The teacher administers a preassessment to students before presenting new content. This strategy exposes students to the most important information in an upcoming presentation, and the teacher can use preassessment results to gain an understanding of which students have a lot of prior knowledge about upcoming content and which do not.

Technology Links

- Use learner response systems or voting websites (such as www.polleverywhere.com) to pretest students. Display the results anonymously in class so students can identify what they already know and what they need to review. Save the results and compare them to assessment data during and at the end of a unit.

- Use online questionnaires or surveys to quickly gather information about class interests or attitudes toward a topic.

Content

- Ask students to visit websites related to upcoming topics. Assign specific websites or ask students to explore on their own to identify information they think is intriguing, confusing, or exciting. Have students share what they found with the class.

- Use text messages or a class website, blog, or wiki to post preview questions or stories related to the content. Websites such as http://swaggle.mobi and www.wetxt.com allow text messages to be sent to a specific list of phones. These sites can also collect responses sent from students' phones so they can be used for previewing activities in class.

Element 9: What do I typically do to chunk content into digestible bites?

Strategies

Presenting content in small chunks

The teacher chunks content into small, digestible bites for students. If presenting new declarative knowledge, the chunks are comprised of concepts and details that logically go together. If presenting new procedural knowledge, the chunks are comprised of steps in a process that go together.

Using preassessment data to vary the size of each chunk

If students scored well in a specific area on a preassessment, the teacher presents that information as part of a larger chunk. When presenting information about which students displayed misconceptions or little prior knowledge on the preassessment, the teacher can use smaller chunks.

Chunk processing

The teacher has students work together to process chunks of information. In groups of three, students decide who will be member A, member B, and member C. The teacher presents the first chunk of information, and member A summarizes it. Members B and C add to what A has already said, and each group identifies elements of the chunk they are still confused about. The teacher takes questions from the whole class to clarify these confusions and then asks each group to predict what the next chunk will be about. The teacher presents the next chunk, and groups repeat the process, except that member B summarizes and members A and C add information. After the teacher presents the third chunk, groups repeat the process again, with member C summarizing, and members A and B adding information.

Technology Links

- Divide presentations into appropriate chunks by inserting slides between sections that prompt students to stop and process what they just learned.

- Use learner response systems or voting websites (such as www.polleverywhere.com) to monitor students' levels of understanding. Use the data to determine if the class is ready for the next chunk.

Content

Element 10: What do I typically do to help students process new information?

Strategies

Perspective analysis (Marzano, 1992)

The teacher asks students to consider multiple perspectives on new knowledge using perspective analysis. This strategy involves five steps, each with a corresponding question:

1. **Identify your position on a controversial topic**—What do I believe about this?

2. **Determine the reasoning behind your position**—Why do I believe that?

3. **Identify an opposing position**—What is another way of looking at this?

4. **Describe the reasoning behind the opposing position**—Why might someone else hold a different opinion?

5. **When you are finished, summarize what you have learned**—What have I learned?

Thinking hats (de Bono, 1999)

The teacher asks students to process new information by imagining themselves wearing any one of six different-colored thinking hats. Depending on the hat they wear, students look at new knowledge in a slightly different way, as follows:

- **White hat** (neutral and objective perspectives)—When wearing the white hat, students examine facts and figures related to the new information without drawing conclusions or interpreting them.

- **Red hat** (emotional perspectives)—When wearing the red hat, students express how they feel about the new information, but should still refrain from judging either the topic or their feelings.

- **Black hat** (cautious or careful perspectives)—When wearing the black hat, students look for weaknesses or risks that stem from new information.

- **Yellow hat** (optimistic perspectives)—When wearing the yellow hat, students look for positive and valuable aspects of new information.

- **Green hat** (creative perspectives)—When wearing the green hat, students use the new knowledge to generate new ideas or create novel solutions to problems using the new information.

- **Blue hat** (organizational perspectives)—When wearing the blue hat, students reflect on their thinking processes and decide what perspectives they would like to take (in other words, what hats they would like to put on) as they interact with new information.

Collaborative processing

The teacher asks students to meet in small groups and summarize the information just presented, ask clarifying questions about the information just presented, or make predictions about upcoming information. After allowing the students to interact in small groups, the teacher can lead the whole class in a discussion of their summaries, questions, and predictions.

Jigsaw cooperative learning

After identifying a number of specific important aspects of the content (for example, five important causes of World War I), the teacher asks students to create groups with the same number of members ("Please organize yourselves into groups of five"). Once students are in their groups, the teacher assigns each student a topic about which he or she will become an "expert." In the example, each student would be assigned one of the five causes of World War I to study.

Once students each have their expert topic, groups disband and students with the same expert topic meet together to investigate the topic, share their findings, ask questions of each other and the teacher, and discuss their ideas. In the example, all students studying cause 1 would meet together, all students studying cause 2 would meet together, and so on.

After each student has become an expert on their topic, the original groups re-form and students each present their expert knowledge to the other members of the group. Other group members can ask questions of the expert or the teacher as they learn the new information.

Reciprocal teaching

Small groups of students, with one student designated as the discussion leader, use this strategy to interact with new information. Before the teacher presents a chunk of new information, members of the group generate predictions about the content. After the teacher presents the chunk of content, the discussion leader asks the group questions about the information presented, and the members of the group discuss each question. After the questions have been discussed, someone from the group (not the discussion leader) summarizes the content presented so far, and the members of the group make predictions about the upcoming chunk of content, beginning the cycle again. The role of discussion leader should rotate from student to student so each student has the opportunity to generate questions about the content and practice facilitating the group's discussion.

Concept attainment

The teacher asks students to identify, compare, and contrast examples and nonexamples of a concept. Examples of a concept should clearly display the attributes of the concept, and nonexamples should clearly not have attributes of the concept. The teacher can also present a group of items to students, designating each item as an example or nonexample of a "mystery concept." Students guess the mystery concept by studying the presented examples and nonexamples.

Technology Links

- Use online resources (such as www.google.com/earth/) and interactive whiteboard tools (such as math tools, drawing tools, or mark-up tools) to help students process information interactively.

- Send processing questions about new topics to students as text messages. Websites such as http://swaggle.mobi and www.wetxt.com allow text messages to be sent to a specific list of phones. These sites can also collect responses sent from students' phones so they can be used for processing activities in class.

- Post questions for the class on an interactive whiteboard or projector screen. After allowing students to discuss them in groups, ask them to write their thoughts on the whiteboard, enter their ideas on a shared Internet site, or produce short audio or video presentations to post on a class website, blog, or wiki.

- Record and post initial presentations of new content online, ask students to listen to or view them *before* class (for example, as homework), and use class time to process the new information.

- Work with the district and school to create electronic collections of processing resources for topics that are taught every year. These collections might include specific processing activities or processing questions for student discussions.

Element 11: What do I typically do to help students elaborate on new information?

Strategies

General inferential questions

The teacher uses two kinds of general inferential questions: (1) default questions and (2) reasoned inference questions. *Default questions* ask students to use their background knowledge to answer questions. In short, students "default" to what they already know to come up with an answer. *Reasoned inference questions* require students to reason and draw conclusions or make predictions about information presented in a critical-input experience. The teacher presents explicit information that the students use as the premise from which they draw conclusions.

Elaborative interrogation

After a student answers a question, the teacher probes the answer by asking elaborative questions such as the following:

- How do you know/why do you believe that to be true?

- What are some typical characteristics or behaviors you would expect of _____?

- What would you expect to happen if _____?

The first question helps students provide evidence to support their conclusions; the second question helps students make generalizations about categories of persons, places, things, or events; and the third question helps students make if/then generalizations about the content (for example, If you change _____, then _____ will happen).

Technology Links

- Send elaboration questions to students' phones using text messages. Websites such as http:// swaggle.mobi and www.wetxt.com allow text messages to be sent to a specific list of phones. These sites can also collect responses sent from students' phones so they can be used for class discussions.

- Ask students to use wikis and other collaborative websites to collectively elaborate on questions the teacher posts.

Element 12: What do I typically do to help students record and represent knowledge?

Strategies

Informal outline

Students use indentation to indicate the relative importance of ideas. They justify big ideas at the left of the paper, and indent and list details under the big idea to which they pertain. The following example shows an informal outline for information about different types of memory (see fig. C.3).

Working Memory
- What we are paying attention to right now
- May or may not be remembered later
- Can only handle a small amount of information at a time

Short-Term Memory
- Where we hold recent events and relatively new information
- Larger storage space than the working memory
- Not everything in the short-term memory will be permanently retained

Long-Term Memory
- The largest part of the memory
- Where all of our childhood memories are stored
- Information in the long-term memory is always remembered

Figure C.3: Informal outline

Combination notes, pictures, and summary

Students record written notes about the content in the left-hand column of a chart, pictographs or pictorial representations of the content in the right-hand column, and a summary of the content in the lower section of the chart (see fig. C.4).

Notes	Pictures
Summary:	

Figure C.4: Combination notes, pictures, and summary.

Graphic organizers

Students record their knowledge using nonlinguistic organizers that correspond to specific patterns commonly found in information. These nonlinguistic representations can be combined with other note-taking strategies (like combination notes, pictures, and summary). Figure C.5 shows several common graphic organizers.

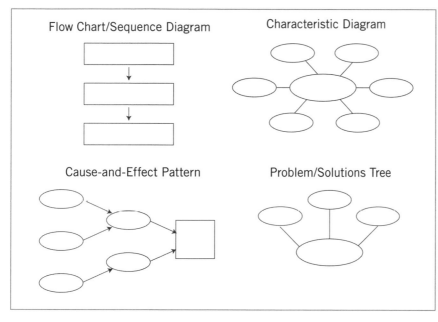

Figure C.5: Graphic organizers.

Free-flowing web

Students place big ideas in central circles and then use lines to connect big ideas to smaller circles with important details about each big idea. The following example shows a free-flowing web for the topic of pollution (see fig. C.6).

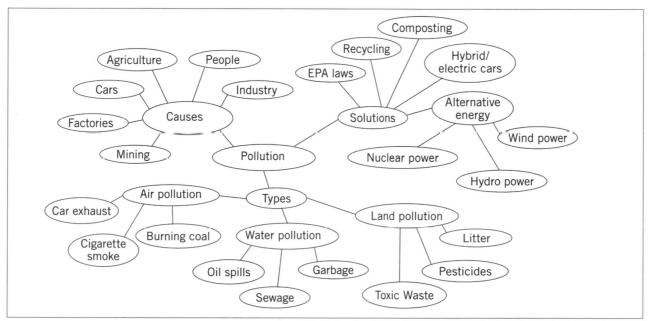

Figure C.6: Free-flowing web on pollution.

Academic notebooks

Students organize compilations of their notes to provide a permanent record of their thinking and make corrections to their thinking as they review previous entries. Students should date their entries and record reactions, questions, answers, and assessments of their progress. Students can also make entries reflecting their conclusions and insights.

Dramatic enactments

Students role-play characters or act out scenes, processes, or events. They can also use their bodies to create symbols for concepts such as radius, diameter, and circumference.

Rhyming pegwords

Students use this strategy to remember a list of facts or information. The method uses a set of concrete images that rhyme with the numbers one through ten, such as the following.

One is a bun.	Six is a stack of sticks.
Two is a shoe.	Seven is heaven.
Three is a tree.	Eight is a gate.
Four is a door.	Nine is a line.
Five is a hive.	Ten is a hen.

To remember a fact or piece of information, a student associates it with one of the concrete images. For example, a student might want to remember the following information about ancient Egyptian civilization:

- Egyptian civilization developed along the Nile River in Africa.
- The Egyptians used a system of writing called hieroglyphics.
- The Egyptians built the pyramids as burial places for their pharaohs.

To remember these facts, the student might connect them to the image for the number one, a bun. He or she might picture a hot dog bun with the Nile River flowing through the center of it, hieroglyphics written on the side of it, and pyramids sitting on top of it. The image is easier to remember than the list of facts.

Link strategy

Students use this strategy to remember facts or information by first creating symbols or substitutes for important ideas and then linking those symbols or substitutes together in a narrative. A symbol is an image that reminds one of important information, like a rainbow to represent the concept of an arc. A substitute is a word that is easy to picture and sounds like the information one is trying to remember, like the word *ark* (a big boat) to remember the concept of the arc of a circle.

Technology Links

- Use images, organizers, and templates provided with presentation software (such as PowerPoint, Prezi, or interactive whiteboard software) to present ideas to students and guide their note-taking.

- To support a variety of learning styles, provide an array of websites that represent the content using different visual and graphic formats.

- Provide students with technology tools they can use to record and represent their understanding of new knowledge (for example, www.inspiration.com or https://bubbl.us).

Content

Element 13: What do I typically do to help students reflect on their learning?

Strategies

Reflective journals

Students use a portion of their academic notebooks to respond to reflection questions such as the following:

- What predictions did you make about today's lesson that were correct? Which predictions were incorrect?

- What information in today's lesson was easy for you to understand? What information was difficult?

- How well do you understand the major ideas we are studying?

- What did you do well today?

- What could you have done better today?

Think logs

Students reflect on specific cognitive skills (for example, classification, drawing inferences, decision making, creative thinking, and self-regulation) that were emphasized during a lesson. Students can respond to prompts such as the following:

- How might you explain classification to a friend?

- Describe an inference you drew today.

- With what aspects of the decision-making process are you most comfortable? With what aspects are you least comfortable?

- What might be the components of a self-regulation plan for your own learning?

Exit slips

At the end of a lesson, students respond to specific reflective questions before they leave the room. Examples of questions students might respond to include the following:

- What do you consider the main ideas of today's lesson?

- What do you feel most and least sure about?

- Do you have specific questions about today's lesson?

- With which aspects of today's classwork were you successful?

Knowledge comparison

Students compare their current levels of knowledge on a topic, or levels of competence with a procedure, to their previous levels of knowledge or competence. Students can use diagrams or flowcharts to show the progression of their knowledge gain.

Two-column notes

Students use two-column notes as an extended reflection activity at the end of a lesson. In the left-hand column, students record facts or other information that they found interesting from the lesson. In the right-hand column, they record their reactions, questions, and extended ideas related to the facts or information in the left-hand column.

Technology Links

- Use a class website, blog, or wiki to capture and post ideas generated in class.

- Use an online survey tool (such as www.surveymonkey.com) to collect student reflections.

- Encourage students to post their reflections using websites such as www.wiffiti.com or www.todaysmeet.com. Websites such as www.photobucket.com allow students to post pictures that exemplify what they have learned.

Content

Design Question: What will I do to help students practice and deepen their understanding of new knowledge?

Element 14: What do I typically do to review content?

Strategies

Cloze activities

The teacher presents previously learned information to students with pieces missing and asks them to fill in the missing pieces.

Summaries

The teacher prepares a summary and asks students to review it or asks students to write quick summaries of previously learned information. These summaries can be short, and a discussion of what each student remembered or thought important from their previous learning might follow.

Presented problems

The teacher presents students with a problem that requires them to use previously learned information in order to solve it.

Demonstration

The teacher asks students to demonstrate a skill or procedure that requires them to use previously learned information to complete.

Brief practice test or exercise

The teacher asks students to complete an exercise that prompts them to remember and apply previously learned information.

Questioning

The teacher asks questions that require students to recall, recognize, or apply previously learned information. These questions might also ask students to make inferences or decisions based on the previously learned information.

Technology Links

- Post key slides from presentations on a class website, or display them in class to guide students' review.

- Ask students to record audio or video of their thoughts about new content. Post these recordings to a class website, blog, or wiki so students can watch or listen to them to review the content.

- Send students review questions by text message or post them to a class website. Websites such as http://swaggle.mobi and www.wetxt.com allow text messages to be sent to a specific list of phones. These sites can also collect responses sent from students' phones so they can be used for review in class.

Element 15: What do I typically do to organize students to practice and deepen knowledge?

Strategies

Perspective analysis (Marzano, 1992)

The teacher helps students practice and deepen their knowledge of a topic using perspective analysis. This strategy involves five steps, each with a corresponding question:

1. **Identify your position on a controversial topic**—What do I believe about this?

2. **Determine the reasoning behind your position**—Why do I believe that?

3. **Identify an opposing position**—What is another way of looking at this?

4. **Describe the reasoning behind the opposing position**—Why might someone else hold a different opinion?

5. **When you are finished, summarize what you have learned**—What have I learned?

Thinking hats (de Bono, 1999)

The teacher asks students to deepen their knowledge of a topic by imagining themselves wearing any one of six different-colored thinking hats. Depending on the hat they wear, students look at new knowledge in a slightly different way, as follows:

- **White hat** (neutral and objective perspectives)—When wearing the white hat, students examine facts and figures related to the new information without drawing conclusions or interpreting them.

- **Red hat** (emotional perspectives)—When wearing the red hat, students express how they feel about the new information, but should still refrain from judging either the topic or their feelings.

- **Black hat** (cautious or careful perspectives)—When wearing the black hat, students look for weaknesses or risks that stem from new information.

- **Yellow hat** (optimistic perspectives)—When wearing the yellow hat, students look for positive and valuable aspects of new information.

- **Green hat** (creative perspectives)—When wearing the green hat, students use the new knowledge to generate new ideas or create novel solutions to problems using the new information.

- **Blue hat** (organizational perspectives)—When wearing the blue hat, students reflect on their thinking processes and decide what perspectives they would like to take (in other words, what hats they would like to put on) as they interact with new information.

Cooperative learning

Students complete practice activities or answer questions independently and then meet in small groups to check their answers with their peers' answers. This gives students a second opportunity to describe how they approached problems and hear alternative approaches that other students used.

Content

Cooperative comparisons

Students work in groups to answer comparison questions such as the following:

- How does our current performance compare to our performance when we started learning the strategy or process?

- How could we classify different techniques for improving our performance with this strategy or process?

- If we were going to coach others to learn this strategy or process, what metaphors or analogies might be helpful to them?

Pair-check (Kagan & Kagan, 2009)

In groups of four, students form pairs (two pairs per group) and designate who will be partner A and who will be partner B. Using a set of exercises, problems, or questions, partner A works on the first exercise, problem, or question while partner B coaches when necessary and praises partner A's work when complete. For the second exercise, problem, or question, the partners reverse roles. Then, the pair checks their answers with the other pair in their group. The goal is for all four group members to reach consensus about each solution. If solutions do not match, group members discuss and coach each other until they reach a common solution. They repeat the process, with consensus achieved after every two exercises, problems, or questions.

Think-pair-share and think-pair-square (Kagan & Kagan, 2009)

After grouping students in pairs, the teacher presents a problem. Students think about the problem individually for a predetermined amount of time. Then students each share their thoughts, ideas, and possible solutions with their partner. Partners discuss and come to a consensus about their solution. The teacher then asks pairs to share what they decided with the class. In a variation (think-pair-square), pairs confer with another pair (making a group of four) and come to a consensus in that group as well before sharing with the whole class.

Student tournaments

The teacher organizes students into teams that then compete in various academic games. The teacher might keep track of each team's points over the course of a unit and provide a tangible reward or recognition to the top one or two teams. Team members should be remixed after each unit to ensure that students have the opportunity to work with a variety of other students.

Error analysis and peer feedback

In pairs, one partner watches the other complete a process or perform a task. Using evaluation criteria the teacher provides, one partner analyzes the other's performance and offers feedback about successes, errors, or missteps.

Performances and peer critiques

The teacher asks students to complete culminating performances when learning procedural knowledge. These performances might conclude with peer review activities in which other students offer praise, ask questions, and give suggestions for improvement.

Inside-outside circle (Kagan & Kagan, 2009)

Students form two concentric circles with an equal number of students in each circle. Students forming the inner circle stand facing outward, and students forming the outward circle stand facing inward (so that each person in the inner circle faces a person in the outer circle). The teacher asks a question or presents a problem, and students discuss their thoughts, answers, and solutions with the person facing them. On a signal from the teacher, each person in the inner circle takes one step to the left, so that everyone now faces a new partner. Partners again compare answers and solutions, after which the teacher asks individuals to share answers or solutions with the group. The teacher might also ask students to share what they discussed with their partners and how it changed (or didn't change) their thinking.

Technology Links

- Introduce students to websites that facilitate collaboration. Some websites are designed to facilitate online conversations, while others allow students to collect information and work together to produce papers and presentations (for example, www.wikispaces.com or https://docs.google.com).

- Have students create video or audio recordings describing how they worked together to practice or deepen their knowledge. Archive these and use them to give subsequent classes ideas about how to work together.

Content

Element 16: What do I typically do to use homework?

Strategies

Preview homework

The teacher asks students to read a passage of text or review media that introduces a concept or idea they will study in class. The teacher might ask students to keep a list of their questions, observations, or connections as they read or review the content. In class, the teacher might have students share their lists and discuss each others' ideas.

Homework to deepen knowledge

The teacher asks students to complete an assignment that helps them compare, contrast, or classify specific aspects of the content. The teacher might also have students create analogies or metaphors involving specific aspects of the content. If using this homework strategy, the teacher should ensure that students each have a thorough understanding of the concepts they are being asked to work with.

Homework to practice a process or skill

The teacher asks students who have demonstrated the ability to independently perform a process or skill in class to practice that process or skill independently in order to increase their fluency, speed, and accuracy with the process or skill.

Parent-assisted homework

To assist students with homework, parents or family members ask reflective questions or listen to students give an oral summary of material they read. To help students develop fluency with skills or procedures, parents might also time them if they are trying to get faster with a specific skill or process. Parents should act as supporters, not teachers, when assisting with homework, and should have a clear idea of their role and what is expected of them.

Technology Links

- Post resources (presentations, videos, or audio recordings) that were used during class on a class website, blog, or wiki so students can access them while they work on homework.

- Provide recommendations of content-related websites that students can use as resources. Encourage and teach students to explore and discover new relevant websites on their own.

- Invite students to post questions and ideas that arise as they complete their homework on a class website, blog, or wiki.

- Create opportunities for students to chat online about their homework as they are completing it.

- When appropriate, encourage students to use their cell phones to capture pictures that exemplify content or that might help them analyze and solve problems.

Element 17: What do I typically do to help students examine similarities and differences?

Strategies

Sentence stem comparisons

Students complete sentence stems that ask them to compare and contrast various people, places, events, concepts, or processes. These comparisons can be general or specific, as follows:

General—House cats are similar to lions because _____ . House cats are different than lions because _____ .

Specific—Sherlock Holmes and Gandalf are both characters who enjoy solving mysteries, but they are different because _____ .

Venn diagrams

Students use these visual tools to compare and contrast two or three people, places, events, concepts, or processes. Students write similarities where circles intersect and they write characteristics unique to an object where the circles do not intersect. Venn diagrams can be used for specific, general, abstract, or concrete comparisons.

Double-bubble diagram

Students use this type of diagram to compare the attributes of two people, places, events, concepts, or processes. They write the two things being compared in large circles on the left and right sides of a page. They list common attributes in smaller circles in the center of the page that connect to both large circles. They write unique attributes in smaller circles at the edges of the page that connect only to the larger circle to which they apply.

Comparison matrix

Students identify elements they wish to compare and write them at the top of each column in a grid. Next, using a matrix like the one following, students identify attributes they wish to compare and write them in the rows. Then, in each cell, students record how the elements are similar (there may be similar entries in multiple cells) and different (these will be unique to a cell). Finally, students summarize what they learned by comparing the elements (see table C.5).

Table C.5: Comparison Matrix

	Element 1	Element 2	Element 3
Attribute 1	Similarities: Differences:	Similarities: Differences:	Similarities: Differences:

Continued on next page →

	Element 1	Element 2	Element 3
Attribute 2	Similarities: Differences:	Similarities: Differences:	Similarities: Differences:
Attribute 3	Similarities: Differences:	Similarities: Differences:	Similarities: Differences:
Summary:			

Classification chart

The teacher creates a chart with several categories listed across the top and asks students to fill in examples that fit in each category. Students can periodically pair up or form groups to share their charts with their peers, discuss and explain why they classified items as they did, and modify their charts after hearing others' perspectives.

Student-generated classification patterns

The teacher asks students to find representative examples of different concepts and sort them into categories based on what they have learned in class. Students then present their conclusions to the class and explain why they selected the examples they did and why they sorted them as they did.

Similes

Students state comparisons using *like* or *as.* They might include an explanation of why one object is like the other and can revise their similes after discussing them with their peers.

Metaphors

Students state comparisons using metaphors. In a metaphor, comparisons are stated as direct relationships—one thing is another. For example, life is a journey. Metaphors are sometimes abstract and can be extended to include more than one comparison. Students should explain why their metaphors are appropriate.

Sentence stem analogies

Students use sentence stems to create comparisons that describe specific relationships between two items or concepts. Analogies always take this form: "*Item 1* is to *item 2* as *item 3* is to *item 4.*" For example, when presented with the stem: "Quarterback is to _____ as pitcher is to _____," a student might create the following analogy:

Quarterback is to receiver as pitcher is to catcher, because the quarterback throws the ball to the receiver, and the pitcher throws the ball to the catcher.

The student might extend this analogy to further analyze the relationship between football and baseball:

An interception is to football as a hit is to baseball, because in both cases, the ball's course is altered before it reaches its intended target.

The teacher might also present students with the first two terms of an analogy and ask them to fill in the second two terms, for example: "A coach is to an athlete as _____ is to _____."

Visual analogies

Students use visual organizers to help them make analogies. Figure C.7 helps students create an analogy and specify the type of relationship being expressed by the analogy.

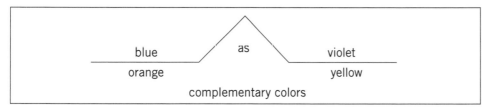

Figure C.7: Visual analogy.

Technology Links

- Work with the district and school to create electronic collections of comparison resources and organizers. By using a common set of resources, organizers, and activities for comparing and classifying, teachers can focus on content rather than on teaching new systems or processes for comparisons.

- Ask students to use their cell phones or cameras to take pictures of examples and nonexamples of concepts being studied. Students can post these to a class website and the teacher can use them during class discussions.

Content

Element 18: What do I typically do to help students examine errors in reasoning?

Strategies

Identifying errors of faulty logic

Students find and analyze errors of faulty logic including contradiction, accident, false cause, begging the question, evading the issue, arguing from ignorance, composition, and division. Marzano and Brown (2009) defined these errors in the following ways (p. 95):

- **Contradiction**—presenting conflicting information

- **Accident**—failing to recognize that an argument is based on an exception to a rule

- **False cause**—confusing a temporal (time) order of events with causality or oversimplifying the reasons behind some event or occurrence

- **Begging the question**—making a claim and then arguing for the claim by using statements that are simply the equivalent of the original claim

- **Evading the issue**—changing the topic to avoid addressing the issue

- **Arguing from ignorance**—arguing that a claim is justified simply because its opposite has not been proven true

- **Composition**—asserting something about a whole that is true of only its parts

- **Division**—asserting about all of the parts something that is generally, but not always, true of the whole

Identifying errors of attack

Students find and analyze errors of attack including poisoning the well, arguing against the person, and appealing to force. Marzano and Brown (2009) defined these errors in the following ways (p. 96):

- **Poisoning the well**—being so completely committed to a position that you explain away absolutely everything that is offered in opposition to your position

- **Arguing against the person**—rejecting a claim using derogatory facts (real or alleged) about the person who is making the claim

- **Appealing to force**—using threats to establish the validity of a claim

Identifying errors of weak reference

Students find and analyze errors of weak reference including using sources that reflect biases, using sources that lack credibility, appealing to authority, appealing to the people, and appealing to emotion. Marzano and Brown (2009) defined these errors in the following ways (p. 96):

- **Sources that reflect biases**—consistently accepting information that supports what we already believe to be true or consistently rejecting information that goes against what we believe to be true

- **Sources that lack credibility**—using a source that is not reputable for a given topic

- **Appealing to authority**—invoking authority as the last word on an issue

- **Appealing to the people**—attempting to justify a claim based on its popularity

- **Appealing to emotion**—using a "sob story" as proof for a claim

Identifying errors of misinformation

Students find and analyze errors of misinformation including confusing the facts and misapplying a concept or generalization. Marzano and Brown (2009) defined these errors in the following ways (p. 96):

- **Confusing the facts**—using information that seems to be factual but that has been changed in such a way that it is no longer accurate

- **Misapplying a concept or generalization**—misunderstanding or wrongly applying a concept or generalization to support a claim

Practicing identifying errors in logic

The teacher uses practice exercises to help students identify errors in logic. The teacher can create his or her own exercises or use those found in *Teaching and Assessing 21st Century Skills* (Marzano & Heflebower, 2012) or online at **marzanoresearch.com/classroomstrategies**.

Finding errors in the media

The teacher provides students with footage of political debates, televised interviews, commercials, advertisements, newspaper articles, blogs, and other sources and asks them to find and analyze errors in reasoning that underlie the messages therein.

Examining support for claims

Students examine the support provided for a claim by analyzing the grounds, backing, and qualifiers that support it, as follows:

- **Grounds**—initial evidence for a claim. Students should analyze claims to see if they provide grounds that answer the question, Why is this claim true? Grounds might be common knowledge, expert opinion, experimental evidence, or factual information.

- **Backing**—additional information about grounds that helps establish their validity.

- **Qualifiers**—exceptions to claims. The number of qualifiers needed for a claim can help determine the certainty of a claim.

Statistical limitations

Students find and analyze errors that commonly occur when using statistical data to support a claim. The five major types of statistical limitations for students to be aware of are (1) regression toward the mean, (2) conjunction, (3) base rates, (4) the limits of extrapolation, and (5) the cumulative nature of probabilistic events. Marzano and Brown (2009) defined these limitations in the following ways (pp. 127–128):

1. **Regression toward the mean**—being aware that an extreme score on a measure is most commonly followed by a more moderate score that is closer to the mean

2. **Errors of conjunction**—being aware that it is less likely that two or more independent events will occur simultaneously than that they will occur in isolation

3. **Keeping aware of base rates**—using the general or typical patterns of occurrences in a category of events as the basis on which to predict what will happen in a specific situation

4. **Understanding the limits of extrapolation**—realizing that using trends to make predictions—extrapolating—is a useful practice as long as the prediction does not extend beyond the data for which trends have been observed

5. **Adjusting estimates of risk to account for the cumulative nature of probabilistic events**—realizing that even though the probability of a risky event might be highly unlikely, the probability of the event occurring increases with time and the number of events

Technology Links

- Work with the district and school to create electronic collections of resources to help students find errors in reasoning (for example, a common list of errors in reasoning with definitions and examples). The use of a common language from class to class will help students recognize and label errors more easily.

- Use audio and video clips from the news media as examples of errors in reasoning. Ask students to find and label the errors, and then ask them to rerecord their own versions of the clip with the errors eliminated.

Element 19: What do I typically do to help students practice skills, strategies, and processes?

Strategies

Close monitoring

When students are learning a new skill, the teacher provides a highly structured environment and monitors student actions very closely to correct early errors or misunderstandings. As students become more adept with a skill, strategy, or process, the teacher encourages them to monitor their own progress and evaluate their own performances.

Frequent structured practice

When students are learning a new skill or process, the teacher first provides a clear demonstration of the skill or process. After this demonstration, students should have frequent opportunities to practice discrete elements of the skill or process and the process as a whole in situations where they have a high probability of success. Students should experience success multiple times before moving away from this type of practice.

Varied practice

Once students have engaged in frequent structured practice, they begin practicing a skill or process in more challenging situations. Students should still experience success, but they might be required to work a bit harder than was necessary during frequent structured practice. During this type of practice, the teacher should encourage students to monitor their progress with the skill or process and to identify their strengths or weaknesses.

Fluency practice

Once students are comfortable with a skill or process and have experienced success with it in a wide range of situations, they engage in independent practice whereby they focus on performing the skill or process skillfully, accurately, quickly, and automatically. The teacher assigns this type of practice with a skill or process as homework. Students keep self-monitoring charts to track their progress and improvement over time.

Worked examples

While students are practicing skills and processes, the teacher provides them with problems or examples that have already been worked out so they receive a clear image of the correct procedure.

Practice sessions prior to testing

The teacher sets up a practice schedule to ensure that students each have a chance to review and practice skills and processes before they are tested or retested on them.

Technology Links

- Search the Internet for example problems or situations at varying levels of difficulty for student practice.

- Provide students with access to audio and video recordings that review important steps and information that students will need as they practice a skill or strategy.

- As students practice a skill or strategy, invite them to post questions or issues to a class website, blog, or wiki. Other students or the teacher can offer help or explain a step of the process in more detail. Teachers can also use these questions to detect patterns of issues or errors that should be addressed with the whole class.

Element 20: What do I typically do to help students revise knowledge?

Strategies

Academic notebook entries

The teacher asks students to make new entries in their academic notebooks after a critical-input experience, after group work or processing, or after reviewing and correcting homework. Over the course of a unit, and during related units, students re-examine their notebooks to correct inaccuracies or incomplete information.

Academic notebook review

Students use their academic notebooks to identify the important vocabulary terms, big ideas and concepts, generalizations, and understandings they should study for an exam or quiz. Students can also use their academic notebooks to generate questions.

Peer feedback

Students trade academic notebooks and respond in writing to each other's entries. Students might answer questions such as the following:

- What methods did this student use to represent information that were especially clear, concise, and appropriate for the information being recorded (for example, graphic organizers, flowcharts, summaries, pictures, or pictographs)?

- What information did this student record that I did not record in my academic notebook?

- What do I consider to be the most important information recorded here?

- What is one thing this student could improve on in recording knowledge in his or her academic notebook?

Assignment revision

The teacher makes comments on students' assignments but records their scores only in the gradebook (not on the assignments). When returning the assignment, the teacher can offer students the opportunity to revise their assignments according to the feedback given and resubmit it to try to get a higher score. Students who choose not to resubmit the assignment can simply accept their initial score, but students who resubmit a revised assignment should have their score for the revised assignment recorded.

Technology Links

- Use electronic academic notebooks to ensure that students do not lose their notebooks, forget to bring them to class, or leave them at home. These also make it easier for students to edit; revise; request or provide feedback; add information, media, or graphics; and share ideas. Make sure that students are mindful about what they include in their notebooks (to avoid excessive copying and pasting from the Internet or other sources).

- Use an interactive whiteboard or similar software to make group revisions to initial ideas.

Content

Element 21: What do I typically do to organize students for cognitively complex tasks?

Strategies

Student-designed tasks

Students design their own cognitively complex tasks that address class or personal learning goals. To begin, students answer the question, What are your initial questions and predictions about this content or information? Next, students respond to the following stimulus questions in order to identify the type of task that best addresses their question or prediction:

Relative to my questions and predictions, is there an important . . .

- Hypothesis I want to test?

- Problem I want to study?

- Decision I want to examine?

- Concept I want to examine?

- Event I want to study?

- Hypothetical or future event I want to examine?

The first option applies to experimental inquiry tasks, the second applies to problem-solving tasks, the third indicates that the students should complete a decision-making task, and the final three correspond to the three types of investigation tasks: definitional investigation, historical investigation, and projective investigation.

Cooperative learning

The teacher uses the following guidelines to govern the use of cooperative learning during cognitively complex tasks:

- The teacher should design structures for group and individual accountability.

- The teacher should provide ongoing coaching of students' interpersonal and group skills (for example, active listening, conflict resolution, restraining impulsivity, summarizing and paraphrasing, and time management).

- The teacher should specify clear roles and responsibilities for all group members. Group roles should rotate so all students have the opportunity to fill various roles (such as facilitator, summarizer, questioner, and so on).

- The teacher should use a variety of grouping criteria, grouping structures (such as formal and informal groups, ad hoc groups, long-term groups, and others), and grouping sizes (for example, whole-class instruction, group work, individual instruction, and independent learning), and he or she should ensure that the grouping practices make sense in the larger scheme of classroom activities and instructional segments.

Academic notebook charts, graphs, and tables

Students track their progress on class or personal learning goals using a bar or line graph kept in a section of their academic notebooks.

Think logs

Students use think logs to reflect on the specific cognitive skills (for example, classification, drawing inferences, decision making, creative thinking, and self-regulation) they are learning as they complete cognitively complex tasks. Students respond to prompts such as the following:

- How might you explain classification to a friend?

- Describe an inference you drew today.

- With what aspects of the decision-making process are you most comfortable? With what aspects are you least comfortable?

- What might be the components of a self-regulation plan for your own learning?

Journals

Students keep task-specific journals (or designate a section of their academic notebooks) to record reflections on their learning as they complete cognitively complex tasks. They might answer questions such as the following:

- What is the purpose of your cognitively complex task?

- To what extent has your cognitively complex task enhanced your achievement of the unit learning goals?

- What questions did your cognitively complex task raise for you today?

- What problems did you encounter while working on your cognitively complex task today?

Peer response groups

Students work with peers to give and receive feedback on their cognitively complex tasks. To ensure equal participation and consistent feedback, the teacher assigns roles to students and uses scoring scales or checklists to ensure similar standards for each member of the group.

Self-evaluations

After completing a cognitively complex task, students engage in a formal self-evaluation process using data from their academic notebooks, final products or performances, and peer or teacher feedback. If appropriate, the teacher might ask the students to suggest what score or grade they think they deserve for their project.

Content

Peer tutoring

Advanced students volunteer to help students who need just a little assistance to move up to the next level. Advanced students should probably not tutor severely struggling students (who need intensive help from the teacher), but the teacher might pair them with students who need only a small amount of help or guidance to achieve competence or proficiency.

Technology Links

- Direct students to websites that encourage collaboration. Some websites are designed to facilitate online conversations, while others allow students to collect information and work together to produce papers and presentations (for example, www.wikispaces.com or https://docs.google.com).

- Ask students to keep think logs and journals online or on a school server. This allows the teacher to monitor student entries and provide feedback when necessary.

- Encourage students to explore websites related to the content in order to find ideas for cognitively complex tasks that interest them or to find different perspectives and issues related to the content.

Element 22: What do I typically do to engage students in cognitively complex tasks involving hypothesis generation and testing?

Strategies

Experimental-inquiry tasks

The teacher uses experimental-inquiry tasks to teach students how to make predictions, test them, examine the results, evaluate the results, and reflect on the process. Observations, experiments, surveys, and interviews are all appropriate data-collection techniques for this type of task. The teacher can ask students to answer the following questions as they engage in experimental-inquiry tasks:

- What is my prediction?

- How will I test my prediction?

- What do I expect to see if my prediction is correct?

- What actually happened?

- Did my prediction come true?

- How has my thinking changed?

Problem-solving tasks

The teacher uses problem-solving tasks to teach students how to set a goal, identify obstacles or constraints to reaching that goal, find solutions, predict which solution is most likely to work, test their prediction, examine the results, evaluate the results, and reflect on the process. The teacher asks students to answer the following questions as they engage in problem-solving tasks:

- What is the goal?

- What obstacle or constraint makes it difficult to accomplish the goal?

- What are some ways I might overcome the obstacle or constraint?

- Which solution do I predict will work best and why?

- What actually happened?

- Do the results fit with my original prediction?

- If not, how should my thinking change regarding the problem?

Decision-making tasks

The teacher uses decision-making tasks to teach students how to identify possible alternatives, outline the criteria for which each alternative will be judged, apply the criteria to each alternative, and select the most appropriate alternative. Students can use a decision-making matrix such as the following to complete decision-making tasks (see table C.6, page 138).

Content

Table C.6: Decision-Making Matrix

Criteria	Alternatives							
0–Does not meet the criterion at all 1–Meets criterion slightly 2–Meets criterion 3–Strongly meets criterion								
Total								

Students answer the following questions as they engage in decision-making tasks:

- What alternatives am I considering?

- What criteria am I using to select among alternatives?

- What do I predict will be the best alternative?

- Which alternatives came out on top?

- Do the results fit with my original prediction?

- If not, how should my thinking change?

Investigation tasks

The teacher uses investigation tasks to teach students how to identify a concept, past event, or future hypothetical event to be investigated; identify what is already known about the subject of investigation; identify confusions or contradictions; and develop a plausible resolution to the confusion or contradictions. The teacher asks students to answer the following questions as they engage in investigation tasks:

- Am I focusing on something that has to be defined better, something that happened in the past, or something that might possibly happen?

- What do I think I will find out?

- What is known about my subject?

- What confusions or contradictions exist about my subject?

- What do I think is the resolution to these confusions and contradictions?

- Did my findings fit with my original prediction?

- If not, how should my thinking change?

Technology Links

- Work with the district and school to create electronic collections of templates, mini-lessons, and other tools used for experimental-inquiry, decision-making, problem-solving, or investigation tasks. This database might also include exemplars of successful student tasks.

- Use the Internet with students to explore different perspectives on content to generate ideas for cognitively complex tasks. For example, a teacher might search for important decisions throughout history to design investigation tasks, or a student might look for examples of interesting phenomena to explore in an experimental-inquiry task.

- Save students' work on cognitively complex tasks (such as written products, video or audio recordings, and pictures), and share these exemplars with students who are designing or beginning work on their own tasks.

Content

Element 23: What do I typically do to provide resources and guidance?

Strategies

Providing support for claims

When students make statements or come to conclusions, the teacher asks them to provide grounds, backing, and qualifiers for their claims, as follows:

- **Grounds**—initial evidence for a claim. Students should provide grounds that answer the question, Why do you think your claim is true? Students might use common knowledge, expert opinion, experimental evidence, and factual information as grounds for their claim.

- **Backing**—additional information about grounds that helps establish their validity.

- **Qualifiers**—exceptions to claims. The number of qualifiers needed for a claim can help determine the certainty of a claim.

The teacher can ask younger students to simply come up with a new idea and then explain why they think their new idea is a good one.

Examining claims for errors

The teacher prompts students to examine their claims for the errors of faulty logic (see page 128), attack (see page 128), weak reference (see page 128), and misinformation (see page 129). Additionally, there are several errors that commonly occur when using statistical data to support a claim; the five major types of statistical limitations for students to be aware of are (1) regression toward the mean, (2) conjunction, (3) base rates, (4) the limits of extrapolation, and (5) the cumulative nature of risk. Students can examine their use of statistical information by looking for common limits or errors. Marzano and Brown (2009) defined these limitations in the following ways (pp. 127–128):

1. **Regression toward the mean**—being aware that an extreme score on a measure is most commonly followed by a more moderate score that is closer to the mean

2. **Errors of conjunction**—being aware that it is less likely that two or more independent events will occur simultaneously than that they will occur in isolation

3. **Keeping aware of base rates**—using the general or typical patterns of occurrences in a category of events as the basis on which to predict what will happen in a specific situation

4. **Understanding the limits of extrapolation**—realizing that using trends to make predictions—extrapolating—is a useful practice as long as the prediction does not extend beyond the data for which trends have been observed

5. **Adjusting estimates of risk to account for the cumulative nature of probabilistic events**—realizing that even though the probability of a risky event might be highly unlikely, the probability of the event occurring increases with time and the number of events

Scoring scales

The teacher asks students to use a scale to monitor their progress toward a learning goal over the course of a cognitively complex task. The scale should contain the target learning goal, a simpler learning goal, and a more complex learning goal.

Interviews

The teacher conducts interviews with students to keep track of their progress as they work on cognitively complex tasks and projects. The teacher might use a checklist or scoring scale to guide each interview and to help the students plan their next steps.

Circulating around the room

The teacher walks around the room while students work, allowing them to easily request assistance.

Expressions and gestures

The teacher uses nonverbal expressions and gestures while providing guidance such as kneeling by a student's desk, using hand gestures while explaining something to a student, making eye contact with a student, nodding while a student is explaining his or her need, and asking questions to gain a clear idea of what a student needs help with.

Collecting assessment information

The teacher examines student assessments to anticipate student needs and make helpful resources immediately available. Students who are not comfortable asking for resources (or who are not able to determine what type of resources or help they need) can benefit from easily available or offered resources.

Feedback

The teacher offers feedback to students about correct or incorrect answers, tasks performed well, corrections needed, insightful comments, and levels of effort expended.

Technology Links

- Encourage students to send email or text messages to request help and guidance. Many students are more comfortable using electronic formats to explain their needs or request assistance.

- Ask students to keep logs, journals, and academic notebooks online or on a school server. Monitor student entries in order to provide feedback and assistance when necessary.

- Encourage students to use technology resources as they design products. For example, if a student is interested in using animation tools, the student might use that medium to communicate findings and conclusions from a cognitively complex task.

Content

Lesson Segments Enacted on the Spot

> *Design Question: What will I do to engage students?*

Element 24: What do I typically do to notice when students are not engaged?

Strategies

Scanning the room

The teacher scans the room to detect students whose levels of attention and engagement are low. The teacher might do this during whole- and small-group instruction, during independent and seatwork time, and during group-work time.

Monitoring levels of attention

If the teacher identifies a student or a small group of students with low levels of attention and engagement, the teacher engages the whole class in an activity to reengage, or he or she might use proximity, questioning, or eye contact to help those students reengage.

Measuring engagement

The teacher periodically asks students to signal their level of engagement. For example, each student might have three cards—a red card that signifies high engagement, a green card that signifies medium engagement, and a yellow card that signifies "need help." Students each display the card that represents their level of engagement at a particular time.

Technology Links

- Use technology tools to engage students and to get their attention. Keep in mind that although technology can attract students' attention easily, it does not necessarily sustain it. Technology should be used in concert with effective instructional strategies.

- Use learner response systems or voting websites (such as www.polleverywhere.com) to ask students about their levels of engagement. Use the data collected to adjust student engagement.

Element 25: What do I typically do to use academic games?

Strategies

What Is the Question?

The teacher creates and displays a matrix with content-based categories across the top and point categories (generally 100, 200, 300, 400, and 500) down the side. This can be done using a bulletin board, an overhead transparency, or PowerPoint. The teacher also creates clues (words, pictures, or a combination of the two) and puts one in each matrix cell, with more difficult clues corresponding to higher point values.

A student or team selects a category and point value. The teacher reveals the corresponding clue. The student answering must state a question for which the clue would be the answer. The teacher decides if a student's question represents an adequate understanding of the concept or term. If the student answers correctly, his or her team gets the points for the question and the same student picks the next category and level. If the student answers incorrectly, a student on the other team gets a chance to answer. If he or she answers correctly, that team gets the points and the next pick; if incorrect, no points are awarded and the original team picks next.

Name That Category

The teacher creates a game board that looks like a pyramid divided into sections with various categories and point values.

The teacher organizes students into teams with one clue giver and one or more guessers. Teams sit so that clue givers face the game board and guessers face the opposite direction. The teacher reveals one category on the game board (the rest remain covered). The clue giver must list words that fit in that category until teammates correctly identify the category name. As soon as one team has correctly identified the first category, the teacher reveals the next one.

Talk a Mile a Minute

The teacher prepares a set of cards, each with a category and list of items that fit in that category (for example, the shapes category card might have *square, circle, rectangle, triangle, right triangle, oval,* and *diamond* listed as words). The teacher organizes students into teams, and each team designates one team member as the talker. The teacher gives a card to each team. The talker tries to get his or her team to say each of the words by quickly describing them. The talker cannot use any of the words in the category title or any rhyming words. The talker keeps talking until the team members identify all of the terms on the card. If team members are having trouble with a particular term, the talker can skip it and come back to it later. The first few teams to identify all the terms receive points. Afterward, the teacher might lead a discussion of which words were hard to guess and how the successful talkers represented those words.

Classroom Feud

The teacher constructs at least one question for every student in the class. Questions can be multiple choice, fill-in-the-blank, or short answer.

On the Spot

The teacher organizes students into teams, and they take turns being the responder for their team. The teacher presents a question to a responder who has fifteen seconds to confer with team members and identify the team's answer. The responder tells the team's answer to the teacher. If correct, that team receives a point. If incorrect, the opposing team has the opportunity to answer. That team's most recent responder acts as responder for his or her group and has fifteen seconds to confer and answer the question. If correct, that team receives a point. If incorrect, no point is awarded. When every student on both teams has functioned as the responder, the team with the most points wins.

Which One Doesn't Belong?

The teacher creates word groups containing three terms that are similar and one term that is different. Students work independently or in groups. The teacher displays one word group at a time. Students have a set amount of time to pick out the term that does not belong and write down why they think that term is different. This game can be played formally (keeping track of points) or informally (if the teacher stops during a presentation to offer four words to the class and asks them to identify which one doesn't belong).

Inconsequential competition

The teacher uses any type of inconsequential competition (including academic games like those previously described) to increase student engagement. The teacher should clearly delineate roles in student groups and change group membership systematically (for example, after each unit) so that students with a high degree of content mastery are regularly paired with those who have lower content mastery. The teacher might consider giving a tangible reward to the top two or more teams at the end of a unit. This strategy can be used to review vocabulary terms, spelling words, literary terms and elements, historical facts, and dates. It can also be used to highlight different perspectives and points of view, key content, competing theories and hypotheses, and different approaches to mathematical problem solving.

Turning questions into games

The teacher turns questions into impromptu games by forming students into four equally sized groups before asking a series of questions during a lesson. Each group can name itself, if desired. After the teacher asks a question, group members talk together for one minute and record their answer on a response card. On the teacher's signal, each group holds up its answer. The teacher keeps a record on the board of the groups that selected the correct answer. After the series of questions, the teacher acknowledges the team with the highest point total.

Vocabulary review games

The teacher uses the book *Vocabulary Games for the Classroom* (Carleton & Marzano, 2010), which contains thirteen games for vocabulary development. They include the following:

1. Word Harvest

2. Name It!

3. Puzzle Stories

4. Two of a Kind

5. Opposites Attract

6. Magic Letter, Magic Word

7. Definition, Shmefinition

8. Which One Doesn't Belong?

9. Who Am I?

10. Where Am I?

11. Create a Category

12. What Is the Question?

13. Classroom Feud

Technology Links

- Use presentation or specialized software to create and run academic games.

- Incorporate learner response systems or voting websites (such as www.polleverywhere.com) into academic games to increase student participation.

- Search the Internet for games and game-like activities to use in or adapt for the classroom.

Element 26: What do I typically do to manage response rates?

Strategies

Random names

The teacher writes each student's name on a separate slip of paper or tongue depressor and selects one at random after asking a question. The teacher should put the selected name back into the jar or hat before the next question.

Hand signals

Students use a thumbs-up to indicate they understand the content being addressed, a thumbs-down to indicate they do not understand, and a flat palm to indicate they understand some of the content but are also confused about some of the content. Students can also use hand signals to indicate responses to multiple-choice questions. For example, one finger indicates that response A is correct, two fingers indicate response B, three fingers indicate response C, and four fingers indicate response D.

Response cards

Students write their answers on small (for example, 12 × 12–inch) whiteboards or chalkboards and reveal them to the teacher simultaneously.

Response chaining

After a student responds to a question, the teacher asks a second student to explain why the initial answer was correct, partially correct, or incorrect. The teacher might also ask the second student to paraphrase the initial answer before responding. The teacher can call on a third student to respond to the second student's response.

Paired response

Students confer in pairs to answer a question. The teacher then calls on a pair. One student can verbalize the answer for the pair, or both can contribute.

Choral response

The teacher presents target information in a clear and concise statement and asks the class to repeat the information as a group. The goal is to form an "imprint" of important information.

Wait time

The teacher allows a pause of at least three seconds after posing a question. The teacher also allows for a pause of at least three seconds if a student stops speaking in the middle of an answer and teaches students to allow a three-second pause between student answers.

Elaborative interrogation

After a student answers a question, the teacher probes the answer by asking, "How do you know that to be true?" and "Why is that so?" The teacher might also ask the student to provide evidence to support his or her conclusions.

Multiple types of questions

The teacher uses a combination of retrieval, analytical, predictive, interpretive, and evaluative questions such as the following:

- **Retrieval questions**—These require students to recognize, recall, and execute knowledge that was directly taught.

- **Analytical questions**—These require students to take information apart and determine how the parts relate to the whole.

- **Predictive questions**—These require students to form conjectures and hypotheses about what will happen next in a narrative or sequence of information or actions.

- **Interpretive questions**—These require students to make and defend inferences about the intentions of an author.

- **Evaluative questions**—These require students to use criteria to make judgments and assessments of something.

Technology Links

- Use learner response systems or voting websites (such as www.polleverywhere.com) to give more students an opportunity to answer questions and increase students' attention and engagement during questioning.

- Ask students to respond to questions posted on a class website, blog, or wiki. Monitor student participation and the complexity of responses generated.

On the Spot

Element 27: What do I typically do to use physical movement?

Strategies

Stand up and stretch

Periodically, the teacher asks students to stand up and stretch. This is especially useful when students need to change focus, concentration, or engagement, because such activity causes more blood and oxygen to flow to the brain.

Give one, get one

After locating information on a specific topic in their academic notebooks, students stand up and find a partner, carrying their notebooks with them. The pair compares what each student has recorded in his or her academic notebook. Students each share at least one piece of information they recorded that the other student did not. Based on this information, students add to or revise the entries in their notebooks. As time allows, students can find a different partner and repeat the process. The teacher leads a discussion afterward whereby students share new information they collected or how they revised their notebooks to make them more accurate or complete.

Vote with your feet

The teacher posts a sign in each corner of the room identifying answers to a true/false or multiple-choice question or reactions to answers to a question (incorrect, partially correct, totally correct). Students move to the corner that has the sign with their answer. Before discussing the correct answer, the teacher asks one student under each alternative to explain why he or she believes that answer is correct.

Corners activities

The teacher splits the class into four groups, which then rotate to each of the four corners of the classroom to examine four different relevant questions related to key content. The teacher assigns a recorder to stay in each corner to summarize students' comments about that corner's question. At the end, each recorder reads the summary from that corner.

Stand and be counted

After a lesson, students stand and are counted based on their self-assessment of how well they understood the key ideas and concepts presented in the lesson. A scale such as the following can be used (see table C.7).

Table C.7: Student Self-Assessment Scale

4 = I clearly understand all of the major ideas and concepts presented today.
3 = I understand most of the ideas and concepts presented today.
2 = I need help understanding many of the ideas and concepts presented today.
1 = I didn't get any of the ideas and concepts presented today.

Body representations

Students create body representations in which they act out important content or critical aspects of a topic (for example, forming cause-and-effect chains, physically acting out key sequence elements, or representing vocabulary terms).

Drama-related activities

Students act out an event being studied, taking the roles of various participants in the event. This works especially well with historical situations, current events, and events in literature.

Technology Links

- During corners activities, use video or audio recording devices to capture student summaries. Post these recordings on a class website or use them to review information during subsequent class discussions.

- Search the Internet for physical movement activities related to specific content (such as scripts for dramatization activities).

On the Spot

Element 28: What do I typically do to maintain a lively pace?

Strategies

Instructional segments

The teacher ensures that each of the following aspects of management and instruction are well planned and occur in a brisk, but not hurried, fashion:

- **Administrative tasks**—These include handing in assignments, distributing materials, and storing materials after an activity.

- **Presentation of new content**—This requires the teacher to switch back and forth between presenting new content in small chunks and allowing time for students to process newly presented chunks of information.

- **Practicing and deepening understanding of key knowledge and skills**—Through complex reasoning processes, this requires students to interact with the content using problem-solving, decision-making, investigation, experimental-inquiry, systems analysis, and hypothesis-testing processes.

- **Getting organized into groups**—This involves students knowing where to look to find out what group they are in, where to meet with their group, and where to find supplies.

- **Seat work**—This requires students to complete work or activities independently. Students should know which activities they are allowed to engage in once they have completed their seat work, such as helping other students, beginning to work on more advanced content, beginning to work on an activity that addresses the content of the seat work from another perspective, or studying a topic of their own choice.

- **Transitions**—These require students to end one activity and begin the next. The teacher must signal the end of the previous activity, announce the next activity (including when it will start, how long it will take, and when it will end), and cue students to move quickly to the next activity.

Establishing procedures for each of these activities can help students understand what is expected during different parts of a lesson.

Pace modulation

The teacher speeds up or slows down the pace of the lesson to meet the engagement needs of students.

The parking lot

If the teacher or students get stuck or bogged down on the answer to a specific question or a specific issue, the teacher writes the issue in a space on the board called the "parking lot." The teacher and students come back to the issue the next day after everyone has had time to think about it and gather information about it.

Motivational hook/launching activity

The teacher uses anecdotes, video clips, audio clips, newspaper headlines, and other short attention-grabbing media to spark students' attention. The teacher might also present unusual information or personal stories related to the lesson topic.

Technology Links

- Use a timer to help students prepare for, complete, and evaluate their transitions. Interactive whiteboard software usually includes a timer tool, and many timers are available online (for example, www.online-stopwatch.com).

- Use video clips, audio clips, headlines, and other attention grabbers to capture students' attention at the beginning of an instructional segment.

On the Spot

Element 29: What do I typically do to demonstrate intensity and enthusiasm?

Strategies

Direct statements about the importance of content

The teacher directly states why students are expected to learn the content being addressed. Providing real-world examples that require knowledge of the content helps students see the importance of the knowledge and information being presented.

Explicit connections

The teacher makes explicit connections between the content and students' interests, or between the content and local, national, or global events.

Nonlinguistic representations

The teacher uses a variety of nonlinguistic representations to help students visualize connections and patterns in the content. These might include graphic organizers, pictographs, or flowcharts. When referencing nonlinguistic representations, the teacher should display intensity and enthusiasm.

Personal stories

The teacher tells personal stories about the content to make it more accessible to students. The teacher might speak about certain content that was difficult to understand at first or content that provided important personal insights. The teacher might also invite students to tell stories about their personal connections to content.

Verbal and nonverbal signals

The teacher uses verbal signals such as the volume and tone of voice, a verbal emphasis on specific words or phrases, and the rate or speed of speech to communicate intensity and enthusiasm to students. The teacher can also communicate intensity and enthusiasm nonverbally by pausing to build anticipation and excitement, smiling and gesturing, and making eye contact and moving around the room while teaching.

Humor

The teacher uses humor to demonstrate his or her enthusiasm for the content. The teacher might use self-directed humor, funny headlines, silly quotes related to the content, or a class symbol for humor.

Quotations

The teacher uses quotations to add context to the content being presented. Websites such as www.quotationspage.com, www.quotegarden.com, and www.brainyquote.com provide libraries of quotations that can be searched or browsed by subject.

Movie and film clips

The teacher uses clips from films and movies to help students gain a new perspective on content and to demonstrate situations where the information being presented applies to real life.

Technology Links

- Use technology appropriately to add energy to the classroom. Videos, audio recordings, podcasts, and visuals can communicate enthusiasm about the content and can add intensity to presentations or discussions.

- Use colorful, focused, nonlinguistic representations to convey enthusiasm about a topic. Create these using images, organizers, and templates provided with presentation software (such as PowerPoint, Prezi, or interactive whiteboard software). Students can also use animation and sketching tools to generate new nonlinguistic representations.

- Search the Internet to find new ideas, new twists on old ideas, or fresh perspectives that will help renew a zest for teaching.

On the Spot

Element 30: What do I typically do to use friendly controversy?

Strategies

Friendly controversy

Students explain and defend their positions on topics about which they disagree. The teacher asks students to use the following guidelines when engaging in friendly controversy:

- Even if you are anxious to say something, listen when others are talking and wait your turn.

- You may criticize ideas but not people.

- As others speak, try to listen to what they are saying and understand why they think their opinion is accurate.

- When you state your opinion, try to provide evidence or reasons for it.

Class vote

Students vote on a particular issue. Before and after the vote, students discuss the merits of various positions. The teacher might ask students to vote again after the final discussion. To incorporate movement, the teacher might ask students to stand on a particular side of the classroom to represent their initial vote. Undecided students stand in the middle of the room. After each side presents arguments for their point of view, students have the opportunity to switch sides, and the teacher asks undecided students to pick a side to stand on.

Seminars

In groups, students explore a text, video, or other resource that expresses highly opinionated perspectives about a key issue or topic related to the curriculum content. Groups contain three to five members with specific roles: moderator, recorder (for notes and questions), sergeant-at-arms (to keep everyone on task), synthesizers, and group representatives (for whole-class debriefing).

Expert opinions

Students research the opinions of experts who hold contrasting perspectives and points of view about a particular issue or topic. The teacher might use this strategy in a cooperative jigsaw where students each research a particular researcher or thought leader and then report back to the whole group about what they discovered. The class then discusses the merits of the various perspectives and the validity (or lack thereof) of a particular thinker's ideas, positions, and evidence.

Opposite point of view

Students defend the opposite point of view from the one they agree with or support. This can help students with overly dogmatic or rigid attitudes explore the nuances of a particular topic or issue and can reinforce the process of providing evidence to support a claim.

Diagramming perspectives

Students use a Venn diagram to compare various points of view. The diagram might highlight areas of congruence and areas of disagreement between two or three ideas.

Lincoln-Douglas debate

Students practice assuming affirmative or negative positions on an issue and giving supporting evidence for their position. The teacher chooses two teams to debate opposing sides of a specific policy or issue. One side argues in favor of the policy or issue (affirmative team) and the other side argues against it (negative team). Each side gets the opportunity to make an opening argument, cross-examine the opposing side, and present a rebuttal. After the debate, each team evaluates their performance as a group, and students self-evaluate their own performance as a member of the team.

Town hall meeting (Hess, 2009)

To help students see a complex issue from multiple perspectives, the teacher designates specific roles that students assume during a town hall meeting. Roles can be based on the people or groups most likely to have strong opinions about an issue or most likely to be affected by a new policy or change in existing policy. The students participate in an open discussion while the teacher mediates. Students stay in character for their respective roles and argue from that point of view for the duration of the discussion. The students then participate in a debriefing whereby they evaluate their own performances and the discussion as a whole.

Legal model (Hess, 2009)

Students critically examine how Supreme Court decisions affect policy as they form their opinions and arguments based on textual evidence from past Supreme Court cases. Each student completes a "ticket" or outline of the essential arguments that each Supreme Court justice made in the case being studied. Students must complete their tickets in order to participate in the discussion and may use them throughout the discussion as a reference guide. The teacher leads a discussion of the case being studied. Using questions that focus on the facts, opinions, and ideas of the case, the teacher helps students articulate their arguments based on the textual evidence they have read. At the end, students participate in a debriefing to evaluate their individual and group performance.

Technology Links

- Use learner response systems or voting websites (such as www.polleverywhere.com) to encourage students to take a position on the issues being discussed.

- Use an interactive whiteboard or other projection device to record students' positions on controversial issues. Also record and display support for students' positions. After discussing issues, the class can group these positions or modify the support to reflect their new learning.

- Ask students to present their positions on an issue in audio or video recordings and post them on a class website, blog, or wiki so other students can watch them before class. Use class time to analyze various positions more deeply.

- Use audio and video recordings (from the Internet or from previous students) about an issue to present alternative positions students might not have considered.

On the Spot

Element 31: What do I typically do to provide opportunities for students to talk about themselves?

Strategies

Interest surveys

The teacher uses interest surveys at the beginning of the year or the beginning of a unit to learn about student interests and goals.

Student learning profiles

The teacher uses student learning profiles to collect self-reported information from students about their preferred learning activities and styles (such as creative, analytical, practical, or mixed), the circumstances and conditions under which they learn best, and ways in which they prefer to express themselves (for example, writing, oral communication, physical expression, artistic media, and others). The teacher might create student learning profiles using formal inventories or informal discussions and surveys.

Life connections

During instruction, the teacher schedules breaks during which students are asked to find connections between the content and their personal experiences and interests. Students can look for and explain similarities and differences between their interests and experiences and the content being studied. Students might also complete analogies comparing aspects of their experiences and interests to elements of the content. Last, students can create nonlinguistic representations (such as graphic organizers, pictographs, or figures) that express relationships between the content being studied and their personal interests and experiences.

Informal linkages during class discussion

As topics are discussed in class, the teacher refers to a previously complied list of student interests. If a topic comes up in a class discussion that relates to a particular student's interest, the teacher makes that connection and says, "Robert, you're interested in astronomy, aren't you? What do you think about the information we just read and the new information about Pluto?"

Technology Links

- Use survey websites or learner response systems to collect information about students' interests quickly and efficiently.

- Encourage students to create personal blogs on a class website. Students can share experiences, ideas, positions, concerns, and audio or video recordings that will help their teacher and peers get to know them.

- Ask students to post or send text messages of personal examples of the content.

Element 32: What do I typically do to present unusual or intriguing information?

Strategies

Teacher-presented information

The teacher presents unusual or intriguing information to capture students' attention. Facts related to the content are preferred, but any unusual information can attract students' attention and help them feel interested in what the teacher is about to say.

Webquests

Students explore the Internet and find a range of obscure but interesting facts and ideas associated with the content being studied.

One-minute headlines

Students quickly share the most unusual (but factual) information they discovered about a particular topic.

Believe it or not

Students create an electronic database of unusual or little known information about the content being studied. This can be preserved from one year to the next, with each class reading previous contributions, correcting misconceptions where appropriate, and adding their own unusual information.

History files

Students research different historical perceptions in the content areas being studied. For example, medical facts have changed a great deal since the time of Hippocrates, and comparing one fact (such as the role of blood in the body) throughout history can yield new insights for students.

Guest speakers and firsthand consultants

Students understand real-world applications of the content being learned by listening to guests share experiences from their careers.

Technology Links

- Text intriguing ideas or interesting information to students before class to stimulate their curiosity and pique their interest in content.

- Use technology (such as Skype) to bring experts and guest speakers into the classroom.

- Design webquests that allow students to discover unusual or intriguing information about the content.

On the Spot

Design Question: What will I do to recognize and acknowledge adherence or lack of adherence to rules and procedures?

Element 33: What do I typically do to demonstrate withitness?

Strategies

Being proactive

Before students arrive, the teacher mentally reviews what might go wrong with specific students in specific classes and how to address those problems. The teacher also tries to be aware of incidents that have happened outside of class that could affect student behavior in class. In addition, the teacher considers students who are passive, aggressive, perfectionists, socially inept, or who have attention problems. Before class starts, the teacher talks privately to potentially disruptive students to make them feel welcome and review expectations for the day. If appropriate, the teacher and student might select a prearranged cue that the teacher can use to signal inappropriate behavior. For example, the teacher might make a small mark on a notepad on the student's desk or tap twice on the desktop if the student's behavior is becoming disruptive or unacceptable.

Occupying the whole room physically and visually

While teaching, the teacher visually scans the classroom, noting the behaviors of individuals or groups of students. If possible, the teacher should make eye contact with each student and should spend time in each quadrant of the room on a regular basis.

Noticing potential problems

The teacher watches for small groups of students huddled together talking intensely; one or more students not engaging in a class activity for an extended period of time; students in a specific area looking at each other and smiling; members of the class looking at a specific location and smiling; students giggling or smiling whenever the teacher looks at or walks near a particular part of the room; or whispering, giggling, or unusual noises when the teacher's back is toward the class.

Series of graduated actions

When noticing disruptive behavior, the teacher makes eye contact with those students involved in the incident or who exhibit the behavior. This should elicit the attention of the suspected students; it may also elicit the attention of other students. The offending students should understand that the teacher has noticed their behavior and it is not acceptable.

If the problem persists, the teacher moves in the direction of the offending students while continuing to address the entire class. The teacher should eventually stand right next to the offending student or students and use nonverbal cues to communicate to the offending students that they need to stop their inappropriate behavior and join in what the class is doing. The teacher should communicate that their participation is welcome and needed.

If the behavior persists, the teacher talks to the offending students quietly and privately. The teacher should request (not demand), in a positive way, that they reengage with what the class is doing and reiterate that their participation is welcome and needed.

Finally, if the behavior does not stop, the teacher stops the class and confronts the offending behavior, staying calm and polite, but explicitly stating the consequences that will ensue if the current behavior continues, while communicating that the students have a decision to make.

Technology Links

- Video record a variety of lessons and examine the video to determine the level of withitness displayed in the clip. Use a 360° video camera to capture footage of all corners of the classroom.

- Ask students to watch footage of a lesson and identify on-task and off-task behavior.

On the Spot

Element 34: What do I typically do to apply consequences for lack of adherence to rules and procedures?

Strategies

Verbal cues

The teacher says a student's name, quietly reminds a student that he or she is not following a rule or procedure, quietly states the expected appropriate behavior, or simply tells a student to stop the current behavior. The teacher might also use comments such as, "Bill, think about what you are doing right now" or "Mary, is what you are doing helping you focus your attention?"

Pregnant pause

The teacher stops teaching in response to recurring disruptive behavior. This will create an uncomfortable silence that will direct the attention in the room toward the misbehaving student. This can be a powerful motivator for a student to adjust his or her behavior. However, if the student's goal in misbehaving was to attract attention, this strategy can backfire. The teacher should be prepared to verbally confront the student in front of the group if necessary.

Nonverbal cues

The teacher uses eye contact, proximity, subtle gestures (such as shaking the head "no," putting a finger on the lips, tapping a student's desk, giving a thumbs-down, or raising eyebrows) to signal to students that their behavior is inappropriate.

Time-out

The teacher asks an offending student to go to a designated place (inside or outside the classroom) until the student is ready to resume regular classroom activities. The teacher might use a graduated process for sending students to time-out: (1) warning; (2) time-out inside classroom, where the student can continue to attend to the academic activities that are occurring; and (3) time-out outside classroom. If the student leaves the classroom for a time-out, the teacher must ensure that the student is still supervised and the student should develop a concrete action plan specifying what he or she will do differently upon returning to the classroom.

Overcorrection

The teacher requires a student who has behaved destructively to make things better than they were before the student acted to destroy them. For example, if a student destroyed class property, the student would need to repair what was destroyed and then improve additional class property. If a student interrupted the class's opportunity to learn, the student would need to learn the material independently and then assist the rest of the class in learning the material.

Interdependent group contingency

The teacher gives the entire class positive consequences only if every student in the class meets a certain behavioral standard. This type of group contingency can be used to reinforce positive group behavior and extinguish negative group behaviors, but should be used carefully, especially at the secondary level where students have a well-developed sense of fairness. Several strategies that use interdependent group contingency are as follows:

- **Marble jar**—Usually used at the elementary level, the teacher adds a marble to a jar for good class behavior and removes a marble from the jar for inappropriate class behavior. When the jar is full, the class earns a tangible reward or privilege.

- **Tally marks**—The teacher puts a tally mark on the board when the class behaves appropriately. Alternatively, the teacher might give a tally mark to individual groups or teams that display appropriate behavior. When either the class or an individual team has received a previously agreed-upon number of tally marks, they earn a tangible reward or privilege.

- **Countdown**—The teacher and students identify a certain number of "slips in protocol" considered acceptable during a specific time interval (such as a class period or day). The teacher makes a mark on the board every time a student fails to follow the target behavior. If fewer marks are tallied than the prearranged number, the whole class retains a privilege or earns a reward.

- **Group grades**—The teacher and students agree that every student in a group will be assigned the group's grade as their individual grade. When using this strategy, the teacher should ensure that each member of the group contributes equally to the final outcome or product.

Home contingency

To help an individual student perceive that his or her teacher and parents or guardians are unified in their attempt to help the student control his or her classroom behavior, the teacher meets with the student and parents or guardians to identify and discuss the student's use of inappropriate behavior in class. With input from the teacher and parents or guardians, the student should identify positive and negative consequences associated with his or her behavior in class. The consequences the student identified can then be implemented both in the classroom and at home. The teacher should communicate with the student's parents or guardians about the student's daily behavior.

Planning for high-intensity situations

The teacher takes the following steps when recognizing that a student is out of control:

1. Determine the level of intensity or crisis that the situation represents. Determine the student's level of control, the availability of outside resources (such as an administrator, counselor, or team teacher), and the level of risk to other students in the room.

2. The teacher should step back from the situation and calm himself or herself. Dealing with a high-intensity situation while agitated or scared may only worsen the situation.

3. The teacher should actively listen to the student and plan subsequent actions. While the student is speaking, the teacher might paraphrase what he or she is saying to let the student know that he or she is being heard. The teacher should continue to actively listen to the student until the student calms down.

4. When the student is calm, the teacher can repeat a simple verbal request such as, "Please join me in the hallway to discuss this further."

On the Spot

Overall disciplinary plan

The teacher creates an overall plan for dealing with disciplinary situations. It might include developing relationships with students, exhibiting withitness, articulating positive and negative consequences for behavior, and creating guidelines for dealing with high-intensity situations. The teacher's disciplinary plan might include considerations such as the following (see table C.8).

Table C.8: Overall Disciplinary Plan

Developing relationships with students	Exhibiting withitness	Articulating positive and negative consequences for behavior	Dealing with high-intensity situations
Seek to improve relationships with all students, especially those who tend to be disruptive in class.	List typical responses to student misbehavior. Analyze the list and determine which responses are effective and which are not.	Make sure that students can describe appropriate and inappropriate behavior. Meet with students to point out specific behaviors that need to be curtailed. Help students develop explicit plans to curtail inappropriate behavior and refine the plan as needed. Isolate offending students from the class until they make a commitment to appropriate behavior.	Develop an action plan for responding to high-intensity situations. Know when to involve administrators to help avoid or deal with high-intensity situations.

Technology Links

- Use emails, phone calls, and text messages to allow teachers, students, and parents to express their perspectives and feelings prior to a face-to-face discussion.

- Ask disruptive students to watch a video of their conduct during class to see how their behavior interfered with the class's learning. Consider accompanying descriptions of appropriate behavior with a video of appropriate behavior.

Element 35: What do I typically do to acknowledge adherence to rules and procedures?

Strategies

Verbal affirmations

The teacher uses short verbal affirmations such as *thank you, good job, that's great*, or *very good*. The teacher might also have short conversations or write notes to students to acknowledge their adherence to rules and procedures. The teacher should describe exactly what the student did that constituted adhering to a rule or procedure and how the behavior contributed to the proper functioning of the class. The teacher might also contrast the student's current behavior with past behavior that failed to adhere to a rule or procedure.

Nonverbal affirmations

The teacher uses a smile, a wink, a nod of the head, a thumbs-up sign, an OK sign (thumb and forefinger loop), a pantomimed tip of the hat, a pat on the back, or a high five to acknowledge students' adherence to rules and procedures.

Tangible recognition

The teacher uses privileges, activities, or items as a reward for positive behavior. Any use of tangible recognition should be accompanied by a thorough class discussion of the rationale behind the system to ensure it is not perceived as a type of bribe or form of coercion. The following privileges and activities might serve as tangible rewards:

- **Friday Fun Club**—This is usually used at the elementary level. Students who have earned membership in the club get to play a fun, educational game for the last hour of school on Friday.

- **Reward field trips**—These are usually used at the secondary level. Students who have no or few discipline referrals are allowed to go on a special field trip.

- **Recognition**—This can be used as a tangible reward. Teachers might display a class poster with the names of students who have met a certain standard of excellence, or students might post thank-you messages to each other or to teachers on a common bulletin board. Posting a list of students who have achieved a certain level of knowledge gain on a learning goal can also serve as a tangible reward.

Token economies

The teacher uses a system in which students receive a token, chit, or points when they meet expectations. They can then exchange these tokens, chits, or points for privileges, activities, or items.

Daily recognition forms

The teacher awards each student a starting score at the beginning of class (for example, 20 points) for a prearranged set of expectations (for example, 4 points for punctuality, 4 points for preparation, 4 points for on-task behavior, 4 points for respectfulness, and 4 points for work completion). If a student fails to meet a particular expectation, some or all of the points associated with that expectation are taken away. The teacher can use a tracking sheet placed on each student's desk to keep track of points throughout the day or class period. At the end of the period or day, students tally their total points, and the teacher records daily totals in a ledger. Students who achieve certain point levels earn privileges, activities, or items.

Color-coded behavior

The teacher gives each student three cards (red card = unacceptable behavior, yellow card = acceptable behavior with room for improvement, green card = exceptional adherence to rules and procedures) to keep on his or her desktop. All students begin the day or period with the green card on top. If a student's behavior warrants it, the teacher changes the exposed card to indicate the level of behavior being exhibited. Students whose behavior has warranted a change to yellow or red may work to have the green card reinstated by displaying appropriate behavior.

Many elementary teachers use a variation of this strategy involving a poster that shows a color (red, yellow, or green) for each student. Students each begin the day on green, and the teacher asks them to change their color if their behavior warrants it.

Certificates

The teacher uses reward certificates to increase parental involvement and awareness of behavior at school. Blank certificates can be personalized with a student's name and the reason for the reward, while preprinted certificates that correspond to specific desired behaviors can be used to quickly reward positive behavior.

Phone calls, emails, and notes

The teacher makes phone calls and sends emails or notes to a student's parents or guardians to recognize positive behavior. The teacher might make a goal of one positive phone call every afternoon. The teacher can also compose individual or group emails and notes to the parents or guardians of students who behaved appropriately during a particular week. All communication should be specific about how positive behavior reinforced a positive classroom environment and climate.

Technology Links

- Use emails, text messages, and phone calls to ensure that students and parents regularly receive positive messages.

- Show students videos of themselves acting appropriately during an activity or presentation and celebrate their effort.

Design Question: What will I do to establish and maintain effective relationships with students?

Element 36: What do I typically do to understand students' interests and backgrounds?

Strategies

Student background surveys

The teacher uses background surveys at the beginning of the year or the beginning of a unit to learn about each student's background, interests, and goals. They might include questions such as the following:

- Where were you born?

- How many brothers and sisters do you have?

- What are some things about your family that make you proud?

- What kinds of things did you do over the summer or on vacation that you enjoyed?

- What would you do if you knew you wouldn't fail?

- Do you have any hobbies (collecting things, artistic endeavors, building things)? If so, what are they?

- Do you participate in sports? If so, which sport(s)? What do like best about playing that sport?

- Do you take lessons of any kind (music, art, singing, dance, speech)? If so, what kind?

- What is your favorite book, game, movie, video or computer game, or television show?

- If you had to describe yourself in a sentence or two, what might you say that would help a person learn something about your personal interests?

The teacher might also ask students to complete sentence stems such as the following:

- During my free time I like to _____.

- One thing I really like to do with my friends is _____.

- I really enjoy _____.

- My family enjoys _____.

- If I had a month of Saturdays, I'd spend most of my time _____.

- Someday I'd like to be _____.

- The subject I like most in school is _____.

- I like this subject best because _____.

Opinion questionnaires

The teacher uses opinion questionnaires to find out about student perspectives on classroom topics.

On the Spot

Individual teacher-student conferences

The teacher uses individual teacher-student conferences as one-on-one opportunities to ask probing questions to more deeply understand student interests, perspectives, and experiences.

Parent-teacher conferences

During parent-teacher conferences, the teacher asks about and listens for critical details regarding students and their recent life experiences. These might include family events or vacations, transition points for parents or siblings (such as graduations, marriages, or job changes), and plans to move to a new home or a different school.

School newspaper, newsletter, or bulletin

The teacher reads school publications to learn about student involvement in athletic events (such as track and swim meets; basketball, baseball, or football games; or awards won), debates, club events, school performances, and community volunteer activities.

Informal class interviews

The teacher asks students to share what is happening in their lives or what things students are talking about that teachers should be aware of.

Investigating student culture

The teacher works to discover information that students know by becoming familiar with popular recording artists and their works, noticing popular places where students like to gather, taking note of local events that are significant to students, and being aware of rivalries between different groups of students. They might also notice popular terms and phrases students often use.

Autobiographical metaphors and analogies

Students construct metaphors that compare academic content with their own lives. These can be simple and concrete, or they can involve more complex patterns and processes. Students can also construct analogies between the content and their lives. These may or may not accompany nonlinguistic representations.

Six-word autobiographies

Students write an autobiography in exactly six words, and the teacher leads a discussion in which students share and explain their autobiographies.

Independent investigations

Students research a topic of interest to them and report back to the class about what they found and learned.

Quotes

Students collect and share quotes that describe their personalities and interests.

Commenting on student achievements or areas of importance

The teacher communicates interest in students by noticing and commenting on individual accomplishments and important events in their lives. The following are potential areas of achievement or importance to students (see table C.9).

Table C.9: Potential Areas of Achievement or Importance to Students

In-school achievements	Achievements outside of school	Important events
• Achievements in other classes • Assignments done well • High-quality presentations • Roles in class (leader, helper, facilitator) • Student government • Achievements in clubs or athletics • Academic recognitions received • Artistic or dramatic accomplishments	• Community service • Volunteering • Socially responsible actions • Awards received	• Changes in parents' jobs • Changes in family structures (births, deaths, marriages, divorces) • Vacations

Lineups

Students line up or sit in groups in ways that reveal their likes and dislikes or preferences. The teacher might use questions such as, Would you rather . . . ? and Which word describes you best?

Individual student learning goals

Students identify something that interests them and relates to the teacher-identified learning goals. Students can state their learning goals using the following formats:

When this unit is completed, I will better understand _____.

When this unit is completed, I will be able to _____.

Students use the following scale to track their progress on individual learning goals (see table C.10).

Table C.10: Student Self-Assessment Scale for Individual Learning Goals

> 4 = I did even better than the goal I set.
> 3 = I accomplished my goal.
> 2 = I didn't accomplish everything I wanted to, but I learned quite a bit.
> 1 = I tried, but I didn't really learn much.
> 0 = I didn't really try to accomplish my goal.

On the Spot

Technology Links

- Encourage students to keep online journals or blogs. Take time to respond to their entries or, with their permission, refer to their comments during class. Use explicit rules and procedures for peer feedback, so students can also respond to each other.

- Create electronic class newspapers and bulletins that highlight positive student accomplishments and school and community events that might interest students.

- Start wikis or other collaborative websites that focus on student interests. For example, if a number of students are interested in sports, help them create a website where they can share ideas and make connections between sports and the content being studied in class.

- Integrate student-created technology into lessons. For example, if a student produces video games or loves to create animations, encourage them to create resources related to the content and use those resources during lessons.

Element 37: What do I typically do to use verbal and nonverbal behaviors that indicate affection for students?

Strategies

Greeting students at the classroom door

The teacher greets students at the door using their first names. The teacher might also ask students how they are feeling and make positive comments about their learning or achievements.

Informal conferences

The teacher finds time to talk informally with students—give compliments, ask for student opinions, mention student successes, and pass on positive comments from other teachers.

Attending after-school functions

The teacher shows affection and interest in specific students who may feel alienated by attending after-school activities in which the student participates. If attending, the teacher should let the student know ahead of time and then make an effort to connect with the student at the event, if possible. While this takes time from the teacher's nonwork sphere, it can be helpful in future interactions with the student.

Greeting students by name outside of school

To show affection, the teacher greets students by name when encountering them at neighborhood venues such as the grocery store, movie theater, or shopping mall. This interaction need not be lengthy, and can be as simple as saying, "Hi, Emily. It's good to see you. Have a good day!"

Giving students special responsibilities or leadership roles in the classroom

To indicate affection for students, the teacher assigns them specific tasks in the classroom, such as caring for a class pet or collecting assignments. If a student's previous actions have warranted it, the teacher might give the student a leadership role on a project or ask him or her to take responsibility for a specific task on a field trip (delivering the lunches to the lunch location, for example).

Scheduled interaction

The teacher creates a schedule that ensures regular interaction with each student by selecting a few students each day to seek out and talk to. The teacher might interact with students in the lunchroom, during breaks between classes, or right after school.

Photo bulletin board

The teacher creates a bulletin board with a photo of each student and asks students to post their thoughts about the class, their personal goals, and other information about themselves and their interests underneath their photos. Photos and information might be changed periodically, depending on the topic of study.

On the Spot

Physical behaviors

The teacher uses appropriate physical signs of encouragement such as smiles, hugs, and high fives to communicate interest in students. Patting a student on the back or putting a hand on a student's shoulder can also communicate interest or concern for a student. While talking to a student, the teacher makes eye contact, stands close to the student (enough to communicate concern or interest without invading their personal space), or looks interested in what they have to say.

Humor

The teacher uses playful banter, jokes, or self-directed humor to build relationships with students. The teacher might also use historical and popular sayings to make a point, or incorporate cartoons, jokes, puns, and plays on words into instruction to incorporate humor in the classroom.

Technology Links

- Add slides to the beginning of presentations to highlight special events in students' lives (birthdays or upcoming athletic events, performances, or concerts). Take a few moments at the beginning of class to recognize and appreciate students.

- Create a website where students can post compliments or thank-you messages to each other and to the teacher.

Element 38: What do I typically do to display objectivity and control?

Strategies

Self-reflection

The teacher self-reflects daily about consistency when enforcing the positive and negative consequences associated with the established rules and procedures. Questions the teacher might consider include the following:

- Did I provide proper acknowledgement when students followed the rules and procedures?

- Did I use proper consequences when students did not follow rules and procedures?

- Did I take every opportunity today to provide positive and negative consequences for student behavior?

- Did I strike a nice balance between positive and negative consequences as needed?

The teacher should also consider how to progressively increase expectations for students to control their own behavior.

Self-monitoring

The teacher monitors his or her emotions in the classroom to avoid displaying counterproductive emotions such as anger, frustration, or hesitation. Before class each day, the teacher mentally reviews all of the students, noting those who might cause problems. The teacher should then identify specific negative thoughts and emotions toward those students by asking, "How do I feel about [student's name]?" Then, the teacher tries to identify events in the past that may be the source of the negative thoughts and feelings toward specific students by asking, "Why do I feel that way?" Finally, the teacher seeks to reframe negative beliefs about students by recognizing that student misbehavior usually has little to do with a specific teacher and by identifying explicit reasons the student might have misbehaved in the past that do not imply disrespect or aggression toward the teacher.

Identifying emotional triggers

The teacher takes time to think of emotional triggers that make it hard to maintain emotional objectivity, such as personal events or certain times of the school year. The teacher can then take extra steps to support emotional objectivity when emotional triggers are present.

Self-care

To focus on self-care, the teacher sits in a comfortable chair, practices deep breathing exercises, or uses guided imagery to create a "private retreat" at the end of each day. The teacher might also maintain a healthy sense of humor about negative events or encounters with students and could seek out funny movies and television shows to lessen tension. The teacher could also treat himself or herself to a reward on a particularly difficult day to help maintain a healthy perspective.

On the Spot

Assertiveness

To be assertive, the teacher stands up for his or her legitimate rights in ways that make it difficult for others to ignore or circumvent them. Assertive people are more likely to maintain a cool exterior in a variety of situations.

Maintaining a cool exterior

The teacher uses the following guidelines to remain calm and cool when dealing with conflict:

- Use assertive body language (for example, eye contact, erect posture, and appropriate distance from listeners).

- Match facial expression with the content of the message being presented to students.

- Use an appropriate tone of voice that does not indicate emotion (use a pitch slightly but not greatly elevated from normal classroom speech).

- Listen to legitimate explanations.

- Avoid being diverted by students who deny, argue, or blame others for their conduct.

When addressing a particularly agitated student, the teacher can practice the following:

- Speak in a calm and respectful tone of voice.

- Use active listening and speaking strategies.

- Maintain an appropriate distance from the student.

- Seek to project a neutral facial expression.

- Comment on the student's behavior, rather than the student's perceived motives.

- Avoid behaviors that provoke fear and anger from students, such as pointing a finger or shaking a fist, raising the voice, moving toward or hovering over the student, squinting the eyes, glaring or staring at the student, or ridiculing the student.

Active listening and speaking

The teacher listens to students without agreeing or disagreeing. The teacher should actively focus on what the student is saying and should try to understand the student's viewpoint. The teacher stays neutral in body posture, gestures, and facial expressions. When the student is finished speaking, the teacher acknowledges that he or she heard the student ("I think I understand how you feel/what you think") and then prompts them to go on ("What else is bothering you?"). The teacher repeats this process until the student can't think of anything else to say and is calmer. Finally, the teacher summarizes what he or she heard the student say. At the end of the summary, the teacher asks, "Am I right? Did I hear you completely?" The student will either say yes or will correct the teacher. If the student corrects the teacher, the teacher should restate the summary with the correction incorporated.

Communication styles

The teacher is aware of how the following communication styles may affect communication and emotional reactions:

- **Assertive connector**—"I value our relationship and what you have to say."

- **Apathetic avoider**—"I don't want much of a relationship with you and will put minimal effort into it."

- **Junior therapist**—"I know you better than you know yourself. I know you better than I know myself."

- **Bulldozer**—"I will do whatever it takes to get my way."

- **Hider**—"I am afraid of you and don't want you to know about me."

Unique student needs

The teacher maintains emotional objectivity by being aware of the following five types of students, described by Marzano (2003):

1. Passive
2. Aggressive
3. Attention problems
4. Perfectionistic
5. Socially inept

Technology Links

- When it is difficult to maintain objectivity in person or over the phone, use electronic communication (such as emails or text messages) to select words more carefully.

- Watch video clips of funny teaching situations from television shows and movies to help maintain a humorous and lighthearted perspective.

On the Spot

Design Question: What will I do to communicate high expectations for all students?

Element 39: What do I typically do to demonstrate value and respect for low-expectancy students?

Strategies

Identifying expectation levels for all students

The teacher identifies the expectation level for each student by pretending that each student has completed a comprehensive assessment covering some of the more difficult content addressed in class. On a class list, the teacher writes the level at which he or she expects each student to perform on such an assessment: high, average, or low.

Identifying differential treatment of low-expectancy students

The teacher tracks his or her behavior for several days to increase awareness of differences in affective tone and quality of interaction with specific students. Using an informal observation form, the teacher keeps track of his or her affective tone and quality of interaction with specific students. Some behaviors associated with each area are identified as follows (see table C.11).

Table C.11: Behaviors Associated With Affective Tone and Quality of Interaction

Affective Tone	Quality of Interaction
• Tone of voice • Proximity • Gestures • Eye contact • Smiles • Playful dialogue • Physical contact • Range of questions	• Feedback • Probing for more complex information • Coaching for an answer • Calling on students • Level of questions • Level of response required for a reward (verbal or otherwise)

The teacher then uses the data collected to generate conclusions about differential treatment of low-expectancy students. The teacher should identify specific students who seem to be receiving differential treatment. The teacher might also examine whether he or she has generalized low expectations for certain groups of students because of ethnicity, appearance, verbal patterns, or socioeconomic status. If this is the case, the teacher should actively seek to behave in a manner not controlled by biased patterns of thought. If biased patterns of thought are present, the teacher might try to ascertain the origin of those patterns and seek to suppress the behaviors prompted by them.

Nonverbal and verbal indicators of respect and value

The teacher uses eye contact, smiling, proximity, hand and body gestures, physical contact, and playful dialogue to communicate value and respect for all students. If a teacher recognizes different treatment for low-expectancy students, the teacher should make an effort to use both verbal and non-verbal indicators to show respect and value for low-expectancy students.

Technology Links

- Use electronic communication (such as emails, texts, or posts on class websites) to communicate with all students simultaneously. This prevents a teacher's body language or eye contact from implying that certain messages are only meant for some students.

- Invite students to participate in online chats or to post ideas on a class website, blog, or wiki. Students who hesitate to share their thoughts and ideas verbally in class may feel more comfortable when they can write and reread their responses. Websites such as www.voki.com allow students to create avatars that talk for them.

On the Spot

Element 40: What do I typically do to ask questions of low-expectancy students?

Strategies

Question levels

The teacher asks questions that require students to analyze information, evaluate conclusions, or make inferences. These types of questions are more complex than questions that test recognition or recall of correct answers. Teachers should ensure that they frequently ask low-expectancy students complex questions, even if these students may need help or encouragement to respond.

Response opportunities

The teacher reinforces high expectations for all students by giving them equal response opportunities. The teacher should use strategies that help manage response rates (see page 146) with all students.

Follow-up questioning

If a student is having trouble answering a question, the teacher restates the question, encourages collaboration, gives hints and cues, or lets the student opt out temporarily. If the teacher does allow the student to opt out, it is important to follow up with the student using a different question or in a one-on-one conversation at a later time.

Evidence and support for student answers

To reinforce high expectations for all students, the teacher requires similar levels of evidence and support for answers from every student. If a student makes a claim, the teacher asks him or her to provide grounds and backing for that claim, regardless of whether the student is low or high expectancy. If a student must make inferences in order to answer a question, the teacher asks the student to explain these inferences, regardless of the student's expectation level.

Encouragement

To encourage participation from all members of the class, the teacher attributes ideas and comments to those who offered them. The teacher also thanks each student who asks a question or provides an answer, even if the answer is incorrect. If a student does answer incorrectly, the teacher acknowledges any correct portions of the response and then explains how the incorrect portion could be altered to make it correct. Alternatively, the teacher states the question that the incorrect response would have answered.

Wait time

The teacher provides appropriate wait time after asking a question and appropriate pause time between student answers to allow all students adequate time to process information and formulate responses.

Tracking responses

The teacher calls on students randomly instead of only selecting those who raise their hands (see random names strategy, page 146). The teacher might also place a checkmark on his or her class chart next to the names of students who have answered or been asked questions. To focus on specific students, the teacher circles those students' names on a seating chart and then tracks how often they ask or respond to questions throughout a class period.

Avoiding inappropriate reactions

The teacher encourages low-expectancy students to answer questions and share their thoughts by avoiding inappropriate reactions to student responses. The teacher should avoid any of the following responses:

- Telling students they should have known the answer to a question

- Ignoring a student's response

- Making subjective comments about incorrect answers

- Allowing negative comments from other students

Technology Links

- Use an online random number or name generator to select students to answer questions.

- Post questions to a class website, blog, or wiki before class so students can make sure they are ready to answer them in class.

On the Spot

Element 41: What do I typically do to probe incorrect answers with low-expectancy students?

Strategies

Using an appropriate response process

The teacher responds appropriately to incorrect or incomplete responses by first demonstrating gratitude for the student's response. Next, the teacher points out what is correct and what is incorrect about the student's response. The teacher should emphasize what was correct and acknowledge that the student was headed in the right direction. If the student's response was completely incorrect, the teacher identifies the question that the incorrect response would have answered. Finally, the teacher helps the student answer correctly or complete his or her previous answer by giving the student more time to think, using hints or cues, modifying or restating the original question, or finding a simpler question within the one initially asked. The teacher might also provide the answer to the student and ask the student to elaborate on it, restate it in his or her own words, or provide an example of the answer.

Letting students "off the hook" temporarily

If a student becomes flustered, confused, or embarrassed while answering a question, the teacher lets the student pass temporarily. However, the teacher should return to the same student at a later time (in either a whole-class or one-on-one context) and ask this student to answer a different question or assist with thinking through the initial question when the student feels calmer.

Answer revision

The teacher uses elaborative interrogation techniques to help a student probe his or her answer until the student realizes that it is not defensible. The teacher might respond to a student's incorrect answer with questions such as, How do you know that to be true? and What evidence can you give to support that conclusion?

Think-pair-share (Lyman, 2006)

The teacher uses this structure to allow students to rehearse and correct answers before sharing them in front of the class. First, the teacher asks or displays a question. Then students form pairs, and students tell their partners their best answers to the question. After two to three minutes of discussion in pairs, the teacher calls on a student. That student can provide their own answer to the question, quote their partner's answer, or ask their partner to quote their answer.

Technology Links

- Use email, text messages, or a class website to probe students' answers. Students who may feel overwhelmed by the pressure of defending or elaborating on their answers during a class discussion might be more comfortable composing their answers electronically and submitting them to the teacher for review.

- When using learner response systems or voting websites (such as www.polleverywhere.com), ask students to vote before a discussion and then ask specific students to defend their answers. After discussing the issue and revoting, ask students to explain why they changed their answers.

APPENDIX A

ANSWERS TO COMPREHENSION QUESTIONS

Answers to Chapter 2: Comprehension Questions

1. *Why is a model of effective performance in a domain important to the development of expertise in that domain?*

   A model of effective performance is important to the development of expertise in a domain because it provides options from which an individual can quickly select the best or most effective actions. As an expert's model of performance develops, this individual has more options to choose from and can quickly and accurately decide on the right course of action in a specific situation. More complex models also allow experts to take more variables into consideration.

2. *What is the overall structure of the model of effective teaching presented in this chapter?*

   The model of effective teaching presented in this chapter is taken from the framework in *The Art and Science of Teaching* (Marzano, 2007). It has forty-one elements organized using a set of design questions that teachers can ask themselves periodically to remind them of the elements of effective instruction. These design questions are organized into three broad categories: (1) lesson segments involving routine events, (2) lesson segments addressing content, and (3) lesson segments enacted on the spot.

3. *What is the difference between elements of lesson segments involving routine events, elements of lesson segments addressing content, and elements of lesson segments enacted on the spot?*

   Teachers use routine elements on a regular basis. Content elements involve helping students interact with the information and skills they learn in the classroom. On-the-spot elements are those that the teacher is prepared to use but has not planned to use on a specific day or lesson. The teacher uses these elements as necessary, when the situation calls for them.

4. *How are lessons where students generate and test hypotheses different from the other types of lessons addressing content?*

   When students generate and test hypotheses, they are more self-directed than during other lessons addressing content. Lessons that involve generating and testing hypotheses ask students to apply what they have learned to complete problem-solving, decision-making, investigation, and experimentation tasks. The teacher functions as a resource provider and guide during these lesson segments. The other two types of content lessons involve effectively interacting with new knowledge and practicing and deepening knowledge.

Answers to Chapter 3: Comprehension Questions

1. *Describe the five performance levels from the scales explained in chapter 3: Not Using (0), Beginning (1), Developing (2), Applying (3), and Innovating (4).*

   Not Using (0) describes a teacher who does not use and is unaware of the strategies or behaviors for a specific element of teaching. A Beginning (1) teacher recognizes that strategies or behaviors related to an element are called for and attempts to use them, but he or she executes the strategies incorrectly or with parts missing. The Developing (2) teacher uses strategies or behaviors when they are called for but does so in a mechanistic way, without monitoring their effect on student outcomes. A teacher at the Applying (3) level effectively uses strategies or behaviors related to an element in the classroom while consistently monitoring their effect on student outcomes and making adjustments when necessary. The Innovating (4) teacher adapts, combines, or creates new strategies to meet the specific needs of each student and situation.

2. *Describe the three phases that a teacher goes through when learning a new strategy.*

   When learning a new strategy, a teacher begins in the *cognitive phase*. In this phase, the teacher simply tries to understand what a strategy is and how to properly execute it. The teacher might read about the strategy or watch a colleague use it. During the second phase, the *shaping phase*, the teacher begins to use the strategy. This stage usually involves significant omissions and errors, which the teacher gradually addresses as he or she improves with the strategy. In the shaping phase, the teacher must devote conscious thought to executing the strategy and usually is not aware of the strategy's effect on student outcomes. The third phase, the *autonomous phase*, is when a teacher has developed the use of a strategy to the point of fluency and is able to execute it while monitoring its effect on student outcomes.

3. *Why is it important to select only a few elements to focus on in a given year?*

   A teacher should select two to three elements that he or she has identified as Not Using (0) or Beginning (1) on the personal profile. Trying to focus on more than three elements can be counterproductive, overwhelming, and frustrating. If possible, a teacher should select one element from each of the three types of lesson segments: (1) routine segments, (2) content segments, and (3) on-the-spot segments.

4. *What are the important elements of a good growth goal?*

   A good growth goal should specifically refer to one or more of the forty-one elements of effective teaching. The elements selected should be those for which the teacher self-rated 1 or 0 on the personal profile. The growth goals should include a time frame, the current level of performance on the goal, and the desired level of performance for the goal.

Answers to Chapter 4: Comprehension Questions

1. *How is focused practice different from the common conception of practice?*

   Practice is commonly thought of as performing an action repeatedly. Focused practice differs from this because it involves repetition of a strategy while paying attention to detailed parts or aspects of the strategy that have been targeted for improvement.

2. *What are the benefits of focusing on specific steps of a strategy or developing a protocol for a strategy?*

   For strategies with a specific set of well-defined steps, focusing on one of those steps allows a teacher to perfect his or her performance on parts of the strategy that are crucial to its overall success. Practicing a specific step of a strategy might include developing explicit guidelines for students about how to complete that step of the strategy most effectively.

   If a strategy does not have a well-defined set of steps, a teacher might develop a protocol to guide focused practice of that strategy. A protocol articulates specific actions associated with a strategy that does not have a well-defined set of steps.

3. *What is overlearning, and what role does it play in the development of fluency?*

   Overlearning refers to practice that continues after a person has achieved proficiency. To be fluent with a strategy, a teacher needs to be able to execute the strategy so easily that his or her attention can be focused on monitoring students' reactions to the strategy. Overlearning helps a teacher reach this level of facility with a strategy.

4. *What are the similarities and differences between focused practice at the Applying (3) level and focused practice at the Innovating (4) level?*

   At the Applying (3) level, a teacher's practice focuses on using information gathered from students' reactions to adapt the strategy to meet students' needs more effectively. At the Innovating (4) level, a teacher is fluent with multiple strategies for a specific element of teaching and can integrate different parts of each strategy to create macrostrategies.

Answers to Chapter 5: Comprehension Questions

1. *What are ways to obtain focused feedback?*

   One of the simplest ways to collect data about the development of one's expertise is to keep a reflection log. Teachers simply record observations and impressions about the use of a strategy on a regular basis over a period of time. Teachers might also use video data to determine if they are becoming increasingly expert with a strategy or behavior. Video data are useful because they can be watched multiple times, and the teacher can examine different behaviors or strategies each time. Teachers can administer surveys to their classes to collect feedback from their students and then reflect on the results. Finally, teachers can use student achievement data to obtain feedback about the effect of a specific strategy on student learning.

2. *What guidelines should a teacher follow when watching video of his or her teaching?*

   Research has shown that self-viewing is most useful if the teacher focuses on a specific aspect of his or her performance. The teacher might watch for use of a specific strategy or behavior, examine student reactions to a strategy, or focus on the functioning of the classroom as a whole (for example, classroom organization or student engagement).

3. *How might you go about collecting student achievement data for a specific strategy in your own classroom?*

   Answers will vary, because each classroom is unique. However, the process should begin by identifying two groups of students—a control group and an experimental group. Both groups should be taught the same content in the same way, except that the selected strategy should be used with the experimental group and not with the control group. A pretest and a posttest should be administered to both groups, and the teacher should compare the gain scores for the control group with the gain scores for the experimental group. If the average gain score for the experimental group is higher than the average gain score for the control group, the strategy has had a positive effect on student achievement.

4. *How might a teacher organize and track multiple sources of feedback?*

   Teachers can track feedback events on a graph that shows their growth over time. They should record each feedback event (reflection log, video data, survey responses, or student achievement data) in a journal with a description of why they assigned a certain score to that feedback event.

Answers to Chapter 6: Comprehension Questions

1. *What things should teachers keep in mind when watching videos of other teachers?*

   Teachers should remember that videos of other teachers may not always show effective teaching. While watching videos, teachers should identify what the teacher in the video did well and what the teacher did not do well. Additionally, teachers viewing video can identify strategies that were not used but might have been effective in the situation shown in the video.

2. *How might you use coaching colleagues to enhance your own professional development?*

   Answers will vary, because each school and teacher is unique. Coaching colleagues can be pairs or small groups of teachers who observe each other and meet to share feedback. An entire team or school could also implement coaching colleagues. Coaching colleagues should create a set of norms to govern their interactions.

3. *What is the purpose of instructional rounds?*

   The purpose of instructional rounds is for teachers to enhance their own practice by comparing it to teachers they observe. Instructional rounds are never evaluative. Teachers who agree to instructional rounds visiting their classrooms should be thanked, but observing teachers should not give feedback unless the observed teacher asks for it. At the end of a set of instructional rounds, observers should identify strategies they currently use, strategies they saw other teachers use, questions they now have about their own use of strategies, and new ideas they now have for using strategies in their classrooms.

4. *How might you use instructional rounds in your school?*

   Answers will vary, because each school is different. Instructional rounds require administrative support. The administrator in charge of instructional rounds designates a lead teacher who schedules a time for each teacher in the building to participate in instructional rounds at least once a semester. The lead teacher works with the administrator to arrange coverage for teachers' classes while they participate in instructional rounds. The lead teacher also recruits highly effective teachers who will allow groups to visit their classrooms and facilitates discussions after the observations.

APPENDIX B

TEACHER SCALES FOR REFLECTIVE PRACTICE

This appendix provides scales, teacher evidence, and student evidence for the forty-one elements of *The Art and Science of Teaching* model described in chapter 2. For definitions of the terms used in this appendix, refer to the online appendix, *Glossary for Reflective Practice*, found at **marzanoresearch .com/classroomstrategies**.

Lesson Segments Involving Routine Events

Design Question: What will I do to establish and communicate learning goals, track student progress, and celebrate success?

1. What do I typically do to provide clear learning goals and scales (rubrics)?
The teacher provides a clearly stated learning goal accompanied by a scale or rubric that describes levels of performance relative to the learning goal.

Teacher Evidence

❑ Teacher has a learning goal posted so all students can see it.

❑ The learning goal is a clear statement of knowledge or information as opposed to an activity or assignment.

❑ Teacher makes reference to the learning goal throughout the lesson.

❑ Teacher has a scale or rubric that relates to the learning goal posted so that all students can see it.

❑ Teacher makes reference to the scale or rubric throughout the lesson.

Student Evidence

❑ When asked, students can explain the learning goal for the lesson.

❑ When asked, students can explain how their current activities relate to the learning goal.

❑ When asked, students can explain the meaning of the levels of performance articulated in the scale or rubric.

How Am I Doing?

	4 Innovating	3 Applying	2 Developing	1 Beginning	0 Not Using
Providing clear learning goals and scales (rubrics)	I adapt and create new strategies for unique student needs and situations.	I provide a clearly stated learning goal accompanied by a scale or rubric that describes levels of performance, and I monitor students' understanding of the learning goal and the levels of performance.	I provide a clearly stated learning goal accompanied by a scale or rubric that describes levels of performance, but I do so in a somewhat mechanistic way.	I use the strategy incorrectly or with parts missing.	I should use the strategy, but I don't.

2. What do I typically do to track student progress?

The teacher facilitates tracking of student progress on one or more learning goals using a formative approach to assessment.

Teacher Evidence	Student Evidence
❑ Teacher helps students track their individual progress on the learning goal. ❑ Teacher assigns scores using a scale or rubric that depicts student status relative to the learning goal. ❑ Teacher uses formal and informal means to assign scores to students. ❑ Teacher charts the progress of the entire class on the learning goal.	❑ When asked, students can describe their status relative to the learning goal using the scale or rubric. ❑ Students systematically update their status on the learning goal.

How Am I Doing?

	4 Innovating	3 Applying	2 Developing	1 Beginning	0 Not Using
Tracking student progress	I adapt and create new strategies for unique student needs and situations.	I facilitate tracking of student progress using a formative approach to assessment, and I monitor the extent to which students understand their level of performance.	I facilitate tracking of student progress using a formative approach to assessment, but I do so in a somewhat mechanistic way.	I use the strategy incorrectly or with parts missing.	I should use the strategy, but I don't.

3. What do I typically do to celebrate success?

The teacher provides students with recognition of their current status and their knowledge gain relative to the learning goal.

Teacher Evidence	**Student Evidence**

❑ Teacher acknowledges students who have achieved a certain score on the scale or rubric.
 	
❑ Teacher acknowledges students who have made gains in their knowledge and skill relative to the learning goal.
 	
❑ Teacher acknowledges and celebrates the final status and progress of the entire class.
 	
❑ Teacher uses a variety of ways to celebrate success:
 	
  • Show of hands
 	
  • Certification of success
 	
  • Parent notification
 	
  • Round of applause
	❑ Students show signs of pride regarding their accomplishments in the class.
	
	❑ When asked, students say they want to continue to make progress.

How Am I Doing?

	4 Innovating	3 Applying	2 Developing	1 Beginning	0 Not Using
Celebrating success	I adapt and create new strategies for unique student needs and situations.	I provide students with recognition of their current status and their knowledge gain relative to the learning goal, and I monitor the extent to which students are motivated to enhance their status.	I provide students with recognition of their current status and their knowledge gain relative to the learning goal, but I do so in a somewhat mechanistic way.	I use the strategy incorrectly or with parts missing.	I should use the strategy, but I don't.

Design Question: What will I do to establish and maintain classroom rules and procedures?

4. What do I typically do to establish and maintain classroom rules and procedures?

The teacher reviews expectations regarding rules and procedures to ensure their effective execution.

Teacher Evidence

- ❏ Teacher involves students in designing classroom routines.
- ❏ Teacher uses classroom meetings to review and process rules and procedures.
- ❏ Teacher reminds students of rules and procedures.
- ❏ Teacher asks students to restate or explain rules and procedures.
- ❏ Teacher provides cues or signals when a rule or procedure should be used.

Student Evidence

- ❏ Students follow clear routines during class.
- ❏ When asked, students can describe established rules and procedures.
- ❏ When asked, students describe the classroom as an orderly place.
- ❏ Students recognize cues and signals from the teacher.
- ❏ Students regulate their own behavior.

How Am I Doing?

	4 Innovating	3 Applying	2 Developing	1 Beginning	0 Not Using
Establishing and maintaining classroom rules and procedures	I adapt and create new strategies for unique student needs and situations.	I establish and review expectations regarding rules and procedures, and I monitor the extent to which students understand the rules and procedures.	I establish and review expectations regarding rules and procedures, but I do so in a somewhat mechanistic way.	I use the strategy incorrectly or with parts missing.	I should use the strategy, but I don't.

5. What do I typically do to organize the physical layout of the classroom?

The teacher organizes the physical layout of the classroom to facilitate movement and focus on learning.

Teacher Evidence	Student Evidence
❑ The physical layout of the classroom has clear traffic patterns.	❑ Students move easily about the classroom.
❑ The physical layout of the classroom provides easy access to materials and centers.	❑ Students make use of materials and learning centers.
❑ The classroom is decorated in a way that enhances student learning:	❑ Students attend to examples of their work that are displayed.
• Bulletin boards relate to current content.	❑ Students attend to information on bulletin boards.
• Students' work is displayed.	❑ Students can easily focus on instruction.

How Am I Doing?

	4 Innovating	3 Applying	2 Developing	1 Beginning	0 Not Using
Organizing the physical layout of the classroom	I adapt and create new strategies for unique student needs and situations.	I organize the physical layout of the classroom to facilitate movement and focus on learning, and I monitor the impact of the environment on student learning.	I organize the physical layout of the classroom to facilitate movement and focus on learning, but I do so in a somewhat mechanistic way.	I use the strategy incorrectly or with parts missing.	I should use the strategy, but I don't.

Lesson Segments Addressing Content

Design Question: What will I do to help students effectively interact with new knowledge?

6. What do I typically do to identify critical information?
The teacher identifies a lesson or part of a lesson as involving important information to which students should pay particular attention.

Teacher Evidence	Student Evidence

❑ Teacher begins the lesson by explaining why upcoming content is important.
 	
❑ Teacher tells students to get ready for some important information.
 	
❑ Teacher cues the importance of upcoming information in some indirect fashion:
  • Tone of voice
  • Body position
  • Level of excitement
	❑ When asked, students can describe the level of importance of the information addressed in class.
	
	❑ When asked, students can explain why the content is important to pay attention to.
	
	❑ Students visibly adjust their level of engagement.

How Am I Doing?

	4 Innovating	3 Applying	2 Developing	1 Beginning	0 Not Using
Identifying critical information	I adapt and create new strategies for unique student needs and situations.	I signal to students which content is critical versus noncritical, and I monitor the extent to which students are attending to critical information.	I signal to students which content is critical versus noncritical, but I do so in a somewhat mechanistic way.	I use the strategy incorrectly or with parts missing.	I should use the strategy, but I don't.

7. What do I typically do to organize students to interact with new knowledge?

The teacher organizes students into small groups to facilitate the processing of new information.

Teacher Evidence	Student Evidence
❑ Teacher has established routines for student grouping and student interaction in groups. ❑ Teacher organizes students into ad hoc groups for the lesson: • Pairs • Triads • Small groups up to about five students	❑ Students move to groups in an orderly fashion. ❑ Students appear to understand expectations about appropriate behavior in groups: • Respect opinions of others • Add their perspective to discussions • Ask and answer questions

How Am I Doing?

	4 Innovating	3 Applying	2 Developing	1 Beginning	0 Not Using
Organizing students to interact with new knowledge	I adapt and create new strategies for unique student needs and situations.	I organize students into small groups to facilitate the processing of new knowledge, and I monitor group processing.	I organize students into small groups to facilitate the processing of new knowledge, but I do so in a somewhat mechanistic way.	I use the strategy incorrectly or with parts missing.	I should use the strategy, but I don't.

8. What do I typically do to preview new content?

The teacher engages students in activities that help them link what they already know to the new content about to be addressed and facilitates these linkages.

Teacher Evidence

- ❑ Teacher uses preview questions before reading.
- ❑ Teacher uses K-W-L strategy or variation of it.
- ❑ Teacher asks or reminds students of what they already know about the topic.
- ❑ Teacher provides an advance organizer:
  - • Outline
  - • Graphic organizer
- ❑ Teacher has students brainstorm.
- ❑ Teacher uses an anticipation guide.
- ❑ Teacher uses a motivational hook or launching activity:
  - • Anecdotes
  - • Short selection from video
- ❑ Teacher uses a word splash activity to connect vocabulary to upcoming content.
- ❑ When necessary, the teacher reteaches basic information or skills.

Student Evidence

- ❑ When asked, students can explain linkages with prior knowledge.
- ❑ When asked, students make predictions about upcoming content.
- ❑ When asked, students can provide a purpose for what they are about to learn.
- ❑ Students actively engage in previewing activities.

How Am I Doing?

	4 Innovating	3 Applying	2 Developing	1 Beginning	0 Not Using
Previewing new content	I adapt and create new strategies for unique student needs and situations.	I engage students in learning activities that require them to preview and link new knowledge to what has been addressed, and I monitor the extent to which students are making linkages.	I engage students in learning activities that require them to preview and link new knowledge to what has been addressed, but I do so in a somewhat mechanistic way.	I use the strategy incorrectly or with parts missing.	I should use the strategy, but I don't.

Becoming a Reflective Teacher © 2012 Robert J. Marzano • marzanoresearch.com
Visit **marzanoresearch.com/classroomstrategies** to download this page.

9. What do I typically do to chunk content into digestible bites?

Based on student needs, the teacher breaks the content into small chunks (that is, digestible bites) of information that can be easily processed by students.

Teacher Evidence	Student Evidence
❑ Teacher stops at strategic points in a verbal presentation. ❑ While playing a videotape, the teacher pauses the tape at key junctures. ❑ During a demonstration, the teacher stops at strategic points. ❑ While students are reading information or stories orally as a class, the teacher stops at strategic points.	❑ When asked, students can explain why the teacher is stopping at various points. ❑ Students appear to know what is expected of them when the teacher stops at strategic points.

How Am I Doing?

	4 Innovating	3 Applying	2 Developing	1 Beginning	0 Not Using
Chunking content into digestible bites	I adapt and create new strategies for unique student needs and situations.	I break input experiences into small chunks based on student needs, and I monitor the extent to which chunks are appropriate.	I break input experiences into small chunks based on student needs, but I do so in a somewhat mechanistic way.	I use the strategy incorrectly or with parts missing.	I should use the strategy, but I don't.

10. What do I typically do to help students process new information?

During breaks in the presentation of content, the teacher engages students in actively processing new information.

Teacher Evidence	Student Evidence

❑ Teacher has group members summarize new information.
 	
❑ Teacher employs formal group processing strategies:
  • Jigsaw
  • Reciprocal teaching
  • Concept attainment
	❑ When asked, students can explain what they have just learned.
	
	❑ Students volunteer predictions.
	
	❑ Students voluntarily ask clarification questions.
	
	❑ Groups are actively discussing the content:
	  • Group members ask each other and answer questions about the information.
	  • Group members make predictions about what they expect next.

How Am I Doing?

	4 Innovating	3 Applying	2 Developing	1 Beginning	0 Not Using
Helping students process new information	I adapt and create new strategies for unique student needs and situations.	I engage students in summarizing, predicting, and questioning activities, and I monitor the extent to which the activities enhance students' understanding.	I engage students in summarizing, predicting, and questioning activities, but I do so in a somewhat mechanistic way.	I use the strategy incorrectly or with parts missing.	I should use the strategy, but I don't.

11. What do I typically do to help students elaborate on new information?

The teacher asks questions or engages students in activities that require elaborative inferences that go beyond what was explicitly taught.

Teacher Evidence	Student Evidence
❑ Teacher asks explicit questions that require students to make elaborative inferences about the content.	❑ Students volunteer answers to inferential questions.
❑ Teacher asks students to explain and defend their inferences.	❑ Students provide explanations and "proofs" for inferences.
❑ Teacher presents situations or problems that require inferences.	

How Am I Doing?

	4 Innovating	3 Applying	2 Developing	1 Beginning	0 Not Using
Helping students elaborate on new information	I adapt and create new strategies for unique student needs and situations.	I engage students in answering inferential questions, and I monitor the extent to which students elaborate on what was explicitly taught.	I engage students in answering inferential questions, but I do so in a somewhat mechanistic way.	I use the strategy incorrectly or with parts missing.	I should use the strategy, but I don't.

12. What do I typically do to help students record and represent knowledge?

The teacher engages students in activities that help them record their understanding of new content in linguistic ways and/or represent the content in nonlinguistic ways.

Teacher Evidence

❑ Teacher asks students to summarize the information they have learned.

❑ Teacher asks students to generate notes that identify critical information in the content.

❑ Teacher asks students to create nonlinguistic representations for new content:

- Graphic organizers
- Pictures
- Pictographs
- Flowcharts

❑ Teacher asks students to create mnemonics that organize the content.

Student Evidence

❑ Students' summaries and notes include critical content.

❑ Students' nonlinguistic representations include critical content.

❑ When asked, students can explain the main points of the lesson.

How Am I Doing?

	4 Innovating	3 Applying	2 Developing	1 Beginning	0 Not Using
Helping students record and represent knowledge	I adapt and create new strategies for unique student needs and situations.	I engage students in activities that help them record their understanding of new content in linguistic and/or nonlinguistic ways, and I monitor the extent to which this enhances students' understanding.	I engage students in activities that help them record their understanding of new content in linguistic and/or nonlinguistic ways, but I do so in a somewhat mechanistic way.	I use the strategy incorrectly or with parts missing.	I should use the strategy, but I don't.

13. What do I typically do to help students reflect on their learning?

The teacher engages students in activities that help them reflect on their learning and the learning process.

Teacher Evidence

❑ Teacher asks students to state or record what they are clear about and what they are confused about.

❑ Teacher asks students to state or record how hard they tried.

❑ Teacher asks students to state or record what they might have done to enhance their learning.

Student Evidence

❑ When asked, students can explain what they are clear about and what they are confused about.

❑ When asked, students can describe how hard they tried.

❑ When asked, students can explain what they could have done to enhance their learning.

How Am I Doing?

	4 Innovating	3 Applying	2 Developing	1 Beginning	0 Not Using
Helping students reflect on their learning	I adapt and create new strategies for unique student needs and situations.	I engage students in reflecting on their own learning and the learning process, and I monitor the extent to which students self-assess their understanding and effort.	I engage students in reflecting on their own learning and the learning process, but I do so in a somewhat mechanistic way.	I use the strategy incorrectly or with parts missing.	I should use the strategy, but I don't.

Design Question: What will I do to help students practice and deepen their understanding of new knowledge?

14. What do I typically do to review content?

The teacher engages students in a brief review of content that highlights the critical information.

Teacher Evidence	Student Evidence
❏ Teacher begins the lesson with a brief review of content.	❏ When asked, students can describe the previous content on which the new lesson is based.
❏ Teacher uses specific strategies to review information:	❏ Student responses to class activities indicate that they recall previous content.
• Summary	
• Problem that must be solved using previous information	
• Questions that require a review of content	
• Demonstration	
• Brief practice test or exercise	
❏ When necessary, the teacher reteaches basic information or skills.	

How Am I Doing?

	4 Innovating	3 Applying	2 Developing	1 Beginning	0 Not Using
Reviewing content	I adapt and create new strategies for unique student needs and situations.	I engage students in a brief review of content that highlights the critical information, and I monitor the extent to which students can recall and describe previous content.	I engage students in a brief review of content that highlights the critical information, but I do so in a somewhat mechanistic way.	I use the strategy incorrectly or with parts missing.	I should use the strategy, but I don't.

Becoming a Reflective Teacher © 2012 Robert J. Marzano • marzanoresearch.com
Visit **marzanoresearch.com/classroomstrategies** to download this page.

15. What do I typically do to organize students to practice and deepen knowledge?

The teacher uses grouping in ways that facilitate practicing and deepening knowledge.

Teacher Evidence	Student Evidence

❑ Teacher organizes students into groups with the expressed idea of deepening their knowledge of informational content.
 	
❑ Teacher organizes students into groups with the expressed idea of practicing a skill, strategy, or process.
	❑ When asked, students explain how the group work supports their learning.
	
	❑ While in groups, students interact in explicit ways to deepen their knowledge of informational content or practice a skill, strategy, or process such as the following:
	
	   • Asking each other questions
	
	   • Obtaining feedback from their peers

How Am I Doing?

	4 Innovating	3 Applying	2 Developing	1 Beginning	0 Not Using
Organizing students to practice and deepen knowledge	I adapt and create new strategies for unique student needs and situations.	I organize students into groups to practice and deepen their knowledge, and I monitor the extent to which the group work extends their learning.	I organize students into groups to practice and deepen their knowledge, but I do so in a somewhat mechanistic way.	I use the strategy incorrectly or with parts missing.	I should use the strategy, but I don't.

16. What do I typically do to use homework?

When appropriate (as opposed to routinely), the teacher designs homework to deepen students' knowledge of informational content or practice a skill, strategy, or process.

Teacher Evidence	Student Evidence
❏ Teacher communicates a clear purpose for homework. ❏ Teacher extends an activity that was begun in class to provide students with more time. ❏ Teacher assigns a well-crafted homework assignment that allows students to practice and deepen their knowledge independently.	❏ When asked, students can describe how the homework assignment will deepen their understanding of informational content or help them practice a skill, strategy, or process. ❏ Students ask clarifying questions of the homework that help them understand its purpose.

How Am I Doing?

	4 Innovating	3 Applying	2 Developing	1 Beginning	0 Not Using
Using homework	I adapt and create new strategies for unique student needs and situations.	When appropriate (as opposed to routinely), I assign homework that is designed to deepen knowledge of information or provide practice with a skill, strategy, or process, and I monitor the extent to which students understand the homework.	When appropriate (as opposed to routinely), I assign homework that is designed to deepen knowledge of information or provide practice with a skill, strategy, or process, but I do so in a somewhat mechanistic way.	I use the strategy incorrectly or with parts missing.	I should use the strategy, but I don't.

17. What do I typically do to help students examine similarities and differences?

When the content is informational, the teacher helps students deepen their knowledge by examining similarities and differences.

Teacher Evidence

- ❑ Teacher engages students in activities that require students to examine similarities and differences between content:
  - Comparison activities
  - Classifying activities
  - Analogy activities
  - Metaphor activities
- ❑ Teacher facilitates the use of these activities to help students deepen their understanding of content:
  - Asks students to summarize what they have learned from the activity
  - Asks students to explain how the activity has added to their understanding

Student Evidence

- ❑ Student artifacts indicate that their knowledge has been extended as a result of the activity.
- ❑ When asked about the activity, student responses indicate they have deepened their understanding.
- ❑ When asked, students can explain similarities and differences.
- ❑ Student artifacts indicate they can identify similarities and differences.

How Am I Doing?

	4 Innovating	3 Applying	2 Developing	1 Beginning	0 Not Using
Helping students examine similarities and differences	I adapt and create new strategies for unique student needs and situations.	When content is informational, I engage students in activities that require them to examine similarities and differences, and I monitor the extent to which the students are deepening their knowledge.	When content is informational, I engage students in activities that require them to examine similarities and differences, but I do so in a somewhat mechanistic way.	I use the strategy incorrectly or with parts missing.	I should use the strategy, but I don't.

18. What do I typically do to help students examine errors in reasoning?

When content is informational, the teacher helps students deepen their knowledge by examining their own reasoning or the logic of the information as presented to them.

Teacher Evidence

- ❏ Teacher asks students to examine information for errors or informal fallacies such as:
  - Faulty logic
  - Attack
  - Weak reference
  - Misinformation
- ❏ Teacher asks students to examine the strength of support presented for a claim by looking for the following:
  - Statement of a clear claim
  - Evidence for the claim presented
  - Qualifiers presented showing exceptions to the claim
- ❏ Teacher asks students to examine claims to determine if they contain statistical limitations involving regression, conjunction, base rates, extrapolation, or the cumulative nature of risk.

Student Evidence

- ❏ When asked, students can describe errors or informal fallacies in information.
- ❏ Student artifacts indicate that they can identify errors in reasoning.
- ❏ When asked, students can explain the overall structure of an argument presented to support a claim.
- ❏ When asked, students can describe common statistical errors.

How Am I Doing?

	4 Innovating	3 Applying	2 Developing	1 Beginning	0 Not Using
Helping students examine errors in reasoning	I adapt and create new strategies for unique student needs and situations.	When content is informational, I engage students in activities that require them to examine their own reasoning or the logic of information as presented to them, and I monitor the extent to which students are deepening their knowledge.	When content is informational, I engage students in activities that require them to examine their own reasoning or the logic of information as presented to them, but I do so in a somewhat mechanistic way.	I use the strategy incorrectly or with parts missing.	I should use the strategy, but I don't.

19. What do I typically do to help students practice skills, strategies, and processes?

When the content involves a skill, strategy, or process, the teacher engages students in practice activities that help them develop fluency.

Teacher Evidence	Student Evidence
❏ Teacher engages students in massed and distributed practice activities that are appropriate to their current ability to execute a skill, strategy, or process, such as the following: • Guided practice if students cannot perform the skill, strategy, or process independently • Independent practice if students can perform the skill, strategy, or process independently	❏ Students perform the skill, strategy, or process with increased confidence. ❏ Students perform the skill, strategy, or process with increased competence.

How Am I Doing?

	4 Innovating	3 Applying	2 Developing	1 Beginning	0 Not Using
Helping students practice skills, strategies, and processes	I adapt and create new strategies for unique student needs and situations.	When content involves a skill, strategy, or process, I engage students in practice activities, and I monitor the extent to which the practice is increasing student fluency.	When content involves a skill, strategy, or process, I engage students in practice activities, but I do so in a somewhat mechanistic way.	I use the strategy incorrectly or with parts missing.	I should use the strategy, but I don't.

20. What do I typically do to help students revise knowledge?
The teacher engages students in revision of previous knowledge about content addressed in previous lessons.

Teacher Evidence	Student Evidence
❑ Teacher asks students to examine previous entries in their academic notebooks or notes. ❑ Teacher engages the whole class in an examination of how the current lesson changed perceptions and understandings of previous content. ❑ Teacher has students explain how their understanding has changed.	❑ Students make corrections to information previously recorded about content. ❑ When asked, students can explain previous errors or misconceptions they had about content.

How Am I Doing?

	4 Innovating	3 Applying	2 Developing	1 Beginning	0 Not Using
Helping students revise knowledge	I adapt and create new strategies for unique student needs and situations.	I engage students in revision of previous content, and I monitor the extent to which these revisions deepen students' understanding.	I engage students in revision of previous content, but I do so in a somewhat mechanistic way.	I use the strategy incorrectly or with parts missing.	I should use the strategy, but I don't.

Design Question: What will I do to help students generate and test hypotheses about new knowledge?

21. What do I typically do to organize students for cognitively complex tasks?
The teacher organizes the class in such a way as to facilitate students working on complex tasks that require them to generate and test hypotheses.

Teacher Evidence	Student Evidence
❑ Teacher establishes the need to generate and test hypotheses. ❑ Teacher organizes students into groups to generate and test hypotheses.	❑ When asked, students describe the importance of generating and testing hypotheses about content. ❑ When asked, students explain how groups support their learning. ❑ Students use group activities to help them generate and test hypotheses.

How Am I Doing?

	4 Innovating	3 Applying	2 Developing	1 Beginning	0 Not Using
Organizing students for cognitively complex tasks	I adapt and create new strategies for unique student needs and situations.	I organize students into groups to facilitate working on cognitively complex tasks, and I monitor the extent to which group processes facilitate generating and testing hypotheses.	I organize students into groups to facilitate working on cognitively complex tasks, but I do so in a somewhat mechanistic way.	I use the strategy incorrectly or with parts missing.	I should use the strategy, but I don't.

22. What do I typically do to engage students in cognitively complex tasks involving hypothesis generation and testing?

The teacher engages students in complex tasks (for example, decision-making, problem-solving, experimental-inquiry, and investigation tasks) that require them to generate and test hypotheses.

Teacher Evidence	Student Evidence
❑ Teacher engages students with an explicit decision-making, problem-solving, experimental-inquiry, or investigation task that requires them to generate and test hypotheses. ❑ Teacher facilitates students generating their own individual or group task that requires them to generate and test hypotheses.	❑ Students are clearly working on tasks that require them to generate and test hypotheses. ❑ When asked, students can explain the hypothesis they are testing. ❑ When asked, students can explain whether their hypothesis was confirmed or disconfirmed. ❑ Student artifacts indicate that they can engage in decision-making, problem-solving, experimental-inquiry, or investigation tasks.

How Am I Doing?

	4 Innovating	3 Applying	2 Developing	1 Beginning	0 Not Using
Engaging students in cognitively complex tasks involving hypothesis generation and testing	I adapt and create new strategies for unique student needs and situations.	I engage students in cognitively complex tasks (for example, decision-making, problem-solving, experimental-inquiry, and investigation tasks), and I monitor the extent to which students are generating and testing hypotheses.	I engage students in cognitively complex tasks (for example, decision-making, problem-solving, experimental-inquiry, and investigation tasks), but I do so in a somewhat mechanistic way.	I use the strategy incorrectly or with parts missing.	I should use the strategy, but I don't.

23. What do I typically do to provide resources and guidance?

The teacher acts as resource provider and guide as students engage in cognitively complex tasks.

Teacher Evidence	Student Evidence
❑ Teacher asks students to provide support for their claims.	❑ Students provide grounds, backing, and qualifiers to support their claims.
❑ Teacher asks students to examine their claims for errors in reasoning or statistical limitations.	❑ Students find and correct errors or limitations in their claims.
❑ Teacher makes himself or herself available to students who need guidance or resources by doing the following:	❑ Students seek out the teacher for advice and guidance regarding hypothesis generation and testing tasks.
• Circulating around the room	❑ When asked, students can explain how the teacher provides assistance and guidance for hypothesis generation and testing tasks.
• Providing easy access to himself or herself	
❑ Teacher interacts with students during the class to determine their needs for hypothesis generating and testing tasks.	
❑ Teacher volunteers resources and guidance as needed by the entire class, groups of students, or individual students.	

How Am I Doing?

	4 Innovating	3 Applying	2 Developing	1 Beginning	0 Not Using
Providing resources and guidance	I adapt and create new strategies for unique student needs and situations.	I act as a guide and resource provider as students engage in cognitively complex tasks, and I monitor the extent to which students request and use guidance and resources.	I act as a guide and resource provider as students engage in cognitively complex tasks, but I do so in a somewhat mechanistic way.	I use the strategy incorrectly or with parts missing.	I should use the strategy, but I don't.

Lesson Segments Enacted on the Spot

Design Question: What will I do to engage students?

24. What do I typically do to notice when students are not engaged?

The teacher scans the room, making note of when students are not engaged and taking overt action.

Teacher Evidence

❑ Teacher notices when specific students or groups of students are not engaged.

❑ Teacher notices when the energy level in the room is low.

❑ Teacher takes action to re-engage students.

Student Evidence

❑ Students appear aware of the fact that the teacher is taking note of their level of engagement.

❑ Students try to increase their level of engagement when prompted.

❑ When asked, students explain that the teacher expects high levels of engagement.

How Am I Doing?

	4 Innovating	3 Applying	2 Developing	1 Beginning	0 Not Using
Noticing when students are not engaged	I adapt and create new strategies for unique student needs and situations.	I scan the room, making note of when students are not engaged and taking action, and I monitor the extent to which students re-engage.	I scan the room, making note of when students are not engaged and taking action, but I do so in a somewhat mechanistic way.	I use the strategy incorrectly or with parts missing.	I should use the strategy, but I don't.

25. What do I typically do to use academic games?

The teacher uses academic games and inconsequential competition to maintain student engagement.

Teacher Evidence

- ❑ Teacher uses structured game formats such as:
  - What Is the Question?
  - Name That Category
  - Talk a Mile a Minute
  - Classroom Feud
- ❑ Teacher develops impromptu games, such as making a game out of guessing which answer might be correct for a given question.
- ❑ Teacher uses inconsequential competition along with classroom games.

Student Evidence

- ❑ Students engage in the games with some enthusiasm.
- ❑ When asked, students can explain how the games keep their interest and help them learn or remember content.

How Am I Doing?

	4 Innovating	3 Applying	2 Developing	1 Beginning	0 Not Using
Using academic games	I adapt and create new strategies for unique student needs and situations.	I use academic games and inconsequential competition to maintain student engagement, and I monitor the extent to which students focus on the academic content of the game.	I use academic games and inconsequential competition to maintain student engagement, but I do so in a somewhat mechanistic way.	I use the strategy incorrectly or with parts missing.	I should use the strategy, but I don't.

26. What do I typically do to manage response rates?

The teacher uses response-rate techniques to maintain student engagement in questions.

Teacher Evidence	Student Evidence
❏ Teacher uses wait time. ❏ Teacher uses response cards. ❏ Teacher has students use hand signals to respond to questions. ❏ Teacher uses choral response. ❏ Teacher uses technology to keep track of students' responses. ❏ Teacher uses response chaining.	❏ Multiple students or the entire class respond to questions the teacher poses. ❏ When asked, students can describe their thinking about specific questions the teacher poses.

How Am I Doing?

	4 Innovating	3 Applying	2 Developing	1 Beginning	0 Not Using
Managing response rates	I adapt and create new strategies for unique student needs and situations.	I use response-rate techniques to maintain student engagement in questions, and I monitor the extent to which the techniques keep students engaged.	I use response-rate techniques to maintain student engagement in questions, but I do so in a somewhat mechanistic way.	I use the strategy incorrectly or with parts missing.	I should use the strategy, but I don't.

27. What do I typically do to use physical movement?

The teacher uses physical movement to maintain student engagement.

Teacher Evidence	Student Evidence

❑ Teacher has students stand up and stretch or do related activities when their energy is low.
 	
❑ Teacher uses activities that require students to physically move to respond to questions, such as:
  • Vote with your feet
  • Corners activity
 	
❑ Teacher has students physically act out or model content to increase energy and engagement.
 	
❑ Teacher uses give one, get one activities that require students to move about the room.
	❑ Students engage in the physical activities the teacher designs.
	
	❑ When asked, students can explain how the physical movement keeps their interest and helps them learn.

How Am I Doing?

	4 Innovating	3 Applying	2 Developing	1 Beginning	0 Not Using
Using physical movement	I adapt and create new strategies for unique student needs and situations.	I use physical movement to maintain student engagement, and I monitor the extent to which these activities enhance student engagement.	I use physical movement to maintain student engagement, but I do so in a somewhat mechanistic way.	I use the strategy incorrectly or with parts missing.	I should use the strategy, but I don't.

28. What do I typically do to maintain a lively pace?

The teacher uses pacing techniques to maintain students' engagement.

Teacher Evidence	Student Evidence
❑ Teacher employs crisp transitions from one activity to another.	❑ Students quickly adapt to transitions and re-engage when a new activity begins.
❑ Teacher alters pace appropriately (speeds up or slows down).	❑ When asked about the pace of the class, students describe it as neither too fast nor too slow.

How Am I Doing?

	4 Innovating	3 Applying	2 Developing	1 Beginning	0 Not Using
Maintaining a lively pace	I adapt and create new strategies for unique student needs and situations.	I use pacing techniques to maintain students' engagement, and I monitor the extent to which these techniques keep students engaged.	I use pacing techniques to maintain students' engagement, but I do so in a somewhat mechanistic way.	I use the strategy incorrectly or with parts missing.	I should use the strategy, but I don't.

29. What do I typically do to demonstrate intensity and enthusiasm?

The teacher demonstrates intensity and enthusiasm for the content in a variety of ways.

Teacher Evidence	Student Evidence

❑ Teacher describes personal experiences that relate to the content.
 	
❑ Teacher signals excitement for content with the following:
  • Physical gestures
  • Voice tone
  • Dramatization of information
 	
❑ Teacher overtly adjusts the energy level.
	❑ When asked, students say that the teacher "likes the content" and "likes teaching."
	
	❑ Students' attention levels increase when the teacher demonstrates enthusiasm and intensity for the content.

How Am I Doing?

	4 Innovating	3 Applying	2 Developing	1 Beginning	0 Not Using
Demonstrating intensity and enthusiasm	I adapt and create new strategies for unique student needs and situations.	I demonstrate intensity and enthusiasm for the content in a variety of ways, and I monitor the extent to which students' engagement increases.	I demonstrate intensity and enthusiasm for the content in a variety of ways, but I do so in a somewhat mechanistic way.	I use the strategy incorrectly or with parts missing.	I should use the strategy, but I don't.

30. What do I typically do to use friendly controversy?

The teacher uses friendly controversy techniques to maintain student engagement.

Teacher Evidence	Student Evidence
❑ Teacher structures mini-debates about the content. ❑ Teacher has students examine multiple perspectives and opinions about the content. ❑ Teacher elicits different opinions on content from members of the class.	❑ Students engage in friendly controversy activities with enhanced engagement. ❑ When asked, students describe friendly controversy activities as "stimulating," "fun," and so on. ❑ When asked, students explain how a friendly controversy activity helped them better understand the content.

How Am I Doing?

	4 Innovating	3 Applying	2 Developing	1 Beginning	0 Not Using
Using friendly controversy	I adapt and create new strategies for unique student needs and situations.	I use friendly controversy techniques to maintain student engagement, and I monitor the effect on students' engagement.	I use friendly controversy techniques to maintain student engagement, but I do so in a somewhat mechanistic way.	I use the strategy incorrectly or with parts missing.	I should use the strategy, but I don't.

31. What do I typically do to provide opportunities for students to talk about themselves?

The teacher provides students with opportunities to relate what is being addressed in class to their personal interests.

Teacher Evidence	Student Evidence
❑ Teacher is aware of student interests and makes connections between these interests and class content.	❑ Students engage in activities that require them to make connections between their personal interests and the content.
❑ Teacher structures activities that ask students to make connections between the content and their personal interests.	❑ When asked, students explain how making connections between content and their personal interests engages them and helps them better understand the content.
❑ When students explain how content relates to their personal interests, the teacher appears encouraging and interested.	

How Am I Doing?

	4 Innovating	3 Applying	2 Developing	1 Beginning	0 Not Using
Providing opportunities for students to talk about themselves	I adapt and create new strategies for unique student needs and situations.	I provide students with opportunities to relate what is being addressed in class to their personal interests, and I monitor the extent to which these activities enhance student engagement.	I provide students with opportunities to relate what is being addressed in class to their personal interests, but I do so in a somewhat mechanistic way.	I use the strategy incorrectly or with parts missing.	I should use the strategy, but I don't.

32. What do I typically do to present unusual or intriguing information?

The teacher uses unusual or intriguing information about the content in a manner that enhances student engagement.

Teacher Evidence	Student Evidence
❑ Teacher systematically provides interesting facts and details about the content. ❑ Teacher encourages students to identify interesting information about the content. ❑ Teacher engages students in activities, like "believe it or not," about the content. ❑ Teacher uses guest speakers to provide unusual information about the content. ❑ Teacher tells stories that are related to the content.	❑ Students' attention increases when unusual information is presented about the content. ❑ When asked, students explain how the unusual information makes them more interested in the content.

How Am I Doing?

	4 Innovating	3 Applying	2 Developing	1 Beginning	0 Not Using
Presenting unusual or intriguing information	I adapt and create new strategies for unique student needs and situations.	I use unusual or intriguing information about the content, and I monitor the extent to which this information enhances students' interest in the content.	I use unusual or intriguing information about the content, but I do so in a somewhat mechanistic way.	I use the strategy incorrectly or with parts missing.	I should use the strategy, but I don't.

Design Question: What will I do to recognize and acknowledge adherence or lack of adherence to rules and procedures?

33. What do I typically do to demonstrate withitness?

The teacher uses behaviors associated with withitness to maintain adherence to rules and procedures.

Teacher Evidence	**Student Evidence**
❑ Teacher physically occupies all quadrants of the room. ❑ Teacher scans the entire room, making eye contact with all students. ❑ Teacher recognizes potential sources of disruption and deals with them immediately. ❑ Teacher proactively addresses inflammatory situations.	❑ Students recognize that the teacher is aware of their behavior. ❑ When asked, students describe the teacher as "aware of what is going on" or as someone who "has eyes in the back of his or her head."

How Am I Doing?

	4 Innovating	3 Applying	2 Developing	1 Beginning	0 Not Using
Demonstrating withitness	I adapt and create new strategies for unique student needs and situations.	I use behaviors associated with withitness, and I monitor the effect on students' behavior.	I use behaviors associated with withitness, but I do so in a somewhat mechanistic way.	I use the strategy incorrectly or with parts missing.	I should use the strategy, but I don't.

34. What do I typically do to apply consequences for lack of adherence to rules and procedures?

The teacher consistently and fairly applies consequences for not following rules and procedures.

Teacher Evidence	Student Evidence

❏ Teacher provides nonverbal signals when students' behavior is not appropriate, such as:
 	
  • Eye contact
  • Proximity
  • Tap on the desk
  • Shaking head "no"
 	
❏ Teacher provides verbal signals when students' behavior is not appropriate, such as:
 	
  • Telling students to stop
  • Telling students that their behavior is in violation of a rule or procedure
 	
❏ Teacher uses group contingency consequences when appropriate (that is, the whole group must demonstrate a specific behavior).
 	
❏ Teacher involves the home when appropriate (that is, he or she makes a call home to parents to help extinguish inappropriate behavior).
 	
❏ Teacher uses direct cost consequences when appropriate (for example, a student must fix something he or she has broken).
	❏ Students cease inappropriate behavior when the teacher signals.
	
	❏ Students accept consequences as part of the way class is conducted.
	
	❏ When asked, students describe the teacher as fair in application of rules.

How Am I Doing?

	4 Innovating	3 Applying	2 Developing	1 Beginning	0 Not Using
Applying consequences for lack of adherence to rules and procedures	I adapt and create new strategies for unique student needs and situations.	I apply consequences for not following rules and procedures consistently and fairly, and I monitor the extent to which rules and procedures are followed.	I apply consequences for not following rules and procedures consistently and fairly, but I do so in a somewhat mechanistic way.	I use the strategy incorrectly or with parts missing.	I should use the strategy, but I don't.

35. What do I typically do to acknowledge adherence to rules and procedures?

The teacher consistently and fairly acknowledges adherence to rules and procedures.

Teacher Evidence	Student Evidence
❑ Teacher provides nonverbal signals that a rule or procedure has been followed, such as: • Smile • Nod of head • High five ❑ Teacher gives verbal cues that a rule or procedure has been followed, such as: • Thanking students for following a rule or procedure • Describing student behaviors that adhere to a rule or procedure ❑ Teacher notifies the home when a rule or procedure has been followed. ❑ Teacher uses tangible recognition when a rule or procedure has been followed, such as: • Certificate of merit • Token economies	❑ Students appear appreciative of the teacher acknowledging their positive behavior. ❑ When asked, students describe the teacher as appreciative of their good behavior. ❑ The number of students adhering to rules and procedures increases.

How Am I Doing?

	4 Innovating	3 Applying	2 Developing	1 Beginning	0 Not Using
Acknowledging adherence to rules and procedures	I adapt and create new strategies for unique student needs and situations.	I acknowledge adherence to rules and procedures consistently and fairly, and I monitor the extent to which my actions affect students' behavior.	I acknowledge adherence to rules and procedures consistently and fairly, but I do so in a somewhat mechanistic way.	I use the strategy incorrectly or with parts missing.	I should use the strategy, but I don't.

Design Question: What will I do to establish and maintain effective relationships with students?

36. What do I typically do to understand students' interests and backgrounds?

The teacher uses students' interests and backgrounds to produce a climate of acceptance and community.

Teacher Evidence

❑ Teacher has side discussions with students about events in their lives.

❑ Teacher has discussions with students about topics they are interested in.

❑ Teacher builds student interests into lessons.

Student Evidence

❑ When asked, students describe the teacher as someone who knows them and is interested in them.

❑ Students respond when the teacher demonstrates understanding of their interests and background.

❑ When asked, students say they feel accepted.

How Am I Doing?

	4 Innovating	3 Applying	2 Developing	1 Beginning	0 Not Using
Understanding students' interests and backgrounds	I adapt and create new strategies for unique student needs and situations.	I use students' interests and backgrounds during interactions with students, and I monitor the sense of community in the classroom.	I use students' interests and backgrounds during interactions with students, but I do so in a somewhat mechanistic way.	I use the strategy incorrectly or with parts missing.	I should use the strategy, but I don't.

37. What do I typically do to use verbal and nonverbal behaviors that indicate affection for students?

When appropriate, the teacher uses verbal and nonverbal behaviors that indicate affection for students.

Teacher Evidence	Student Evidence
❏ Teacher compliments students regarding academic and personal accomplishments.	❏ When asked, students describe the teacher as someone who cares for them.
❏ Teacher engages in informal conversations with students that are not related to academics.	❏ Students respond to the teacher's verbal interactions.
❏ Teacher uses humor with students when appropriate.	❏ Students respond to the teacher's nonverbal interactions.
❏ Teacher smiles or nods at students when appropriate.	
❏ Teacher puts a hand on students' shoulders when appropriate.	

How Am I Doing?

	4 Innovating	3 Applying	2 Developing	1 Beginning	0 Not Using
Using verbal and nonverbal behaviors that indicate affection for students	I adapt and create new strategies for unique student needs and situations.	I use verbal and nonverbal behaviors that indicate affection for students, and I monitor the quality of relationships in the classroom.	I use verbal and nonverbal behaviors that indicate affection for students, but I do so in a somewhat mechanistic way.	I use the strategy incorrectly or with parts missing.	I should use the strategy, but I don't.

38. What do I typically do to display objectivity and control?

The teacher behaves in an objective and controlled manner.

Teacher Evidence	Student Evidence
❑ Teacher does not exhibit extremes in positive or negative emotions. ❑ Teacher addresses inflammatory issues and events in a calm and controlled manner. ❑ Teacher interacts with all students in the same calm and controlled fashion. ❑ Teacher does not demonstrate personal offense at student misbehavior.	❑ Students are settled by the teacher's calm demeanor. ❑ When asked, the students describe the teacher as in control of himself or herself and in control of the class. ❑ When asked, students say that the teacher does not hold grudges or take things personally.

How Am I Doing?

	4 Innovating	3 Applying	2 Developing	1 Beginning	0 Not Using
Displaying objectivity and control	I adapt and create new strategies for unique student needs and situations.	I behave in an objective and controlled manner, and I monitor the effect on the classroom climate.	I behave in an objective and controlled manner, but I do so in a somewhat mechanistic way.	I use the strategy incorrectly or with parts missing.	I should use the strategy, but I don't.

Design Question: What will I do to communicate high expectations for all students?

39. What do I typically do to demonstrate value and respect for low-expectancy students?

The teacher exhibits behaviors that demonstrate value and respect for low-expectancy students.

Teacher Evidence

❏ When asked, the teacher can identify the students for whom there have been low expectations and the various ways in which these students have been treated differently from high-expectancy students in the past.

❏ Teacher provides low-expectancy students with nonverbal indications that they are valued and respected, such as:

- Making eye contact
- Smiling
- Making appropriate physical contact

❏ Teacher provides low-expectancy students with verbal indications that they are valued and respected, such as:

- Playful dialogue
- Addressing students in a manner they view as respectful

❏ Teacher does not allow negative comments about low-expectancy students.

Student Evidence

❏ When asked, students say that the teacher cares for all students.

❏ Students treat each other with respect.

How Am I Doing?

	4 Innovating	3 Applying	2 Developing	1 Beginning	0 Not Using
Demonstrating value and respect for low-expectancy students	I adapt and create new strategies for unique student needs and situations.	I exhibit behaviors that demonstrate value and respect for low-expectancy students, and I monitor the impact on low-expectancy students.	I exhibit behaviors that demonstrate value and respect for low-expectancy students, but I do so in a somewhat mechanistic way.	I use the strategy incorrectly or with parts missing.	I should use the strategy, but I don't.

	40. What do I typically do to ask questions of low-expectancy students?

The teacher asks questions of low-expectancy students with the same frequency and depth as with high-expectancy students.

Teacher Evidence	**Student Evidence**
❑ Teacher makes sure low-expectancy students' questions are answered at the same rate as high-expectancy students' questions. ❑ Teacher makes sure low-expectancy students are asked challenging questions at the same rate as high-expectancy students.	❑ When asked, students say the teacher expects everyone to participate. ❑ When asked, students say the teacher asks difficult questions of every student.

How Am I Doing?

	4 **Innovating**	**3** **Applying**	**2** **Developing**	**1** **Beginning**	**0** **Not Using**
Asking questions of low-expectancy students	I adapt and create new strategies for unique student needs and situations.	I ask questions of low-expectancy students with the same frequency and depth as with high-expectancy students, and I monitor the quality of participation of low-expectancy students.	I ask questions of low-expectancy students with the same frequency and depth as with high-expectancy students, but I do so in a somewhat mechanistic way.	I use the strategy incorrectly or with parts missing.	I should use the strategy, but I don't.

41. What do I typically do to probe incorrect answers with low-expectancy students?

The teacher probes incorrect answers of low-expectancy students in the same manner as he or she does with high-expectancy students.

Teacher Evidence	**Student Evidence**
❏ Teacher asks low-expectancy students to further explain their answers when they are incorrect.	❏ When asked, students say that the teacher won't "let you off the hook."
❏ Teacher rephrases questions for low-expectancy students when they provide an incorrect answer.	❏ When asked, students say that the teacher "won't give up on you."
❏ Teacher breaks a question into smaller and simpler parts when a low-expectancy student answers a question incorrectly.	❏ When asked, students say the teacher helps them answer questions successfully.
❏ When low-expectancy students demonstrate frustration, the teacher allows them to collect their thoughts but goes back to them at a later point in time.	

How Am I Doing?

	4 Innovating	3 Applying	2 Developing	1 Beginning	0 Not Using
Probing incorrect answers with low-expectancy students	I adapt and create new strategies for unique student needs and situations.	I probe incorrect answers of low-expectancy students in the same manner as with high-expectancy students, and I monitor the level and quality of responses of low-expectancy students.	I probe incorrect answers of low-expectancy students in the same manner as with high-expectancy students, but I do so in a somewhat mechanistic way.	I use the strategy incorrectly or with parts missing.	I should use the strategy, but I don't.

REFERENCES AND RESOURCES

Ackerman, P. L. (2007). New developments in understanding skilled performance. *Current Directions in Psychological Science, 16,* 235–239.

Ambady, N., & Rosenthal, R. (1992). Thin slices of expressive behavior as predictors of interpersonal consequences: A meta-analysis. *Psychological Bulletin, 111*(2), 256–274.

Ambady, N., & Rosenthal, R. (1993). Half a minute: Predicting teacher evaluations from thin slices of nonverbal behavior and physical attractiveness. *Journal of Personality and Social Psychology, 64*(3), 431–441.

Anzalone, F. M. (2010). Education for the law: Reflective education for the law. In N. Lyons (Ed.), *Handbook of reflection and reflective inquiry: Mapping a way of knowing for professional reflective inquiry* (pp. 85–99). New York: Springer.

Armstrong, V., & Curran, S. (2006). Developing a collaborative model of research using digital video. *Computers and Education, 46*(3), 336–347.

Ball, D. L., & Cohen, D. K. (1999). Developing practice, developing practitioners: Toward a practice-based theory of professional education. In L. Darling-Hammond & G. Sykes (Eds.), *Teaching as the learning profession: Handbook of policy and practice* (pp. 3–32). San Francisco: Jossey-Bass.

Blank, R. K., de las Alas, N., & Smith, C. (2008). *Does teacher professional development have effects on teaching and learning? Evaluation findings from programs in 14 states.* Washington, DC: The Council of Chief State School Officers. Accessed at http://programs.ccsso.org/content/pdfs/cross-state_study_rpt_final.pdf on June 2, 2011.

Bloom, B. S. (1986). "The hands and feet of genius": Automaticity. *Educational Leadership, 43*(5), 70–77.

Bolton, G. (2010). *Reflective practice: Writing and professional development.* Thousand Oaks, CA: SAGE.

Brophy, J. (Ed.). (2004). *Advances in research on teaching: Vol. 10. Using video in teacher education.* Oxford, UK: Elsevier.

Calandra, B., Gurvitch, R., & Lund, J. (2008). An exploratory study of digital video editing as a tool for teacher preparation. *Journal of Technology and Teacher Education, 16*(2), 137–153.

Carleton, L., & Marzano, R. J. (2010). *Vocabulary games for the classroom*. Bloomington, IN: Marzano Research Laboratory.

Carroll, J. B. (1963). A model of school learning. *Teachers College Record, 64,* 723–733.

Cepeda, N. J., Pashler, H., Vul, E., Wixted, J. T., & Rohrer, D. (2006). Distributed practice in verbal recall tasks: A review and quantitative synthesis. *Psychological Bulletin, 132,* 354–380.

Chi, M. T. H. (2006). Laboratory methods for assessing experts' and novices' knowledge. In K. A. Ericsson, N. Charness, P. J. Feltovich, & R. R. Hoffman (Eds.), *The Cambridge handbook of expertise and expert performance* (pp. 167–184). New York: Cambridge University Press.

Cochran-Smith, M., & Lytle, S. L. (1999). The teacher research movement: A decade later. *Educational Researcher, 28*(7), 15–25.

Colvin, G. (2008). *Talent is overrated: What* really *separates world-class performers from everybody else.* New York: Penguin.

Costa, A. L., & Garmston, R. J. (2002). *Cognitive coaching: A foundation for renaissance schools.* Norwood, MA: Christopher-Gordon.

Coyle, D. (2009). *The talent code.* New York: Bantam.

Craig, C., & Olson, M. R. (2002). The development of teachers' narrative authority in knowing communities: A narrative approach to teacher learning. In N. Lyons & V. K. LaBoskey (Eds.), *Narrative inquiry in practice: Advancing the knowledge of teaching* (pp. 115–129). New York: Teachers College Press.

Csikszentmihalyi, M. (1990). *Flow: The psychology of optimal experience.* New York: HarperCollins.

Csikszentmihalyi, M., Rathunde, K., & Whalen, S. (1993). *Talented teenagers: The roots of success and failure.* New York: Cambridge University Press.

Cunningham, A., & Benedetto, S. (2002, March). *Using digital video tools to promote reflective practice.* Paper presented at the Society for Information Technology and Teacher Education International Conference, Nashville, TN. Accessed at www.aace.org/conf/site/pt3/paper_3008_619.pdf on June 8, 2011.

Darling-Hammond, L., & McLaughlin, M. W. (1999). Investing in teaching as a learning profession: Policy problems and prospects. In L. Darling-Hammond & G. Sykes (Eds.), *Teaching as the learning profession: Handbook of policy and practice* (pp. 376–411). San Francisco: Jossey-Bass.

de Bono, E. (1999). *Six thinking hats.* New York: Back Bay Books.

Dewey, J. (1910). *How we think.* Boston: Heath.

Driskell, J. E., Willis, R. P., & Copper, C. (1992). Effect of overlearning on retention. *Journal of Applied Psychology, 77*(5), 615–622.

Durso, F. T., & Dattel, A. R. (2006). Expertise and transportation. In K. A. Ericsson, N. Charness, P. J. Feltovich, & R. R. Hoffman (Eds.), *The Cambridge handbook of expertise and expert performance* (pp. 355–371). New York: Cambridge University Press.

Ericsson, K. A. (1996). The acquisition of expert performance: An introduction to some of the issues. In K. A. Ericsson (Ed.), *The road to excellence: The acquisition of expert performance in the arts and sciences, sports and games* (pp. 1–50). Mahwah, NJ: Erlbaum.

Ericsson, K. A., & Charness, N. (1994). Expert performance: Its structure and acquisition. *American Psychologist, 49*(8), 725–747.

Ericsson, K. A., Krampe, R. T., & Tesch-Romer, C. (1993). The role of deliberate practice in the acquisition of expert performance. *Psychological Review, 100*(3), 363–406.

Ericsson, K. A., Roring, R. W., & Nandagopal, K. (2007). Giftedness and evidence for reproducibly superior performance: An account based on the expert performance framework. *High Ability Studies, 18*(1), 3–56.

Ericsson, K. A., & Smith, J. (1991). Prospects and limits of the empirical study of expertise: An introduction. In K. A. Ericsson & J. Smith, *Toward a general theory of expertise: Prospects and limits* (pp. 1–38). Cambridge, UK: Cambridge University Press.

Farrell, T. S. C. (1999). Reflective practice in an EFL teacher development group. *System, 27,* 157–172.

Farrell, T. S. C. (2004). *Reflective practice in action: 80 reflection breaks for busy teachers.* Thousand Oaks, CA: Corwin Press.

Feltovich, P. J., Prietula, M. J., & Ericsson, K. A. (2006). Studies of expertise from psychological perspectives. In K. A. Ericsson, N. Charness, P. J. Feltovich, & R. R. Hoffman (Eds.), *The Cambridge handbook of expertise and expert performance* (pp. 41–67). New York: Cambridge University Press.

Galbraith, P., & Anstrom, K. (1995). Peer coaching: An effective staff development model for educators of linguistically and culturally diverse students. *Directions in Language and Education, 1*(3), 1–8.

Gaschler, R., & Frensch, P. A. (2007). Is information reduction an item-specific or an item-general process? *International Journal of Psychology, 42*(4), 218–228.

Gobet, F., & Charness, N. (2006). Expertise in chess. In K. A. Ericsson, N. Charness, P. J. Feltovich, & R. R. Hoffman (Eds.), *The Cambridge handbook of expertise and expert performance* (pp. 523–538). New York: Cambridge University Press.

Goldman, R. (2004). Video perspectivity meets wild and crazy teens: A design ethnography. *Cambridge Journal of Education, 34*(2), 157–178.

Gordon, S. P., Nolan, J. F., & Forlenza, V. A. (1995). Peer coaching: A cross-site comparison. *Journal of Personnel Evaluation in Education, 9,* 69–91.

Griswold, S. L. (2005). Videotaped performances: Guiding teacher professional development within a competency based framework (Doctoral dissertation, Capella University). *Dissertation Abstracts International, 65*(10), 3760.

Haft, S. (Producer), Witt, P. J. (Producer), Thomas, T. (Producer), & Weir, P. (Director). (1989). *Dead poets society* [Motion picture]. United States: Touchstone.

Hennessy, S., & Deaney, R. (2009). The impact of collaborative video analysis by practitioners and researchers upon pedagogical thinking and practice: A follow-up study. *Teachers and Teaching: Theory and Practice, 15*(5), 617–638.

Hess, D. E. (2009). *Controversy in the classroom: The democratic power of discussion*. New York: Routledge.

Holt, B. J., & Rainey, S. J. (2002). *An overview of automaticity and implications for training the thinking process* (Research report 1790). Alexandria, VA: U.S. Army Research Institute for the Behavioral and Social Sciences.

James, W. (1890). *Principles of psychology*. New York: Holt.

Jenkins, L., & Hoyer, W. J. (2000). Instance-based automaticity and aging: Acquisition, reacquisition, and long-term retention. *Psychology and Aging, 15,* 551–565.

Joyce, B., & Showers, B. (2002). *Student achievement through staff development* (3rd ed.). Alexandria, VA: Association for Supervision and Curriculum Development.

Kagan, S., & Kagan, M. (2009). *Kagan cooperative learning*. San Clemente, CA: Kagan.

Kim, H. S., Clabo, L. M. L., Burbank, P. & Martins, M. L. D. (2010). Application of critical reflective inquiry in nursing education. In N. Lyons (Ed.), *Handbook of reflection and reflective inquiry: Mapping a way of knowing for professional reflective inquiry* (pp. 159–172). New York: Springer.

Korthagen, F. A. J., & Kessels, J. P. A. M. (1999). Linking theory and practice: Changing the pedagogy of teacher education. *Educational Researcher, 28*(4), 4–17.

Korthagen, F. A. J., & Vasalos, A. (2005). Levels on reflection: Core reflection as a means to enhance professional growth. *Teachers and Teaching: Theory and Practice, 11*(1), 47–71.

Korthagen, F. A. J., & Vasalos, A. (2010). Going to the core: Deepening reflection by connecting the person to the profession. In N. Lyons (Ed.), *Handbook of reflection and reflective inquiry: Mapping a way of knowing for professional reflective inquiry* (pp. 529–552). New York: Springer.

Logan, G. D. (1988). Toward an instance theory of automatization. *Psychological Review, 95,* 492–527.

Logan, G. D. (1992). Shapes of reaction-time distributions and shapes of learning curves: A test of the instance theory of automaticity. *Journal of Experimental Psychology: Learning, Memory, and Cognition, 18,* 883–914.

Logan, G. D., & Etherton, J. L. (1994). What is learned during automatization? The role of attention in constructing an instance. *Journal of Experimental Psychology: Learning, Memory, and Cognition, 20,* 1022–1050.

Lundeberg, M., Koehler, M. J., Zhang, M., Karunaratne, S., McConnell, T. J., & Eberhardt, J. (2008, March). *"It's like a mirror in my face": Using video-analysis in learning communities of science teachers to foster reflection on teaching dilemmas*. Paper presented at the annual meeting of the American Educational Research Association, New York. Accessed at http://pbl.educ.msu.edu/wp-content /uploads/2008/04/lundeberg_et_al_march_2008.pdf on June 8, 2011.

Lyle, J. (2003). Stimulated recall: A report on its use in naturalistic research. *British Educational Research Journal, 29*(6), 861–878.

Lyman, F. (2006). *Think-pair-share SmartCard* [Reference Card]. San Clemente, CA: Kagan.

Lyons, N., & LaBoskey, V. K. (2002). *Narrative inquiry in practice: Advancing the knowledge of teaching*. New York: Teachers College Press.

Marzano, R. J. (1992). *A different kind of classroom: Teaching with dimensions of learning.* Alexandria, VA: Association for Supervision and Curriculum Development.

Marzano, R. J. (with Marzano, J. S., & Pickering, D. J.). (2003). *Classroom management that works: Research-based strategies for every teacher.* Alexandria, VA: Association for Supervision and Curriculum Development.

Marzano, R. J. (2006). *Classroom assessment and grading that work.* Alexandria, VA: Association for Supervision and Curriculum Development.

Marzano, R. J. (2007). *The art and science of teaching: A comprehensive framework for effective instruction.* Alexandria, VA: Association for Supervision and Curriculum Development.

Marzano, R. J. (2009). *Designing and teaching learning goals and objectives.* Bloomington, IN: Marzano Research Laboratory.

Marzano, R. J. (2010). *Formative assessment and standards-based grading.* Bloomington, IN: Marzano Research Laboratory.

Marzano, R. J. (2011). Making the most of instructional rounds. *Educational Leadership, 68*(5), 80–81.

Marzano, R. J., & Brown, J. L. (2009). *A handbook for the art and science of teaching.* Alexandria, VA: Association for Supervision and Curriculum Development.

Marzano, R. J., Frontier, T., & Livingston, D. (2011). *Effective supervision: Supporting the art and science of teaching.* Alexandria, VA: Association for Supervision and Curriculum Development.

Marzano, R. J., Gaddy, B. B., Foseid, M. C., Foseid, M. P., & Marzano, J. S. (2005). *A handbook for classroom management that works.* Alexandria, VA: Association for Supervision and Curriculum Development.

Marzano, R. J., & Heflebower, T. (2012). *Teaching and assessing 21st century skills.* Bloomington, IN: Marzano Research Laboratory.

Marzano, R. J., Norford, J. S., Paynter, D. E., Pickering, D. J., & Gaddy, B. B. (2001). *A handbook for classroom instruction that works.* Alexandria, VA: Association for Supervision and Curriculum Development.

Marzano, R. J., & Pickering, D. J. (with Heflebower, T.). (2011). *The highly engaged classroom.* Bloomington, IN: Marzano Research Laboratory.

Marzano, R. J., Pickering, D. J., & Pollock, J. E. (2001). *Classroom instruction that works: Research-based strategies for increasing student achievement.* Alexandria, VA: Association for Supervision and Curriculum Development.

Mast, J. V., & Ginsburg, H. P. (2010). A child study/lesson study: Developing minds to understand and teach children. In N. Lyons (Ed.), *Handbook of reflection and reflective inquiry: Mapping a way of knowing for professional reflective inquiry* (pp. 257–271). New York: Springer.

McGrath, C. (1997, March 23). Elders on ice. *New York Times Magazine.*

Miyata, H. (2002, December). *A study of developing reflective practices for preservice teachers through a web-based electronic teaching portfolio and video-on-demand assessment program.* Paper presented at the International Conference on Computers in Education, Auckland, New Zealand.

Murphy, M., Dempsey, M., & Halton, C. (2010). Reflective inquiry in social work education. In N. Lyons (Ed.), *Handbook of reflection and reflective inquiry: Mapping a way of knowing for professional reflective inquiry* (pp. 173–188). New York: Springer.

National School Reform Faculty. (2008). *Frequently asked questions (FAQ).* Accessed at www.nsrfharmony.org/faq.html#1 on June 17, 2011.

Nye, B., Konstantopoulos, S., & Hedges, L. V. (2004). How large are teacher effects? *Educational Evaluation and Policy Analysis, 26*(3), 237–257.

Ogle, D. (1986). K-W-L: A teaching model that develops active reading of expository text. *Reading Teacher, 39*(6), 564–570.

Ponticell, J., Olson, G. E., & Charlier, P. S. (1995). Project MASTER: Peer coaching and collaboration as catalysts for professional growth in urban high schools. In M. J. O'Hair & S. J. Odell (Eds.), *Educating teachers for leadership and change: Teacher education yearbook III* (pp. 96–116). Thousand Oaks, CA: Corwin Press.

Posner, M. I., & Rothbart, M. K. (2007). *Educating the human brain.* Washington, DC: American Psychological Association.

Powell, A., Francisco, J., & Maher, C. (2003). An analytical model for studying the development of learners' mathematical ideas and reasoning using videotape data. *Journal of Mathematical Behavior, 22*, 405–435.

Rawson, K. A. (2004). Exploring automaticity in text processing: Syntactic ambiguity as a test case. *Cognitive Psychology, 49*, 333–369.

Rawson, K. A., & Middleton, E. L. (2009). Memory-based processing as a mechanism of automaticity in text comprehension. *Journal of Experimental Psychology: Learning, Memory, and Cognition, 35*, 353–370.

Rawson, K. A., & Touron, D. R. (2009). Age differences and similarities in the shift from computation to retrieval during reading comprehension. *Psychology and Aging, 24*(2), 423–437.

Robbins, P. (1991). *How to plan and implement a peer coaching program.* Alexandria, VA: Association for Supervision and Curriculum Development.

Rosaen, C. L., Lundeberg, M., Cooper, M., Fritzen, A., & Terpstra, M. (2008). Noticing noticing: How does investigation of video records change how teachers reflect on their experiences? *Journal of Teacher Education, 59*(4), 347–360.

Salomon, G., & McDonald, F. (1970). Pretest and posttest reaction to self-viewing one's teaching. *Journal of Educational Psychology, 61*, 280–286.

Schneider, W., & Shiffrin, R. M. (1977). Controlled and automatic human information processing: I. Detection, search, and attention. *Psychological Review, 84*(1), 1–66.

Schön, D. A. (1983). *The reflective practitioner: How professionals think in action.* New York: Basic Books.

Schön, D. A. (1987). *Educating the reflective practitioner.* San Francisco: Jossey-Bass.

Seidel, T., Prenzel, M., Rimmele, R., Schwindt, K., Kobarg, M., Meyer, L., et al. (2005, August). *Do videos really matter? The experimental study LUV on the use of videos in teacher professional development*. Paper presented at the Eleventh Conference of the European Association for Research on Learning and Instruction, Nicosia, Cyprus.

Sheard, M. K., & Harrison, C. (2005, September). *"Video on ice": Exploring the concept of "video-as-method" using Interactive Classroom Explorer*. Paper presented at the British Educational Research Association Annual Conference, Pontypridd, UK.

Shenk, D. (2010). *The genius in all of us: Why everything you've been told about genetics, talent, and IQ is wrong*. New York: Doubleday.

Sherin, M. G. (2001). Developing a professional vision of classroom events. In T. Wood, B. S. Nelson, & J. Warfield (Eds.), *Beyond classical pedagogy: Teaching elementary school mathematics* (pp. 75–93). Mahwah, NJ: Erlbaum.

Sherin, M. G. (2004). New perspectives on the role of video in teacher education. In J. Brophy (Ed.), *Using video in teacher education* (pp. 1–27). New York: Elsevier Science.

Sherin, M. G., & Han, S. (2004). Teacher learning in the context of a video club. *Teaching and Teacher Education, 20*, 163–183.

Sherin, M. G., & van Es, E. A. (2005). Using video to support teachers' ability to notice classroom interactions. *Journal of Technology and Teacher Education, 13*(3), 475–491.

Shiffrin, R. M., & Schneider, W. (1977). Controlled and automatic human information processing: II. Perceptual learning, automatic attending, and a general theory. *Psychological Review, 84*(2), 127–190.

Slater, C. L., & Simmons, D. L. (2001). The design and implementation of a peer coaching program. *American Secondary Education, 29*(3), 67–76.

Sorenson, P. D., Newton, L. R., & Harrison, C. (2006, September). *The professional development of teachers through interaction with digital video*. Paper presented at the British Educational Research Association Annual Conference, Coventry, UK.

Spurgeon, S., & Bowen, J. L. (2002, June). *Digital video/multimedia portfolios as a tool to develop reflective teacher candidates*. Paper presented at the National Educational Computer Conference, San Antonio, TX. Accessed at www.eric.ed.gov/PDFS/ED475953.pdf on June 8, 2011.

Sternberg, R. J., & Horvath, J. A. (1995). A prototype view of expert teaching. *Educational Researcher, 24*(6), 9–17.

Storeygard, J., & Fox, B. (1995). Reflections on video: One teacher's story. *Journal of Staff Development, 16*(3), 25–28.

Swafford, J., Maltsberger, A., Button, K., & Furgerson, P. (1997). Peer coaching for facilitating effective literacy instruction. In C. K. Kinzer, K. A. Hinchman, & D. J. Leu (Eds.), *Inquiries in literacy theory and practice*. Chicago: National Reading Conference.

Touron, D. R., & Hertzog, C. (2004). Distinguishing age differences in knowledge, strategy use, and confidence during strategic skill acquisition. *Psychology and Aging, 19*, 452–466.

van Es, E. A. (2009). Participants' roles in the context of a video club. *Journal of the Learning Sciences, 18*, 100–137.

van Es, E. A., & Sherin, M. G. (2006). How different video club designs support teachers in "learning to notice." *Journal of Computing in Teacher Education, 22*(4), 125–135.

van Manen, M. (1977). Linking ways of knowing with ways of being practical. *Curriculum Inquiry, 6*(3), 205–228.

Weisberg, R. W. (2006). Modes of expertise in creative thinking: Evidence from case studies. In K. A. Ericsson, N. Charness, P. J. Feltovich, & R. R. Hoffman (Eds.), *The Cambridge handbook of expertise and expert performance* (pp. 761–787). New York: Cambridge University Press.

York-Barr, J., Sommers, W. A., Ghere, G. S., & Montie, J. (2006). *Reflective practice to improve schools: An action guide for educators* (2nd ed.). Thousand Oaks, CA: Corwin Press.

Zwart, R. C., Wubbels, T., Bergen, T., & Bolhuis, S. (2009). Which characteristics of a reciprocal peer coaching context affect teacher learning as perceived by teachers and their students? *Journal of Teacher Education, 60*(3), 243–257.

INDEX

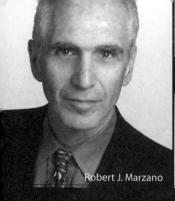
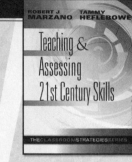